LOVECRAFTIAN PROCEEDINGS

HIPPOCAMPUS PRESS LIBRARY OF CRITICISM

S. T. Joshi, *Primal Sources: Essays on H. P. Lovecraft* (2003)
———, *The Evolution of the Weird Tale* (2004)
———, *Lovecraft and a World in Transition: Collected Essays on H. P. Lovecraft* (2014)
Robert W. Waugh, *The Monster in the Mirror: Looking for H. P. Lovecraft* (2006)
———, *A Monster of Voices: Speaking for H. P. Lovecraft* (2011)
Scott Connors, ed., *The Freedom of Fantastic Things: Selected Criticism on Clark Ashton Smith* (2006)
Ben Szumskyj, ed., *Two-Gun Bob: A Centennial Study of Robert E. Howard* (2006)
S. T. Joshi and Rosemary Pardoe, ed., *Warnings to the Curious: A Sheaf of Criticism on M. R. James* (2007)
Massimo Berruti, *Dim-Remembered Stories: A Critical Study of R. H. Barlow* (2011)
Gary William Crawford, Jim Rockhill, and Brian J. Showers, ed., *Reflections in a Glass Darkly: Essays on J. Sheridan Le Fanu* (2011)
Massimo Berruti, S. T. Joshi, and Sam Gafford, ed., *William Hope Hodgson: Voices from the Borderland: Seven Decades of Criticism on the Master of Cosmic Horror* (2014)
Donald R. Burleson, *Lovecraft: An American Allegory—Selected Essays on H. P. Lovecraft* (2015)
Lovecraft Annual
Dead Reckonings

LOVECRAFTIAN PROCEEDINGS

Papers from NecronomiCon Providence: 2013

Edited by John Michael Sefel and Niels-Viggo S. Hobbs
Robyn Hill, Associate Editor

Hippocampus Press

New York

Copyright © 2015 by Hippocampus Press. The terms "NecronomiCon Providence" and "Dr. Henry Armitage Memorial Scholarship Symposium" are trademarks of the Lovecraft Arts & Sciences Council, Inc., and used by permission. All works are © 2015 by their respective authors.
Cover illustration "The Shadow of His Smile" © by Pete Von Sholly.

Published by Hippocampus Press
P.O. Box 641, New York, NY 10156.
http://www.hippocampuspress.com

All rights reserved.
No part of this work may be reproduced in any form or by any means without the written permission of the publisher.

Cover illustration by Pete Von Sholly
Cover design by Barbara Briggs Silbert.
Hippocampus Press logo designed by Anastasia Damianakos.

First Edition
1 3 5 7 9 8 6 4 2

ISBN 978-1-61498-149-7

Contents

Preface 7
    JOHN MICHAEL SEFEL

Introduction 9
    NIELS-VIGGO S. HOBBS

Poe, Lovecraft, and "the Uncanny": The Horror of the Self 13
    ANTHONY CONRAD CHIEFFALO

"A Stalking Monster": The Influence of Radiation Poisoning on
    H. P. Lovecraft's "The Colour out of Space" 35
    ANDY TROY

Dead Lies Dreaming: H. P. Lovecraft and the Other Side of Modernity 53
    ANDREW LENOIR

Lovecraftian Milton: Prophetic Certainties, Romantic Rebellions, and
    Horrific Imaginings in the Weird Worlds of Milton and Lovecraft 73
    MARCELLO C. RICCIARDI

The Failed Promises of Rationality: Sam J. Lundwall on the
    Individual Lost in an Uncaring and Soulless World 95
    LARS G. E. BACKSTROM

New England's Curator: Colonial Revival in the Travelogue and
    Fiction of H. P. Lovecraft 109
    KENNETH W. LAI

Lovecraft, Fear, and the Medieval Body Frame 125
    PERRY NEIL HARRISON

Attempting to "Untangle" the Mind, Body, and Phallus in Lovecraft's
    "The Thing on the Doorstep" 135
    ZACK REARICK

The Shadow of His Smile: Humor in H. P. Lovecraft's Fiction 151
    STEPHEN WALKER

Monstrous Modernism: H. P. Lovecraft's Theory of the Aesthetic
    in Modernity 165
    JASON RAY CARNEY

Dagon and Derrida: The Modern and Post-Modern in Dialogue in the
    Cthulhu Mythos.. 173
        LYLE ENRIGHT
I and Cthulhu: Using Martin Buber's Ontology of Dialogue to Examine H. P.
    Lovecraft's Cosmic Dread.. 189
        DANIEL HOLMES
Thinking Ecocritically: A Look at Embodiment and Nature in the Fiction
    of H. P. Lovecraft... 201
        CORY WILLARD
Genuine Pagans: A Foray into Lovecraftian Religions 215
        DENNIS P. QUINN
Appendix: Abstracts of Papers Presented at NecronomiCon Providence—
    2013 Emerging Scholarship Symposium 235
        CHAIR: JOHN MICHAEL SEFEL
Index 259

Preface

Recent years have witnessed tremendous growth in the establishment of and respect for serious academic study of weird fiction in general and the works of H. P. Lovecraft in particular. A great deal of thanks is owed to a handful of luminaries in our small but growing community, notably S. T. Joshi and Derrick Hussey, both of whom have been instrumental in bringing this collection to print. As interest in this subject expands, we have seen new symposiums and CFPs cropping up across the nation (and, increasingly, internationally), giving great hope that these delvings into the weird, pulpish, and Cthulhuvian may be here to stay.

If we are to embrace a forward-looking, long-lasting strategy for Lovecraft's improving standing in greater academia, those behind the symposium argue that some form of metaphorical Petri dish is vital to encouraging risk-taking and growth. The areas of Lovecraftian scholarship, research, and writing have always been a home for the tumultuous, for the risky, for the wild-eyed dreamer, and for the long-shot. Whether a graduate student wading into the eldritch waters for the first time or a veteran scholar exploring a new and still formulating theory, Niels and I were eager to create a space for a scholarly conversation that encouraged experimentation, friendly debate, and a general sense of throwing ideas against the wall to see what sticks.

The Dr. Henry Armitage Memorial Scholarship Symposium is meant to supply such a space, and to celebrate emerging scholarship in engaged, spirited conversation. This is not a thesis statement's final stop, but rather a stepping stone. We hope to see many arguments presented here develop into journal articles, chapters, and books—and we know, when that happens, that these testing grounds will have helped launch those efforts. If NecronomiCon Providence is a celebration of the best current Lovecraft goings-on, then this symposium is designed to provide a preview of what's to come.

As the academic discipline of Lovecraft studies emerged over the past several decades, each brave writer, thinker, and publisher was, in their own way, a vanguard of the current movement. As we now settle into a larger, more established identity, we must celebrate and cherish that which led the way, while simultaneously encouraging those who would create their own, unhewn paths. As Lovecraft scholarship grows, we hope the NecronomiCon Providence may provide a welcomed opportunity for community—and, with the Dr. Henry Armitage Memorial Scholarship Symposium, we hope that we might provide a useful space for new ideas, for controversy, for comradeship, and for today's community to build toward tomorrow.

—JOHN MICHAEL SEFEL
Founding Chair
Dr. Henry Armitage Memorial Scholarship Symposium

Introduction

NecronomiCon Providence, 23–25 August 2013, marked something of a return of famed weird fiction author H. P. Lovecraft to his hometown of Providence through a citywide conference and festival that highlighted both the remarkable writer and the city that gave rise to him. Not a typical fan convention in any strict sense, NecronomiCon Providence set out to reshape the concept into something much more meaningful for guests and attendees. It became something that gave a far more immersive experience to all involved, providing attendees with myriad discussions on all manner of Lovecraftian topics and engaging them in frank analysis of the weird fiction genre represented by Lovecraft and the many authors, artists, and academics he inspired. At the core of this effort was a desire to give the convention an approachable scholarly foundation by including talks by experts on various subjects, such as archaeo-astronomy, the darker sides of Rhode Island history, the extremes of biological diversity, and the remarkable architecture of Providence. Additionally, we decided to seek out a broader spectrum of academics, beyond those already well known or well established, in and out of the Lovecraftian community. To this end, we decided to create a symposium modeled closely after the type commonly seen at scientific and liberal arts conferences around the world.

The Lovecraft Arts & Sciences Council (the organizer of NecronomiCon Providence) put out the call for submissions of new academic works early in 2013, and we quickly realized that there are many academics, young and old, professional and independent, who are passionate about their own particular facet of Lovecraftian studies—passionate enough to devote much time to plumbing the depths of all manner of previously unplumbed depths, as you will see with the included works. We had originally called for papers that would explore all aspects of the works and life of the Old Man of Providence, including the influence of history, architecture, science (anthropology, biology, geology, etc.), and popular culture (movies, theater, etc.) on his writing. We hoped to foster exploration of

Lovecraft as a rationalist who created an elaborate cosmic mythology, and how this mythology was influenced by, and has come to influence, numerous other authors and artists before and since.

We received this, and so much more. We were showered with a veritable trove of amazing and novel proposals for presentations, along with the promise of written theses to follow. As a result, we committed to publishing the proceedings of what promised to be an interesting body of work.

One of the best of the many fortunes that befell us in staging the NecronomiCon Providence convention, and in particular the symposium, was a timely email from John Sefel of Baylor University in Texas, who was very keen to help with this symposium in any capacity offered to him. It quickly became evident that John was the ideal person to helm the symposium, and he immediately immersed himself in the task—much to my relief and awe. I simply can't imagine the Emerging Scholarship Symposium, as we then dubbed it, being anywhere near as remarkable without his stewardship. I simply can't thank him enough.

John also shepherded all the papers and began the thankless and arduous task of curating them into both a narrative and a prized relic of NecronomiCon Providence 2013. We strongly feel that all the submissions included here contribute to a greater understanding of Lovecraft and associated authors and artists of weird fiction. The authors approached their respective theses with a great deal of passion and insight. The 2013 Emerging Scholarship Symposium, so named to highlight the novel research presented, was a resounding success (speaking personally, as the executive director of the convention, this is the facet I truly think of most fondly), and we look forward to the new works that 2015 will bring. I'd like to thank the many folks who enjoyed the 2013 symposium talks so immensely that they made it obvious that we need to do it again. And I'd also like to thank our friend Ken Birdwell, who was so impressed with what he saw and heard that he is providing the capital so that not only do we *need* to do another one, but we *can* do another one. For 2015, we have decided to rename the symposium the Dr. Henry Armitage Memorial Scholarship Symposium, in order to give it a bit more gravitas balanced with a tongue-in-cheek, thinly veiled reference to the man who was the caretaker of that most revered and reviled book, the *Necronomicon* itself.

Unlike Dr. Armitage (may he rest in peace in the Dreamlands), whose job was to keep certain tracts of dark knowledge forever sequestered, we very much encourage a full reading of the great works enclosed herein. Deep thanks to Derrick Hussey of Hippocampus Press for offering these works a much-needed home, and to S. T. Joshi for being both the type model for Lovecraftian academics and for his superlative editorial help and oversight. Truly, this was a team effort. Most of all, many thanks to all the authors who submitted their works and poured their hearts and souls into these writings. May their collective sacrifices now be our bounteous reward.

With warmest regards from hoary Providence,

—NIELS-VIGGO S. HOBBS
Director, Lovecraft Arts & Sciences Council

Abbreviations

AT *The Ancient Track: Complete Poetical Works* (Hippocampus Press, 2013)
CE *Collected Essays* (Hippocampus Press, 2004–06; 5 vols.)
CF *Collected Fiction* (Hippocampus Press, 2015–16; 4 vols.)
SL *Selected Letters* (Arkham House, 1965–76; 5 vols.)

Poe, Lovecraft, and "the Uncanny": The Horror of the Self

Anthony Conrad Chieffalo
University of Rhode Island

"The Uncanny" Connection

Lovecraft's goal in his writing was to elevate horror fiction to what he referred to as "cosmic horror." In one of his works of literary criticism, "Supernatural Horror in Literature," Lovecraft creates a detailed chronology regarding what he considers to be the major contributions to horror from "The Dawn of the Horror-Tale" to "The Modern Masters" who were Lovecraft's contemporaries. In its introduction he identifies the characteristics of superior horror fiction as having "that most terrible conception of the human brain—a malign and particular suspension or defeat of those fixed laws of Nature which are our only safeguard against the assaults of chaos and the daemons of unplumbed space" (CE 2.84). Despite the fantastic nature of Lovecraft's work, his conception of fear was utterly realistic. His interpretation of "unplumbed space" was the darkness of a cave, the unfathomable depths of an ocean, or the infinitudes of the universe beyond the grasp of modern science.

For a writer who set many of his stories in mystical realms like the Dreamlands, this perspective is surprisingly narrow. Lovecraft was such a devoted believer in reality determined by science and reason that he viewed writing works of fiction as the only means of escaping from its confinement. To quote Lovecraft, "I choose weird stories because they suit my inclination best—one of my strongest and most persistent wishes being to achieve, momentarily, the illusion of some strange suspension or violation of the galling limitations of time, space, and natural law which forever imprison us" ("Notes on Writing Weird Fiction" [CE 2.175-76]).

Lovecraft's works entertain the notion of the unknown in its relation to horror, but he did not perceive the psychology of horror to the extent that Freud developed the notion in his essay "The Uncanny." Lovecraft's often-quoted adage states: "The oldest and strongest emotion of mankind is fear, and the oldest and strongest kind of fear is fear of the unknown. These facts few psychologists will dispute, and their admitted truth must establish for all time the genuineness and dignity of the weirdly horrible tale as a literary form" ("Supernatural Horror in Literature" [CE 2.82]). Despite noting the significance of the fear of the unknown to the field of psychology, Lovecraft fails to grasp the profound implications of his statement as they relate to a specific understanding of the unknown defined by preeminent psychologist Sigmund Freud.

"The Uncanny" was published in 1919. It invites a fascinating reinterpretation of the unknown as it applies to horror in weird fiction, including Lovecraft's own works and those of authors who inspired him, such as Edgar Allan Poe. Freud's essay defines this mode of horror called "the uncanny" as "that species of the frightening that goes back to what was once well known and had long been familiar" (124).

Freud's essay first provides an etymological analysis of the German definition of the words *heimlich* (familiar, homely) and *unheimlich* (uncanny). Citing the German Dictionary of Jacob and Wilhelm Grimm, Freud directs his reader's attention to a key passage that specifies that "Starting from the homely and the domestic, there is a further development towards the notion of something removed from the eyes of strangers, hidden, secret" (133). The definition for what is "homely" is, paradoxically, also used to convey a sense of privacy, what is withdrawn from knowledge or unconscious. Freud's etymological approach ultimately indicates the ambivalence that emerges between these terms, where the definition of *heimlich* overlaps that of its antonym until the unfamiliar becomes a species of the familiar.

"The Uncanny" continues with specific occurrences of this mode of horror in literary works. To illustrate his theory of the uncanny, Freud relies heavily on a work by German Romantic author E. T. A. Hoffmann, "The Sand-Man." The uncanny element that draws the focus of Freud's interest is that of the Sand-Man himself and the protagonist's relationship to the entity, a creature from folklore that tears out children's eyes in order to feed them to his children, who live on the moon. Relying on such connections between "the monster" and "the father," Freud is able to appropriate Hoffmann's work to fit his psychoanalytical vision.

A focal aspect of this work of uncanny fiction is how the psychological conflict within the protagonist becomes the central conflict of the narrative. The infantile memory of the story and traumatic memory haunt him into his adulthood and result in his eventual suicide. He is unable to reconcile consciousness with subconsciousness. Freud considered Hoffmann to be the "unrivalled master of the uncanny in literature" (141).

Lovecraft viewed psychoanalysis as a force of demystification in relation to literature. According to Lovecraft, an active imagination is required in order to appreciate occurrences of the supernatural in horror fiction, but even the most pragmatic of individuals can appreciate the faculty of the imagination: "the sensitive are always with us, and sometimes a curious streak of fancy invades an obscure corner of the very hardest head; so that no amount of rationalism, reform, or Freudian analysis can quite annul the thrill of the chimney-corner whisper or the lonely wood" (CE 2.83). Lovecraft viewed Freudian analysis as a threat to the imagination rather than an expansion upon creative expression or a means of interpreting such creativity and enriching the experience.

"What lingers of Poe in Lovecraft is his psychological concern" (Burleson 216). Poe famously explored the dark psychology of the individual mind through many of his unreliable narrators, while Lovecraft's cosmic horror was an exploration of the psychological effects that a person experiences when encountering the unknown. Despite Lovecraft's intentions, his works express a concern for psychological interiority in addition to cosmic exteriority. H. P. Lovecraft's works do not represent a new genre of "cosmic horror," but rather an extension of the dark psychology that is found in his precursor: Edgar Allan Poe.

Of the ten sections of "Supernatural Horror in Literature," nine are devoted to literary movements as a whole with fleeting references to such writers as Mary Shelley and Robert Louis Stevenson. Only one is devoted entirely to a single individual, a man who marked a literary dawn for Lovecraft: "It is our good fortune as Americans to be able to claim that dawn as our own, for it came in the person of our illustrious and unfortunate fellow-countryman Edgar Allan Poe" (CE 2.100). Lovecraft classifies Poe's works in terms of their essence of spiritual horror, separating the tales of ratiocination and those "certain others, probably influenced considerably by Hoffmann, [that] possess an extravagance which relegates them to the borderline of the grotesque" (CE 2.102). Lovecraft continues to separate tales of the uncanny from tales of supernatural horror, though Freud's essay asserts the profound relationship between the two that is responsible for the greatest examples of horror fiction.

Lovecraft obsessed over the universality of his cosmic horror subgenre, the pessimistic implication that all human beings are bound to a single and inconsequential fate. This is, as S. T. Joshi states in *The Rise and Fall of the Cthulhu Mythos*, "the notion of human insignificance that is the dominant theme of Lovecraft's overall work" (117). Although Lovecraft often makes reference to horrors that will encompass all mankind, his protagonists are consistently depicted as experiencing their fears in solitude. A psychological conflict arises, becoming the main focus of many of his works. These interior, psychological struggles are reminiscent of the dark psychology that can be traced through the horror prose of Edgar Allan Poe and his renowned mastery of unreliable narrators.

The main conflicts of Lovecraft's often formulaic horror stories are never actually external to the protagonist. As in the works by Poe, the seemingly external events are actually reflections of the internal conflict within the protagonist. The protagonists engage in internalized confrontations as they attempt to conquer the overwhelming fear experienced in these tales. They are battles between the mind and the threat posed by its own thoughts and emotions. The psychological implication of cosmic horror becomes a universal threat that impacts each individual human being on a personal level.

The unknown horrors confronted in Lovecraft's fiction become symbols of the larger confrontation of his protagonists, which is the consistent focus of his writing. This is found in "The Call of Cthulhu," where Henry Anthony Wilcox is plagued by nightmarish visions of Cyclopean locations and the unknowable Cthulhu; for one cannot comprehend Cthulhu without sacrificing his sanity in the process. These are beings that can never be seen or fully recognized. It is an unknown that is at the edge of consciousness, always threatening the mind with its tangible indefiniteness. This paradox is what constitutes the uncanny. It is the incomprehensibility of a thing simultaneously knowable and unknowable. The mind attempts to conquer the deepest and darkest recesses of itself and faces annihilation at the other end of paradox.

The motifs that create the sensation of the uncanny that are proposed by Freud's essay are the concepts of the doppelgänger, the evil eye, and the struggle to maintain one's sanity in the face of this self-horror. These uncanny motifs exist in abundance in the works of Edgar Allan Poe and H. P. Lovecraft, who rely heavily on techniques of this uncanny mode in order to foster fear and dread in their readers rooted deep in the infantile memories of human subconscious. All these recurring elements of the uncanny involve the divisive and conflicted self. The horror aspect of these tales is intrinsically unified with the notion of fear and hatred in relation to the self. A theme of self-loathing or self-horror is born that is embodied in the symbols of the self as evil other. The first of these three symbols is a man's own dark shadow; the loathsome stares back at us from the other side of the mirror.

I, Doppelgänger

A common element of uncanny fiction is the notion of psychological estrangement. Such characters are so detached from their own thoughts and emotions that they can no longer recognize themselves. This phenomenon is represented by duplicating the protagonist and creating a scenario where the two manifestations of a single persona meet. These encounters involve a failure to recognize the "reflection in the mirror." The protagonist is incapable of identifying the doppelgänger as an aspect of himself. It is always perceived as a stranger that is external and unfamiliar to the protagonist. What he never fails to recognize in the doppelgänger is the belief that it poses a threat to the integrity of his existence.

Though Sigmund Freud identifies the motif of the double in "The Uncanny," the concept is perhaps best explicated by Jacques Lacan. Lacan developed a psychoanalytic theory termed the mirror stage. An aspect of an infant's development, this phenomenon involves the recognition of the self in the mirror for the first time. The effect of this occurrence is the formation of the ego as the infant identifies itself in the image:

> I have described . . . the sight in the mirror of the ego ideal, of that being that he first saw appearing in the form of the parent holding him up before the mirror. By clinging to the reference-point of him who looks at him in a mirror, the subject sees appearing, not his ego ideal, but his ideal ego, that point at which he desires to gratify himself in himself. This is the function, the mainspring, the effective instrument constituted by the ego ideal. (Lacan 257)

This process of self-recognition represents a pivotal moment in psychological development where an infant's physical existence converges with its mental existence. The result of this new perspective is ultimately the formation of what become the infant's realizations of its own individuality. This constructed ego is the infant's recognition of an idealized self. It is important to remember the vital distinction between perceived self and true self, as it is at the heart of the symbolic conflict with the doppelgänger.

This mirror stage is not only an early instance of self-recognition, but one of self-analysis and even alienation. "The subject has a relation with his analyst [himself viewed in a reflection] the centre of which is at the level of the privileged signifier known as the ego ideal, in so far as he will feel himself both satisfactory and loved. But there is another function, which institutes an identification of a strangely different kind, and which is introduced by the process of separation" (Lacan 257). In the mirror, the infant becomes divided into both the subject and the analyst. The reflection simultaneously unifies and separates as the infant's self-awareness is only through an acceptance of the reflected other.

Lacan's conception of the complexities of the mirror stage and of self-identification provides a specific context for Freud's notion of the doppelgänger as an aspect of the uncanny. From infancy, the reflection exists as both a representation of the self that is known and the stranger that exists as a fragmentation of identity. The reflection then becomes vilified as it challenges the integrity and uniqueness of the self. Man is a psychologically fractured creature; flawed flesh aspiring toward an ethereal ideal. It is at this point that the self becomes object of resentful fixation.

In Freud's "The Uncanny," the inherent psychological fear of the double is based on the notion that "one becomes co-owner of the other's knowledge, emotions, and experience . . . a person may identify himself with another and so become unsure of his true self; or he may substitute the other's self for his own. The self may thus be duplicated, divided, and interchanged" (141–42). In literary works, the double represents a destabilized sense of identity that has been subject to forces of manipulation. The fracturing of the self serves as a means of portraying an interior, psychological conflict between "who I am" and "who I think I am."

Historically, the double has been seen as an insurance against death. In "The Uncanny," Freud describes the evolution of the notion of the double:

> it seems likely that the 'immortal' soul was the first double of the body. . . . But these ideas arose on the soil of boundless self-love, the primordial narcissism that dominates the mental life of both the child and primitive man, and when this phase is surmounted, the meaning of the 'double' changes: having once been an assurance of immortality, it becomes the uncanny harbinger of death. (142)

The most prominent use of the vilified doppelgänger and "harbinger of death" in Poe's works is found in "William Wilson." The narrator of this tale calls himself William Wilson; the alliteration of the name clearly evokes imagery of the double. This narrator is prone to narcissistic tendencies, which are one of the indications of Freud's notion of "the uncanny." As occurs frequently in Poe's works, the story begins with the "near-death" confession of the narrator. He states: "although temptation may have erewhile existed as great, man was never *thus*, at least, tempted before—certainly never *thus* fell. And is it therefore that he has never thus suffered?" (337). Wilson expresses an aggrandized self-image, separating himself from the entirety of mankind as the *most* tempted, the *most* fallen, and the *most* unfortunate in terms of the suffering that he has endured. This narcissism forms a veil over Wilson's face that prevents him from seeing the truth of his own existence that he is his own worst enemy.

"William Wilson" centers on the childhood event where the narrator recollects living in a boarding school and meeting a particular character among his schoolmates; it is a person "who, although no relation, bore the same Christian and surname as myself;—a circumstance, in fact, little remarkable; for, notwithstanding a noble descent, mine was one of those every-day appellations . . . In this narrative I have therefore designated myself as William Wilson" (341). The fact that the narrator refuses to reveal his real name and adopts a false persona is further indication of how his identity has been compromised.

The duplication of the Wilson identity diminishes its integrity, and the reader can begin to discern how the existence of the double poses a threat to the confidence and stability of William Wilson. This equality is emphasized by ensuing uncanny encounters between these figures:

> I discovered, or fancied I discovered, in his accent, his air, and general appearance, a something which first startled, and then deeply interested me, by bringing to mind dim visions of my earliest infancy—wild, confused and thronging memories of a time when memory herself was yet unborn . . . I could with difficulty shake off the belief of my having been acquainted with the being who stood before me, at some epoch very long ago—some point of the past even infinitely remote. The delusion, however, faded rapidly as it came. (346)

It is fascinating that this work predates Freud by nearly a century yet describes Freud's notion of the experience of the uncanny so perfectly. In this quotation is Freud's obsession with infantile memories as well as the concept of repressed memory. The narrator experiences this uncanny feeling in this passage that is concerned with sensation as much as it is concerned with revelation. It was a feeling that startles, yet interests Wilson as he encounters memories beyond his capacity for memory. This appears to be an acknowledgment of the existence of Wilson's own subconscious. Despite this instance of an uncanny experience, Wilson dismisses it quickly as mere delusion. The narrator approaches self-awareness as the moment of recognizing uncanny memory from infancy as the instant when single identity fractured in two, but fails as is prescribed by the formula of the uncanny tale.

The impossibility of the conscious self to escape the subconscious self, depicted by Wilson's conflict with the doppelgänger, is an exercise in futility. The double becomes synonymous with fate, just as the conclusion of the tale has been ill-fated from Wilson's "near-death" introduction. The emergence of the repressed is unavoidable, and so is the inability of the individual to cope with its return. In the final encounter between Wilson and his double, Wilson plunges his sword through the chest of his archenemy. The ensuing epiphany is an attempt to put revelation to words as idealized self and true self collide:

> A large mirror,—so at first it seemed to me in my confusion—now stood where none had been perceptible before; and, as I stepped up to it in extremity of terror, mine own image, but with features all pale and dabbled in blood, advanced to meet me with a feeble and tottering gait.... Not a thread in all his raiment—not a line in all that marked and singular lineaments of his face which was not, even in the most absolute identity, *mine own!* Thus it appeared, I say, but was not. It was my antagonist—it was Wilson, who then stood before me. (356)

Wilson directly confronts his double and nearly acknowledges that the doppelgänger has been nothing more than his own reflection. Ironically, by identifying Wilson as his antagonist the narrator correctly indicates that he has been his own enemy from the beginning.

The horror of this truth is revealed in the final utterance of the dying double, as he whispers as if speaking through the narrator: "'*You have conquered, and I yield. Yet, henceforward art thou also dead—dead to the World, to Heaven and to Hope! In me didst thou exist—and, in my death, see by this image, which is thine own, how utterly thou hast murdered thyself*'" (356–57). The description of this act as a "murder of the self" evokes a conception of the conflict with the double as a form of suicide. The outcome of self-horror is self-destruction.

The doppelgänger motif is used by H. P. Lovecraft as an extension of the way in which it is found in Edgar Allan Poe. It is a means of depicting inner conflict on a literary battlefield where two selves divided from one are set against one another and assume the roles of protagonist and antagonist. In *The Case of Charles Dexter Ward*, the titular protagonist discovers a portrait bearing a visage of uncanny similarity to himself. He later learns that it is an image of one of his ancestors named Joseph Curwen, an evil wizard who was intent on discovering the secret of immortality. There are many parallels between the accounts describing the life of Ward and his forgotten ancestor. Both are reclusive, studying day and night to delve deeper into the mysteries of life, death, and the infinitudes beyond human comprehension although they lived centuries apart.

Lovecraft begins his tale at a point after its conclusion, as it is aptly titled "Chapter One: A Result and a Prologue." The story is centered on Ward's confrontation with his double, but begins with an opening sentence that relates the recent disappearance of "an exceedingly singular person" (CF 2.215). The true beginning of the tale is when Charles Ward learns of his descent from the infamous Joseph Curwen and becomes obsessed with him: "for every vague rumour that he had heard of Curwen now became something vital to himself, in whom flowed Curwen's blood" (CF 2.264). Lovecraft slowly merges these seemingly distinct identities in the language of his narrative. Surrounding Curwen is the sense of the family's dark secret that has been repressed. However, as Ward traces the clues to this mystery, his existence becomes bound to uncovering the secret. The genealogical connection to Curwen, a blood relative of Ward, is a journey of self-discovery. Here is both the repressed and its subtle emergence encapsulated in the characters of this narrative that are representations of terms defined by Freud's psychoanalysis.

Lovecraft conveys how the familial connection between Ward and Curwen is not the only symbol of their "oneness." When Ward discovers a hidden portrait in the wall of an old building, he is astonished "to confront the bewildered Charles Dexter Ward, dweller in the past, with his own living features in the countenance of his horrible great-great-great-grandfather" (CF 2.273). Soon after, Ward becomes a recluse to society and devotes himself entirely to mysterious research. He makes an acquaintance with an individual called Allen and both set to work "robbing the tombs of all the ages ... in the hopes of recovering from the bygone ashes some vestige of the consciousness and lore which had once animated and informed them" (CF 2.326). Continuously seeking knowledge through the past, as depicted here in the tombs of the long deceased, Ward further reveals his psychosis. What is buried in the past is the equivalent of infantile memory, as what was once known but has been repressed and nearly forgotten. This is a recurring motif in both Poe and Lovecraft as the entombed becomes exhumed, signifying the refusal of the repressed to remain dormant. One can never truly divorce himself from his past or from his reflection. To know thyself is to fear and ultimately hate thyself.

There is a discernible shift in the narrative as the original protagonist of *Charles Dexter Ward* completely vanishes as the "hero" of the tale and is replaced by his physician Dr. Willett. It is Willett who comes to the horrifying revelation that Allen was actually the wizard Joseph Curwen, resurrected from death by Ward. Willett also learns that, at a certain point, Curwen murdered Ward and replaced him in public because of their nearly identical physical similarities. Curwen was then forced to put on an elaborate charade by assuming the roles of both Allen and Ward. Willett deduces all this when Allen and Ward no longer appear in public at the same time: "Who had ever seen Charles and Allen together? Yes, the officials had once, but who later on? Was it not when Allen left that Charles suddenly lost his growing fright and began to live wholly at the bungalow? Curwen–Allen–Ward–in what blasphemous and abominable fusion had two ages and two persons become involved?" (CF 2.356). After making this discovery, Willett tracks down Curwen and, seeing through his disguise, uses a supernatural incantation to destroy him.

As in Poe's "William Wilson," identity is not something that is clearly defined or stable in Lovecraft's *The Case of Charles Dexter Ward*; it is fluid and interchangeable. Lovecraft describes it as a "blasphemous and abominable fusion" of personalities as the identities of Charles Dexter Ward, Allen, and Joseph Curwen become inseparably unified. To reference Lovecraft's focus on history and genealogy in this work in relation to this theory of self-identification and self-revelation, these personalities were never truly separate. The same likeness existed in the past and the present and traversed time to reach an "exceedingly singular" fate. It is a tale of a single ego in Ward that is fragmented by the allure of the past; the secret is buried not only in libraries and tombs but in the blood coursing through his veins.

With both William Wilson and Charles Dexter Ward, the double kills the original in order to replace him and become the single owner of the identity. Wilson's narcissism becomes self-envy that leads to acts of hatred and violent rage against his double, while Charles Dexter Ward delves so far into the myth of his ancestor and the secret in his own blood that he loses himself to the overpowering darkness of his family history. The fantastic elements of these examples of literature create fictional spaces where psychological wars are waged and the questions of human identity and the complexities of the mind are pondered. Poe and Lovecraft tell tales of doom for the individual who attempts to reconcile the known with the unknown and effectively cause his own destruction. Self-awareness is a futile endeavor—a mind-shattering, crawling chaos proposed by Poe and Lovecraft.

The Evil "I"

Freud takes great interest in the aspect of "The Sand-Man" involving the fairy tale of the monstrous father figure who steals the eyes of human children. The eye motif continues throughout the story as the protagonist later encounters the spectacle salesman who is responsible for igniting the suppressed memory in his adulthood. In true Freudian fashion, "The Uncanny" draws attention to the "substitutive relation between the eye and the male member that is manifested in dreams, fantasies, and myths . . . a particularly strong and obscure emotion is aroused by the threat of losing the sexual organ, and that it is this emotion that first gives resonance to the idea of losing other organs" (140). Freud's details of the castration complex supports his reasoning that it is the repressed, infantile fear of losing the male sex organ that is coupled with the fear of the father figure in the notion of the Oedipal complex and is responsible for the sense of uncanny horror in Hoffmann's work.

Freud widens the scope of this notion to encompass another view of the motif of eyes in uncanny literature. Whether the eye serves as an emblem for the castration complex (dismemberment) or as the embodiment of evil, both concepts share the same concern at their core. They both focus on possessiveness and fear of loss: "One of the uncanniest and most widespread superstitions is fear of the 'evil eye' . . . Anyone who possesses something precious, but fragile, is afraid of the envy of others" (146). What is genuinely evil in this sense is this aspect of the self that is consumed with envy and aggressive reaction. There is perhaps no story in literature that captures this notion of the evil eye as effectively as Edgar Allan Poe's "The Tell-Tale Heart."

Poe is the unrivaled master of the unreliable narrator. A common characteristic of this figure is his incapacity for introspection. To quote Jeffrey Folks, "Poe's narrators are always impotent in the face of the injustice they so clearly register. What Poe's personae typically lack is the animating purpose and empathetic feeling to accompany their much vaunted intellect. Too often they seem brilliant thought-generating machines, endlessly emitting theories on all matters but utterly devoid of purpose or feeling" (63). The narrator of "The Tell-Tale Heart" is fixated on his external sensory perception and completely ignorant of his instability: "why *will* you say that I am mad? The disease had sharpened my senses—not destroyed—not dulled them. Above all was the sense of hearing acute. I heard all things in the heaven and in the earth. I heard many things in hell. How, then, am I mad?" (555). Along with this unreliable assertion of the narrator's sanity is a very reliable account of his megalomania. He believes that his senses allow him to hear in heaven and in hell, and he clearly envisions himself as more god than man. In "The Uncanny," Freud associates this method of thinking to a principle called "the omnipotence of thoughts . . . the narcissistic overrating of one's own mental processes" (147). Poe's narrator is simultaneously self-absorbed and self-removed. He is severed from the bounds of reality as he obsesses over the power of mental processes while failing to acknowledge mental instability.

There is no conflict between the narrator and the old man, "for it was not the old man that vexed [him], but his Evil Eye" (556). The narrator detests the thought of being seen. To be seen means to expose oneself to the authority of another and assume a position of naked submission to the bearer of the gaze. The eye is also an instrument of evaluation and judgment, as the narrator indicates when he describes how he conceals the old man's corpse beneath the floorboards: "no human eye—not even *his*—could have detected any thing wrong" (558). The implication is that the narrator's hatred of the eye stems not from its gruesome aspect, but from its symbolic significance. To destroy the eye would put an end to the fear of being seen by another. However, the narrator is unaware of the symbiotic relationship that has formed between his own ego and the old man's eye. "'The Tell-Tale Heart' foregrounds different stages of Ego-Evil as the narrator defines himself through the narcissistic eye, the malicious glare, and the enigmatic gaze of the other. . . . The story opens with the process of 'I see myself seeing you,' featuring the narrator's egoistic positioning of the self and the other" (Ki 27).

What the narrator ultimately hates is the fear of being known. As he is incapable of knowing himself, he cannot bear the thought of being known by another. However, his narcissistic self-obsession is at the heart of this tale as the narrator is defined by how he is perceived by the old man. Though he fears and detests the idea of being seen, he also desires it. "In the Lacanian context, the eye allows the self to see itself as a unified creature and as a judge, hence the eye is related to the imaginary 'identity-building' process. However, as the eye sees what it wants to see, 'sight' or 'insight' can mean bias" (Ki 27). This is how the identity that is constructed by the narrator becomes his own antagonist in the text as it exists behind a barrier of awareness.

The violent murder is, in fact, an act of jealousy as the narrator envies the capacity of the eye to see and know him. It is a power that is not available to the narrator. Despite his claims to possessing godlike sensory abilities, he knows that he can never truly see himself and even fears the thought of what he would find if he were to do so. As stated by Freud: "his envy will reach a particular intensity and then convert this intensity into effective action. What is feared is thus a covert intention to harm, and on the strength of certain indications it is assumed that this intention can command the necessary force" (147). What begins as mere envy builds until it erupts as violent outburst.

The self-destruction of this narrator results from his attempt to suppress the guilt of murder, which manifests itself as the beating of the heart that only the narrator can hear. The "suicide" in this work comes in the form of the narrator's final admission at the conclusion of the story when he confesses to his crime. E. Arthur Robinson suggests that the narrator projects his own persona upon the old man whom he murders. Robinson states that "a major theme . . . is the murderer's psychological identification with the man he kills. . . . The loud yell of the murderer is echoed in the old man's shriek, which the narrator, as though with increasing clairvoyance, later tells the police was his own. Most of all . . . the madman's mistaking his own heartbeat for that of his victim, both before and after the murder" (374). Identity loses its distinctiveness, as was seen with the occurrence of the doppelganger in uncanny fiction. In killing the old man, the narrator is actually satisfying his subconscious desire to kill himself.

The eye is portrayed as an embodiment of evil in Lovecraft's "The Lurking Fear." The aspect of the subterranean creatures that the narrator finds terrifying is their unknowability, as he encounters one and describes it as "a nameless, shapeless abomination which no mind could fully grasp and no pen even partly describe" (CF 1.355). As occurs often in Lovecraft, the monster is defined more by what it is not than what it is. It is defined by what it lacks, as it is both "nameless" and "shapeless." Common with uncanny fiction, however, is the narrator's desire to attempt to know that which cannot be known. He recounts delving into the tunnels of these creatures: "I forgot danger, reason, and cleanliness in my single-minded fever to unearth the lurking fear" (CF 1.365–66). The motif of unearthing the unknown is prevalent in works by Poe and Lovecraft. To unearth is to make visible, to take what was concealed and bring it to the surface where it can be made known. This desire to know coupled with the inability to do so becomes the obsession of the narrator.

When the narrator encounters the beings once again, there is one aspect of them to which he can relate. In the dark tunnels, the narrator discerns "two daemoniac reflections of my expiring lamp; two reflections glowing with a baneful and unmistakable effulgence, and provoking maddeningly nebulous memories. I stopped automatically, though lacking the brain to retreat. The eyes approached . . ." (CF 1.366). The eyes of this unfamiliar creature spark a horrifying familiarity at the core of the narrator's being. Once again, Lovecraft depicts an internal relation with the unknown where fear stimulated from an external source emerges proliferates within the interior of the mind. The implication is that the source of this fear is not actually from literal monsters that the narrator encounters, but from the narrator himself who is haunted most profoundly by the memories that emerge within his own mind.

The fourth and final section of the short story is titled "The Horror in the Eyes." Though the narrator escapes from the creatures, the narrative indicates that he will forever be haunted by his experience. "If heaven is merciful, it will some day efface from my consciousness the sight that I saw, and let me live my last years in peace" (CF 1.371). What had once been the narrator's intense passion of unearthing the unknown becomes a desperate plea to relegate that knowledge to the subconscious recesses of his mind as he seeks to erase that horrifying sight from his consciousness. The revelation at the conclusion of the story is that the eyes of the subterranean creatures are not unlike the dissimilar eyes of the vanished Martense family that had dwelled in the deserted mansion on the mountain long ago. One eye was blue and the other brown. For the narrator, this revelation of the creatures as degenerated humans is "the embodiment of all the snarling chaos and grinning fear that lurk behind life" (CF 1.373). There is nothing more terrifying than to see oneself being seen. The creatures in this case are a perversion of the human ideal that is reflected in their all-too-familiar eyes.

In Lovecraft's "From Beyond," a scientist named Crawford Tillinghast creates a machine that allows him to access realms of consciousness beyond the physical plane of reality. Lovecraft's concept for this work stems from his thorough study of philosophy and science. "The philosophical interest of the tale is noteworthy, for it centres upon an issue of fundamental importance in all modern philosophical speculation since Descartes—the problem of knowledge. How do we know what we know?" (Joshi, "Sources for 'From Beyond'" 367). Like the narrator of "The Tell-Tale Heart," Tillinghast has delusions of godhood. When he proves to the narrator that his machine works and they see the beings that come from beyond, Tillinghast proclaims: "I have harnessed the shadows that stride from world to world to sow death and madness. . . . Space belongs to me, do you hear?" (CF 1.200). It was not supernatural discovery that Lovecraft's mad scientist sought but supernatural godhood and ultimate power over all creation seen and unseen. Once revealed, the unfamiliar does not contain revelation but the horror of truth that was formally and mercifully hidden from coherent perception. To see and know becomes a curse in these works, not a blessing.

The transformation of Tillinghast is described by the narrator: "His eyes were pits of flame, and they glared at me with what I now saw was overwhelming hatred" (CF 1.199). The mad scientist becomes bearer of the evil eye. This power of "new sight" is Tillinghast's obsession. He imposes his desire to see and know the secrets of existence upon the narrator: "You see them? You see them? You see the things that float and flop about you and through you every moment of your life? [. . .] Have I not succeeded in breaking down the barrier; have I not shewn you worlds that no other living men have seen? [. . .] *I want you to see them* [. . .] Look, look, curse you, look!" (CF 1.199–201) The imagery of the eye and of sight in this work reflects Tillinghast's desire to become all-seeing and all-knowing. The nature of this knowledge, however, is deadly: "Lovecraft, while certainly not deploring knowledge as such, is deploring the *misuse* of knowledge or the *effects*—often cataclysmic—that knowledge can have" (Joshi, "'Reality and Knowledge" 110). Tillinghast's ill-fated attempt to achieve omniscience reflects both the misuse of knowledge and the cataclysmic effect of this type of knowledge in the futile attempt to master the universe through mastering the self. Tillinghast is so consumed by his narcissistic obsession that he must possess everything, including the sensory experiences of other human beings as he implores the narrator to see what he wants him to see. The evil eye is the ultimate instrument of control, as it is how the ego dominates the universe through biased interpretation. This is merely the perception of universal control as another aspect of the conflict between true self and perceived self.

Ascending the Mountains of Madness

The structure of many of Poe's short stories involves a final, climactic scene that reveals how the narrator succumbs to the madness that he openly denies throughout the entire tale. This conclusion is equivalent to the death of the protagonist, who is left to endure utter defeat. The narrator's loss of self is embodied in the loss of his sanity. This interior struggle over the sanity of the mind becomes the primary source of self-conflict in these horror tales, as evidenced in Poe's works where the true antagonist is the subconscious self, a trend that is repeated in Lovecraft's tales of psychological horror.

The mind is labyrinthine, infinitely complex. It is this complexity that becomes the fatal flaw for many of Poe's narrators. Unaware of the recesses of their own identity, these narrators can no longer perceive their own emotions. Each becomes lost in the labyrinth of their minds, and this compartmentalization serves as a third motif of the fractured self. When their repressed feelings finally emerge, the narrators no longer recognize them as fundamental aspects of themselves. This is how one's conscience or guilt can become his worst enemy. The focal conflict in each of these stories, regardless of the external conflict, involves the narrator's confrontation with his estranged self. Picture a man chased by a mysterious figure in a maze of mirrors. There is no evading the horrifying visage that looms around every corner and meets his gaze at every turn. They are being pursued by an unknown aspect of themselves: their own reflection. The eye is the tool of knowing that is deceived by the reflection (the double), but it is the mind where self-horror proliferates into debilitating madness.

A most intriguing instance of psychological horror, "The Music of Erich Zann," involves a narrator who discovers a mysterious street in his travels called the Rue d'Auseil. He is entranced by the music that he hears from Erich Zann's apartment. The narrator soon finds himself obsessed with his desire to know the secrets of Erich Zann and his mysterious music. Before his apparent death, Zann scribbles something on a piece of paper that the narrator presumes to be the knowledge he desires. The transaction is interrupted by a gust of wind that carries the knowledge out of the narrator's reach. The narrator ultimately finds himself unable to return to Zann's apartment: "Despite my most careful searches and investigations, I have never since been able to find the Rue d'Auseil. But I am not wholly sorry; either for this or for the loss in undreamable abysses of the closely written sheets which alone could have explained the music of Erich Zann" (CF 1.290). This work directly references the relationship between the known and the unknown in how it centers upon the mystery of the secret and the relationship between the narrator and Zann. It is the representation of a fragmented mind and the will to attain awareness that is coupled with the psychological act of repression.

Carl Buchanan's "'The Music of Erich Zann:' A Psychological Interpretation (or Two)" is an essay that directly applies Freud's theory of "The Uncanny" to Lovecraft's intensely cerebral text: "The adventure of the speaker/narrator who visits Erich Zann's world is like a dream; a typical specimen, in fact, of an anxiety nightmare in which the dreamer is led by an agent to a repressed memory from which the speaker recoils—his own memory, of course, for the things that scare us most lie hidden behind curtained windows in ourselves" (224). The dreamlike atmosphere of "The Music of Erich Zann" is an essential aspect of the tale. The setting becomes a space where the unfamiliar and the familiar converge and intersect. Zann becomes the agent that assists in the narrator's journey into this realm of dreams.

The narrator is intrigued by the music, but he does not recognize it. Buchanan suggests that in this dream space the music takes on a figurative meaning: "It is not, of course, music as we know it, but a symbolic language expressing (and concealing) the secret hidden by Zann. Zann's room, cobwebbed and meager, seems more deserted than inhabited, as befits a rarely visited chamber of memory" (224-25). This language that both expresses and conceals refers to a form of uncanny communication where meaning is both familiar and unfamiliar. It is familiar in that it refers to a point in one's past that is a fundamental aspect of his being identified as Freud's notion of infantile experience. It is simultaneously unfamiliar as the object of repression. As this is a dream world, no meaning can be overtly direct or easily accessed.

In this realm of symbols and hidden meaning, Zann represents a King of Sleep, as indicated by Buchanan:

> Zann himself is transparently the Sandman, or King of Sleep ("Erich" means king), for Zand is Dutch for sand, as Freud points out in his essay on "The Uncanny." This essay, published two years before "Zann," has this definition of the unheimliche (uncanny): "[it is] the name of everything that ought to have remained secret and hidden but has come to light." (225)

This insightful application of Freud's essay reveals Lovecraft's extensive use of symbolism and an apparently conscious application, according to Buchanan, of Freudian theory in one of Lovecraft's works of fiction. The narrator comes into conflict with this "King of Sleep," however, in his inability to communicate with him: "Zann's muteness accompanies musical virtuosity, since his language is not verbal but pre-verbal, direct as is the language of dreams, for the truth must be told, albeit in symbolic guise" (Buchanan 225). In Freudian fashion, the true self that can access forbidden memory is that which exists in a mind liberated from ego, as is the case for the mind when it is in a dream state. Zann inhabits the narrator's edificial dream world and becomes an aspect of true but forbidden self for the narrator.

The music represents a form of uncanny communication, but it is nearly impossible for the narrator to translate as he is detached from his own subconscious. This lack of awareness is common for uncanny protagonists, who are typically incapable of introspection. Likewise, the narrator also exhibits a desire to seek out the unknown and bring it to the surface and make it known: "his curiosity, or we would say, the need to overcome his repression and regain the lost part of himself, makes the student climb the 'last creaking staircase to the peaked garret'" (Buchanan 225). By ascending in this house that is representative of a mind subdivided into floors and rooms, the narrator exhibits the will to know the secret recesses of his mind.

According to Buchanan, the disparity between the "inside" and the "outside" of the home is indicative of the conflict between the familiar or conscious self and the unfamiliar or subconscious self. As the narrator's desire to know the secret of the music within the home heightens, so too does the strength of the mighty wind that pummels the exterior of the building. The narrator's presence with Zann in the interior becomes a means of escaping the storm through the shelter of the conscious mind, though the music stirs the narrator's desire to reconcile the unknown with the known: "Outside is the unconscious: limitless space, like oceans, represents the black or underside of the mind. The sight itself is too horrible to recall; the memory must remain hidden and the narrator flees from it" (Buchanan 226). The conclusion, however, must result in the failure of the protagonist:

> When he awakens, the 'hero's' key to the site is lost, although the maddening music will continue to haunt him, reminding him of something perhaps better forgotten. The papers with their revelation must be lost, as the old man must 'die' and the location of the very street must be suppressed, as is the too-horrible scene. The student's mind remains at war within itself, but that is not an unusual condition. (Buchanan 227)

The narrator fails to realize that to know Zann's secret would mean to know his unadulterated self for the first time. The war within the self is not an unusual condition because it is at the core of uncanny literature, centered on the notion that the true self cannot be known and that the attempt of doing so leads only to self-destruction or madness in the sight of indescribable abominations that affront the limited faculties of simple-minded human beings incapable of knowing who *they* are, let alone beings who exist beyond the boundaries of space and time.

Lovecraft's "The Music of Erich Zann" becomes a psychological allegory on par with Poe's "The Fall of the House of Usher." It is "a tale of psychological terror as well as fantasy, and a reasonable interpretation that satisfies and should enhance Lovecraft's literary reputation: it properly belongs beside 'A Cask of Amontillado' or 'The Tell-Tale Heart' as a superbly wrought extended metaphor of the repression of guilt and its attendant horrors" (Buchanan 228). The quality of Lovecraft's prose stems not from his personal conception of cosmic horror as a tale where the mind experiences the supernatural and attempts to endure the onslaught of senses that are beyond limited human faculties, but from the uncanny truth of the terrifying unknowns that exist within the human subconscious.

Fear Himself

Lovecraft's "The Call of Cthulhu," opens with the statement that "The most merciful thing in the world, I think, is the inability of the human mind to correlate all its contents. We live on a placid island of ignorance in the midst of black seas of infinity, and it was not meant that we should voyage far" (CF 2.21). The complexity of the human mind is explored by works of uncanny horror that bridge the gap between general conceptions of the self and psychological revelation. As Poe was a successor to Hoffmann in his development of the uncanny into a horror of the self, so too did Lovecraft further Poe's psychology of fear. These are works that illustrate the deepest and most internalized fears of a human being, which stem from the friction between the conscious self and the subconscious self. The true source of fear in these works is that of human ignorance: man can never truly know himself. These works illustrate the futile endeavor of the attempt to achieve self-awareness that results in fear and hatred of an identity in relation to itself. What Lovecraft calls "cosmic horror" may be more appropriately classified as "self-horror."

Works Cited

Buchanan, Carl. "'The Music of Erich Zann:' A Psychological Interpretation (or Two)." In *A Century Less a Dream: Selected Criticism on H. P. Lovecraft*, ed. Scott Connors. Holicong, PA: Wildside Press, 2002. 224–29.

Burleson, Donald R. *H. P. Lovecraft: A Critical Study*. Westport, CT: Greenwood Press, 1983.

Folks, Jeffrey. "Poe and the *Cogito*." *Southern Literary Journal* 42 (2009): 57–72.

Freud, Sigmund. *The Uncanny*. Tr. David McLintock. New York: Penguin, 2003.

Joshi, S. T. "'Reality' and Knowledge: Some Notes on the Aesthetic Thought of H. P. Lovecraft." In *Lovecraft and a World in Transition: Collected Essays on H. P. Lovecraft*. New York: Hippocampus Press, 2014. 105–14.

———. *The Rise and Fall of the Cthulhu Mythos*. Poplar Bluff, MO: Mythos Books, 2008.

———. "The Sources for 'From Beyond.'" In *Lovecraft and a World in Transition: Collected Essays on H. P. Lovecraft*. New York: Hippocampus Press, 2014. 367–71.

Ki, Magdalen Wing-Chi. "Ego-Evil and 'The Tell-Tale Heart.'" *Renascence* 61 (2008): 25–38.

Lacan, Jaques. *Seminars of Jacques Lacan: The Four Fundamental Concepts of Psychoanalysis.* New York: W. W. Norton, 1998.

Poe, Edgar Allan. *Poetry, Tales, and Selected Essays.* New York: Library of America, 1996.

Robinson, E. Arthur. "Poe's 'The Tell-Tale Heart.'" *Nineteenth-Century Fiction* 19 (1965): 369–78.

"A Stalking Monster": The Influence of Radiation Poisoning on H. P. Lovecraft's "The Colour out of Space"

Andy Troy
Independent Scholar

In the years following the publication of H. P. Lovecraft's 1927 short story "The Colour out of Space," especially after World War II's destructive and momentous atomic bombs dropped on Hiroshima and Nagasaki, armchair reviewers have noted the similarities between the alien creature's decaying influence and the rapid deterioration of high-dose radiation poisoning.

This comparison was made as early as 1945, the very year of the bombings, when Edmund Wilson, one of Lovecraft's first, and fiercest, posthumous critics, wrote that "the story called 'The Colour out of Space' more or less predicts the effects of the atom bomb" (Wilson 49). The sentiment that Lovecraft somehow "prophesied" atomic warfare is now so widespread that it is featured on the back jacket copy of the Ballantine/Del Rey edition, which states that "a horror from the skies—far worse than any nuclear fallout—transforms a man into a monster" (*Best of H. P. Lovecraft*). But the reader should not, in modern hindsight, dismiss the scientific elements of "The Colour out of Space" as merely coincidental or arbitrary.[1]

---

1. Consider the incorrect assertions of online posts found on the Chronicles Network forums, the H. P. Lovecraft Literary Podcast forums, and Grim Reviews as a few informal examples. I, Brian [Brian G. Turner], "Colour out of Space," *Science Fiction Fantasy Chronicles*, 21 April 2004, http://www.sffchronicles.co.uk/forum/1806-colour-out-of-space.html; Talleyrand, 13 November 2010 (10:42 a.m.), comment on Genus Unknown, "Episode 59—The Colour out of Space—Part 1," *H. P. Lovecraft Literary Podcast Forums*, November 11, 2010, http://hppodcraft.com/forums/index.php?topic=471.0; and Grim Blogger, "H. P. Lovecraft: Prophet of the Nuclear Age?," *Grim Reviews* (blog), 27 March 2011, http://grimreviews.blogspot.com/2011/03/hp-lovecraft-prophet-of-nuclear-age.html.

I contend that Lovecraft purposefully syncretized various scientific disciplines—chiefly chemistry, biology, and anatomy—into a fictional study of radiation poisoning that preceded formal recognition by several months, and widespread admission of its danger by years. While Lovecraft did not entirely break new ground in the field, he does seem to be the first writer, in "Colour," to correlate several different branches of radiation studies into a cohesive whole. Scientifically speaking, the extraterrestrial Colour (as I shall hereafter refer to it) is portrayed in the story as a wholly alien force, unfathomable to the "wise men" (597) from Miskatonic University. Whether in its initial stage as a meteorite on Nahum Gardner's farm or its later form of a sentient gas, the Colour is deliberately written to confound our understanding of natural laws. Steven J. Mariconda asserts in "The Subversion of Sense in 'The Colour out of Space'" that the power of the story comes from its "subtle contradictions" (20). Lovecraft's use of science serves to reinforce this point, with the scientists attempting to classify the Colour as it contradicts them at every turn. But a careful reading of "The Colour out of Space," in comparison to scientific texts of the day, demonstrates that a radioactive substance, and the subsequent havoc it would wreak on the environment and the organisms on the Gardner farm, provides the only solution to the identity of the Colour.

In this article I will show the different ways in which Lovecraft incorporated contemporary scientific research into the narrative of "The Colour out of Space," especially as it relates to radiation studies. With differing schools of thought existing on the topic in Lovecraft's time, the story presents a multifaceted view of radiation: as a popular and scientific curiosity; as a boon, or at times a detriment, to manufacture; and finally as a dire threat to human health and safety. Most important to this latter issue is the so-called Radium Girls scandal of the 1920s, when the industrial dangers of radium, "discovered" in the bodies of dialpainters in New Jersey, became central to the discussion of radioactivity's place in society, and in "Colour" as well. Through the lens of the Radium Girls, it is evident that "The Colour out of Space" is actually, thematically speaking, a story about industrial radiation poisoning.

Scholars have pointed to various weird tales, including *The Terror* and "Novel of the White Powder," both by Arthur Machen, "The Damned Thing" by Ambrose Bierce, and "The Willows" by Algernon Blackwood, as possible inspirations for the Colour. But although these stories detail mysterious countryside attacks, a wasting disease caused by poison, inexplicable color properties, and eerie trees, respectively, they are unsatisfactory at explaining Lovecraft's creation of a true alien. It is unlikely that he simply mashed together elements of his favorite stories, as evidenced by his carefully constructed atmosphere and verisimilitude in other areas of "Colour." The stories listed above all have a common element: their horrific antagonists are all given motives (however otherworldly) and clear-cut characteristics, neither of which can be said about the Colour. So *just what is the Colour?*

Despite all the laboratory activity and chemical jargon on the part of the scientists in the story, there is one notable property that Lovecraft seems to have deliberately omitted: radioactivity. By March 1927, much scientific study had been done on radioactive elements, from their early discovery and classification to their rapid exposure and exploitation by various industries. Prior to Hermann Joseph Muller's July 1927 paper on genetic mutations caused by radiation, there was no widespread recognition in the scientific community of possible permanent damage from exposure to such materials. And yet there was, ever since the Curies' initial research, clear evidence of damage both large and small to living things. Early experiments in the 1890s by Curie, Becquerel, and Rutherford were instigated by the excitement of a new scientific field with possible health and energy benefits. In his book *Deadly Sunshine,* David Harvie states that "the possibility that radium might have therapeutic benefits similar to those of X-rays was intriguing, and a number of the Curies' colleagues encouraged them in that thinking. However, they also knew that radium salts in close skin contact produced discolouring, and sometimes blisters similar to burns, and that if the exposure was extended, ulceration occurred" (50). Much like Nahum Gardner, early radium researchers were able to "connect events," and yet continued their dangerous experiments regardless. There was also, as Harvie notes, an ongoing public debate about the validity and safety of radium; "the idea caught hold in the public's imagination that a single radioactive atom would inevitably make adjacent atoms radioactive, initiating an unstoppable global chain reaction [. . .] The 'Rays of Life' faction celebrated the seemingly magical benefits; and the 'Death Ray' brigade characterized the mystery 'energies' as inevitably malevolent" (Harvie 57). We shall see how Lovecraft uses this real-world dichotomy—knowledge of danger versus acting on that knowledge—to ironic effect later, as it becomes clear that his inspiration draws from the broad history of radiation studies.

There is a distinct link between the graying, brittle sickness caused by the Colour and the real effects of radiation burns. These mutations are most noticeable in the Gardners' cows and swine, since they are closely fed, watched, and guarded. When the pigs grow "inordinately fat, then suddenly [begin] to undergo loathsome changes which no one could explain" (604), Lovecraft draws to the fore of the story the logical dilemma of the Colour's nature. Earlier, the "men of science" (598) were baffled by chemical properties they found unexplainable. Now, the common farmers are confronted by this same problem on another level. When the cow's milk begins "to be bad" (602), Nahum moves them upland, which seems to solve the problem temporarily. But although they are protected from the poisoned soil, all the livestock become affected nevertheless. Lovecraft describes it thus: "It was very inexplicable, for they had never been fed from the tainted vegetation [. . .] There could be no question of poison, for all the cases occurred in a locked and undisturbed barn. No bites of prowling things could have brought the virus, for *what live beast of earth can pass through solid obstacles*" (604; emphasis added). Here all the possible solutions are brought to light, and they are found wanting. The spoiled vegetables cannot be killing the animals, nor can it be a deliberate chemical sabotage. A germ or virus is briefly considered, but even the Gardners realize that a vector is needed for such an infection. Again, the unspoken agent of destruction is here the correct solution: waves of radiation can penetrate solid substances, just as X-rays are used for medical purposes.

Since the experiments of Becquerel and Rutherford at the turn of the century, the penetrative properties of radiation were well known in science books and popular journals. There is even a prominent article, salaciously titled "Are Modern X-Rays a Public Danger?" in the October 1921 issue of *Popular Science* addressing the penetrative ability of radiation. The author, the French radiologist Gaston Contremoulins, warns of the dangers of "radiodermatitis" on patients, practitioners, and even bystanders near radioactive elements. He describes this condition as "a skin lesion [. . .] caused by the skin absorbing a large quantity of radiations" (29). Furthermore, Contremoulins notes a second, chronic effect that occurs "deep beneath the skin upon the active cells that are the most vulnerable. It is principally the internal secretion glands that are affected. Among those who continually receive even weak doses, a gradual lessening of vitality takes place, leading slowly to a physiological impoverishment that inevitably carries them off sooner or later" (29). I shall return to this loss of vitality later, but it suffices to demonstrate that Lovecraft was familiar with the penetrative abilities of radiation. The animals in "Colour" undergo similar, if fictionally exaggerated, stages of living decay. Before the aforementioned grey brittleness sets in, the swine are noticed to be "falling to pieces" as they die, with their faces showing signs of "singular alterations" (604). This poisoning affects the cows similarly; Lovecraft writes that "certain areas or sometimes the whole body would be uncannily shrivelled or compressed, and atrocious collapses or disintegrations were common" (604). These mysterious wounds are nearly identical in description to Contremoulin's "lesions," and analogous injuries on the Gardner family's bodies are even more closely tied to the realities of industrial disease. It is in the human aspect of "Colour" that Lovecraft most deftly, and most clearly, relates the horror story of radiation poisoning.

The most prominent radioactive incident of the 1920s had a vast impact on both perceptions of the safety of radium and industrial exposure to it. From 1917 to 1926, the U.S. Radium Corporation, based in Orange, New Jersey, used a radium-based self-luminescent paint for watch dials (branded as "Undark" in print advertisements). This manufacture employed working-class women to brush the radioactive paint onto watch numbers; in the process, their skin and clothes became coated with radium dust, but, most importantly, the women pointed their brush tips *using their lips*, and ingested a large amount of the paint. Most, if not all, of the workers developed anemia, fragile and broken bones, and necrosis of the jaw; an unknown number died of directly related causes. Claudia Clark's book *Radium Girls* is the chief resource for this unfortunate history as it unfolded, and the combination of time, place, and circumstance surrounding the Radium Girls scandal was unequivocally a primary source for the radiation poisoning in "The Colour out of Space."

As has been mentioned earlier, there was a startling disconnect in the 1920s between the scientifically recognized dangers of radiation exposure and its continued practical and popular use. A study by Thomas Ordway from a 1916 *Scientific American* (a periodical Lovecraft is known to have read and corresponded with, at least circa 1906; see Joshi 120) warns of "changes in the fingers of radiologists in London, Vienna, and Germany. The skin grew thick, 'horny' and the nails brittle; fingers became numb or painful, clumsy, and sensitive to heat and pressure" (quoted in Clark 59). There is a great deal of emphasis to be placed on the word "brittle," as we note the explicit connections between the Radium Girls history and the disintegration of the Gardner family. These connections are not just a source of inspiration but indeed the third underlying *theme* of "The Colour out of Space," aside from Lovecraft's stated intentions of creating an atmospheric study and a truly alien life-form. The hidden story of "Colour" is that of industrial radiation poisoning.

The only impediment, before we continue, is to ask how Lovecraft would have known of the Radium Girls scandal. For one, he was living in Brooklyn from 1924 to 1926, when the stories of ill and dying dial-painters were first hitting newsstands in the *New York Times* and the *Providence Evening Bulletin*. Lovecraft is known to have read the former while in New York—he searched the classified ads every Sunday for employment (Joshi 507-8) and found travel destinations in its editorial pages (Joshi 524)—and he maintained a subscription to the latter for many years (Joshi 619). The *Bulletin* ran the article "Five Deaths Laid to Radium Poison" on Monday, 22 June 1925, which gives the basics of the dial-painting case, including the term "radium necrosis" and the theory that the poison entered the girls' systems through the practice of lip-pointing. There is even, unique to this article, a wager by the factory's owner, William Bailey, that he will ingest "in one dose all the radium that is used on all the watch dials produced at any one plant in a month." This ludicrously high dose of acute radium poisoning was clearly never followed through on, although its effect may be felt in the climax of "Colour." The remainder of the pertinent articles I shall consult are from the *New York Times*, which, although Lovecraft seems to have preferred the more conservative *Bulletin*, was still a timely source of scientific news for him; on Friday, 14 March 1930, for example, it included the first notice of the discovery of Pluto, which led to the planet's inclusion in "The Whisperer in Darkness" (Joshi 761).

Lovecraft also took several trips to New Jersey during his residence in Brooklyn, where he was alternately inspired and depressed by the sights he found there. He took at least four overnight walks through the antiquarian destination of Elizabeth, starting in October 1924 (Joshi 596). These sojourns took him remarkably close to the site of the U.S. Radium dialpainting factory in East Orange; Elizabeth is only ten miles distant, while Springfield, part of another all-night tour that August (Joshi 604-5), is a scant three miles away. In fact, on 30 August 1925, Lovecraft noted the presence of Paterson's "hideous factory section" (quoted in Joshi 605) across the river (presumably the Passaic), the same industrial sprawl that extended south to Orange's chemical plants. Furthermore, Joshi explicitly links Lovecraft's experience of the New Jersey landscape with the story's "west of Arkham" atmosphere, specifically his trip through the Palisades to Buttermilk Falls that same August (Joshi 672). Thus, Lovecraft was familiar with the manufacturing areas of New Jersey and would have recognized them as the same sites of the radiation poisoning headlines earlier that year.

It would have been simple for Lovecraft to write the Colour as a malevolent alien entity intent on destroying humanity. In doing otherwise, he not only deepens the mystery of the creature's nature but also the cosmic tragedy at the center of the story. The Gardners are innocent victims of an alien feeding, but they are especially tragic because there is no clear *reason* for its occurrence. This sentiment is directly connected to, and inspired by, the events surrounding the dialpainting factory in New Jersey. Although decades of hindsight have allowed historians to view the U.S. Radium Corporation as the "villains" of the Radium Girls story, contemporary media at first portrayed U.S. Radium as cooperating with investigations and being equally confounded as to what could be causing its workers' illnesses. For the first few years of the scandal, Clark argues, "no person or institution was villainous, evil—just the inanimate element radium" (130). The victims, young women often with strong family ties, "were seen as particularly innocent and undeserving" (Clark 130) of their fates. This quirk of the Radium Girls reportage—the media's strategy of soliciting sympathy through innocence and high tragedy—is a key thematic element in "The Colour out of Space" as well. Consider Clark's assessment of the "tragic" element of the Radium Girls scandal:

> "Fate" implied that no one was at fault. With fate the culprit, there was no one and nothing at which to be angry. This raised another issue. The "sob stories" in the press presented the women as innocent victims of a horrible fate, but this emphasis on fate avoided placing blame at anyone's door—for instance, linking the dialpainters' suffering with decisions made by their employer. Radium was a stalking monster. (Clark 130)

This emphasis on a lurking predator—and the fatalistic attitude toward its predations—can be seen explicitly in Lovecraft's narrative. As the Gardner family continues to degrade, there can be seen "something of stolid resignation about them all, as if they walked half in another world between lines of nameless guards to a certain and familiar doom" (604). And even more of a link than this surreal imagery can be found several pages later, as Nahum raves to Ammi Pierce that "something was creeping and creeping and waiting to be seen and felt and heard [. . .] It must all be a judgment of some sort; though he could not fancy what for, since he had always walked uprightly in the Lord's ways so far as he knew" (606). There has never been in Lovecraft's work a more undeserving "fate" than that which befalls the Gardner family, and it is in direct correlation to the media's sentimental treatment of the Radium Girls and their plight.

This kind of narrative compassion, even *pity*, is a rarity in Lovecraft's cosmic works. But the utter *dissolution* of self in "Colour" is influenced by the Radium Girls scandal, as it affected the victims socially, mentally, and bodily. Claudia Clark writes of the breadth of "the tragedy of their victimization" (131) in media publicity in two important ways. Firstly, as women, wives, and mothers, the dial-painters were considered "particularly pathetic figures" (132) in the sensationalist journals, as they were often rendered "unfit to marry or to bear children" (130) by the poisoning. The second way in which contemporary journalism spun the Radium Girls story was graphically, through an early form of body horror. Because the symptoms of radiation poisoning were similar to other industrial diseases, this allowed newspapers to expound on the finer details of the victims' suffering. Although the earliest accounts of May 1925 only report Dr. Frederick Hoffman's presentation to the American Medical Association ("New Radium Disease"), by June the *New York Times* had moved on to graphic narratives of the girl's treatment. "When a tooth was pulled it was found that the gum would not heal and necrosis of the edge of the jawbone developed" ("New Radium Disease"), the 20 June 1925 article says of one victim's visit to a dentist. It continues by itemizing the victims and their ailments. Such meticulous accounts continue throughout the Radium Girls saga in the *New York Times*.[2] Clark's astute assessment of the "themes" of the Radium Girls story, such as they are for a non-fictitious occurrence, is striking in its accuracy to "The Colour out of Space," as follows: "Like a horror story, the dialpainters' narrative began with innocent young women who were unknowingly stalked by an invisible, heartless enemy. At moments of their greatest happiness, newly married, newly with child, the women were struck down. Their disease had no known cure and meant certain death" (133). These two components of the Radium Girls

---

2. See "Plans to Safeguard Radium Handlers"; "Radium and Gas as Death Cause Open New Issue."

legend, as it quickly became in the American imagination, are firmly enmeshed in Lovecraft's thematic treatment of the Gardners in "Colour."

The mental ailments suffered by the dial-painters and other industrial workers form another link to the Gardner family; the Gardners' symptoms function either as direct corollaries to the 1925-26 reports of radiation poisoning or symptoms of earlier recognized industrial diseases. The first hint of the Colour's influence on the Gardners is an idiopathic "reserve or melancholy" among them, contributing to "poorer health and a feeling of vague disquiet" (Clark 61). This malaise continues for weeks of "moments when consciousness seemed half to slip away" (Clark 63). One of the earliest, and most predominant, symptoms of radiation poisoning in Lovecraft's day was malaise and anemia, as he would have read in the 20 June 1925 issue of the *New York Times*. It details the death of the dial-painter Sarah Maillefer, which was ruled by Dr. Harrison Martland, a central figure in the Radium Girls saga,[3] as "pernicious anemia." In the same article, several other girls are listed with their cause of death as "anemia." These symptoms are listed even more explicitly three days later in the *Times* article "Plans to Safeguard Radium Handlers." A former founder of U.S. Radium Corporation, Dr. Sabin von Sochocky, admits to the gamut of maladies that were attributed to working with radium, including "a rheumatic condition, anemia, debility, a condition similar to pyorrhea and malaise." This malaise, already familiar to researchers like Contremoulins, was not unique to radiation poisoning. One of the many reasons it was failed to be recognized as a distinct, separate industrial disease for years was its similarity to earlier maladies. Claudia Clark points to phosphorus poisoning as the first suspected culprit in the New Jersey factory, with its three major components being anemia, brittle bones (again we see terms familiar from "Colour") and "phossy jaw, whereby phosphorus fumes attacked the gums in mouths with carious teeth; symptoms included tooth loss, gum swelling, necrosis (decay) of the jaw bone, facial disfiguration, and terrible pain" (Clark 18). The 20 June 1925 *Times* article explicitly mentions this ailment, when Dr. Frederick Hoffman states that "'these women developed what at first closely resembled phosphorus necrosis.'" It is also important that the theory given in the article bears a striking re-

---

3. Claudia Clark argues against Martland's importance to the "discovery" of radiation poisoning, but that is a matter for industrial historians to contend.

semblance to the effects of the Colour, in that "there is a slow accumulation of poison in the organs, *which at first stimulates* until it reaches a point where a rapid physical breakdown results" (my emphasis). Despite this early attempt at an etiology, radiation remained, like the Colour itself, an unexplainable killer.

The other major industrial hazard of the time, which also seems to exert an influence on the nature of the Colour, is mercury poisoning. Clark outlines the malady's main symptoms as "malaise, depression, headaches, nervousness, insomnia, loss of appetite, loose teeth and ulcerated gums, sometimes a slight anemia. [. . .] Melancholia is common, as are other psychological symptoms such as loss of memory or hallucination" (19). Here is a clearer outline of the origin of the troubling psychological effect the Colour has on the Gardner family. Nabby Gardner, especially, is mentally transformed by its influence, with "the poor woman scream[ing] about things in the air which she could not describe. [. . .] Things moved and changed and fluttered, and ears tingled to impulses which were not wholly sounds" (CF 2.380). Within a month (note the time-lapse, implying a chronic exposure), Mrs. Gardner has "ceased to speak and crawl[s] on all fours, and before that month was over Nahum got the mad notion that she was slightly luminous in the dark" (CF 2.380). There can be little doubt that this passage reads not only as a semi-autobiographical account of Lovecraft's mother's illness—who hallucinated that "weird and fantastic creatures [. . .] rushed out from behind buildings and from corners at dark" (Clara Hess, cited in Joshi 301)—but also as a poignant depiction of a victim of mercury poisoning. This likely also draws from a striking article which appeared in the *Providence Evening Bulletin*, on the same day as the "Five Deaths Laid to Radium Poison" piece, about a disturbing incident of industrial lead poisoning. Eight workers died at a leaded gasoline factory, with the gruesome detail noted that their first symptom of exposure was "a hallucination of winged insects, and employees of the plant have dubbed it 'the House of the Butterflies' [. . .] The person affected is said to pause at his work and, gazing intently into space, to snatch at something not there" ("Eight Said to Have Died in Lead Plant"). This not only hearkens to Nabby Gardner's unsettling visions, but also to her taciturn son Zenas, who will "do nothing but stare into space" (CF 2.383). The Gardners' malaise and hallucinations eventually turn into a mercuric loss of appetite as they eat "their meagre and ill-cooked meals and [do] their thankless and monotonous chores through the aimless days" (CF 2.381).

When Ammi braves a visit to the Gardner farmhouse, we finally witness the bodily disintegrations caused by the Colour, namely those of Nabby and Nahum. Their two deaths are the climax of the tale and they represent Lovecraft's final restatement of the terrifying effects of radiation poisoning. We have already been told of the transformation of the livestock into gray, brittle things, but to see it happening to humans adds an extra dimension of horror, just as the Radium Girls scandal brought to the public mind the hitherto laboratory-bound dangers of radium. That the "blasphemous monstrosity" in the attic, as Ammi terms the decaying and almost-dead Nabby, "very slowly and perceptibly move[s] as it continue[s] to crumble" (CF 2.385) is a masterstroke on Lovecraft's part. Rather than a swift monster or an inanimate corpse, Nabby lingers miserably between life and death, waiting to die in the same way the "doomed" dial-painters lived out their remaining years. After dispatching of Nabby, Ammi is faced with the nightmare of his friend Nahum disintegrating before his eyes. It is here that we are finally given an explicit, graphic description of the Colour's ravaging of a human body:

> Whether it had crawled or whether it had been dragged by any external force, Ammi could not say; but the death had been at it. Everything had happened in the last half-hour, but collapse, greying, and disintegration were already far advanced. There was a horrible brittleness, and dry fragments were scaling off. Ammi could not touch it, but looked horrifiedly into the distorted parody that had been a face. "What was it, Nahum—what was it?" he whispered, and the cleft, bulging lips were just able to crackle out a final answer. (CF 2.387)

This passage is the ultimate rendition of the Radium Girls scenario, with each and every detail of Nahum's death corresponding to earlier symptoms of radiation poisoning noted by Contremoulins (the greying and split skin), *Scientific American* (the brittleness and scaling), and the deaths of the dialpainters themselves. It is especially important to notice the "bulging lips" as being nearly identical to the trademark Radium Girls symptom, an abscessed jaw. Lovecraft reiterates this explicitly when, after Nahum gives his dying words, the body part of Nahum "which spoke could speak no more because it had completely caved in" (CF 2.388). Here Lovecraft does not write about a collapsed hand reaching out for Ammi, or eyeballs falling from their sockets, perhaps. That Nahum's *jawbone* caves in is confirmation of radium necrosis; every symptom that has preceded his decaying demise in "Colour" has not been a coincidence or a tidied-up hodgepodge of scientific grotesqueries. Nearly *every* victim of industrial radiation poisoning in the 1920s had necrosis of the jaw as their primary, and most visible, symptom, brought on by radium accumulating in the jawbone and causing infection and bone decay.

It is also significant that Lovecraft distinguishes here between chronic exposure to the Colour's influence (in Nabby's case) and the acutely high dose of alien radiation that Nahum receives, since all the symptoms that ravage the latter occur "in the last half-hour" of his life. In the story's denouement, after Ammi retrieves help from Arkham, Lovecraft again makes the distinction between chronic and acute exposure to radiation. Ammi's momentary encounter with the Colour in the attic is contrasted with its amplified form shining from the well, as follows:

> Ammi had restrained the driver on impulse, forgetting how uninjured he himself was after the clammy brushing of that coloured vapour in the attic room, but perhaps it is just as well that he acted as he did. No one will ever know what was abroad that night; and though the blasphemy from beyond *had not so far hurt any human of unweakened mind*, there is no telling what it might not have done at that last moment. (CF 2.392; my emphasis)

Thus the Colour first weakens the mind of its victims (just as the earlier-mentioned industrial diseases initially manifest themselves in psychological symptoms) before preying on their bodies. The final characteristic that Lovecraft gives the Colour is its ability to linger in the earth of the Gardner farm, even after the main "body" of the thing has sped off into the cosmos. Witnessing what no others do, Ammi sees "something feebly rise, only to sink down again" and knows that "this last faint remnant must still lurk down there in the well" (CF 2.397). This remnant is, of course, representative of the rate of decay, or half-life, of all radioactive elements including radium. The scientists investigating the dial-painters' deaths knew of this property, attributing jaw necrosis to the emission of "alpha particles from radium's radioactive decay" (Clark 98) in the bone. The public was also well aware of radium's decay producing radon gas—the radioactive ingredient in all "radium water" solutions. Thus this notion, that the Colour's taint might remain long after its physical disappearance, is not a fluke but another subtle tweaking of actual scientific fact.

Using all these points, Ammi, and, by extension, the narrator, is able to work out what amounts to a functioning etiology of the Colour's corruptive influence. By further extrapolation, this shows how Lovecraft himself synthesized radiation poisoning in a single story. Though Ammi attributes the alien being's radioactivity to it being "some'at from beyond"—and he repeats this phrase twice more, calling it "the blasphemy from beyond" and later muttering that "it come from beyond" (CF 2.394)[4]—it is clear that, although the being itself remains insubstantial and incomprehensible, its *effects* can be understood through the application of contemporary scientific study. By stripping away the obvious labels of "radioactivity," "necrosis," etc., Lovecraft obfuscates the Colour's true nature; it is not completely "from beyond" as Ammi would believe, but somewhat within the scope of current science. This is not to say that radioactivity accounts for every aspect of the Colour's being. Even as Lovecraft allows us to begin to understand the results of the creature's presence near Arkham, there are no clues in "The Colour out of Space" as to its origins, its intent, or its biology. The notion that the alien being is radioactive does not lessen its mystery or its cosmic threat; it instead deepens our understanding of the dangers of its ominous arrival, and persistent remaining, on Earth.

The depictions of corruption and death so rampant in "The Colour out of Space," having been influenced by Lovecraft's views on contemporary occupational diseases, imply that there is something inherently wrong or unnatural about these maladies. Indeed, because many of their symptoms mirror Lovecraft's own family experiences with sickness—his father's syphilitic paresis, his mother's hysteria and hallucinations, and his own bouts of weakness and melancholy—these accounts, especially the Radium Girls scandal, may have had a personal effect on him. The newspaper coverage of the dialpainters' stories was intentionally manipulated to make radium the "stalking monster" rather than the corporate powers who wielded it, and Lovecraft's formulation of a literal radiation monster is a direct response to this interpretation. The Colour's inexplicable nature, as well as its permanent threat to Earth, is proof that Lovecraft was not merely mimicking the media's portrayal of radiation poisoning, but escalating it to apocalyptic proportions. There is in this way a hint of satire to "The

---

4. This drives home Joshi's argument for a likely predecessor to "Colour" in Lovecraft's oeuvre, namely the story "From Beyond." See S. T. Joshi, "The Sources for 'From Beyond'" (*Crypt of Cthulhu*, Eastertide 1986), in *Lovecraft and a World in Transition* (New York: Hippocampus Press, 2014), 367–71.

Colour out of Space," which is at once a mockery of the concept of radium as a "death ray" and a horrifying realization of that same notion.

Lovecraft intended to highlight the hypocrisy of the public's view of radiation, the silly but dangerous belief that irradiated water, fertilizer, and medical nostrums were actually beneficial when used correctly, despite the overwhelming contrary evidence of decades. Scientists of Lovecraft's day were, in fact, either willfully ignoring radiation's harmful properties or were too busy touting it as a curative to notice. The general public, as well as regulatory and government agencies, also took little heed of what few serious warnings came from the scientific community. As far back as 1910, there were prominent front-page newspaper articles in the *Times*, cautioning that "clinical workers with radium may ultimately find that instead of curing what they think is cancer, they have succeeded in producing cancer" ("Danger in Using Radium"). Even the same *week* that the supposedly unexpected and shocking Radium Girls story came to light in the *Times*, the *Providence Evening Bulletin* ran the headline that "Radium Is Expected to Turn on Thieves." Police staked out emergency rooms for a group of crooks in possession of radium, as they knew "the radium would prove the undoing of the thieves, because of its powerful rays which have fatally burned many scientists experimenting with it." Bizarrely, there is no such glib acknowledgment of the extreme danger of radiation in other media, or at previous times. If radium was supposedly well-known for its fatal properties, that did not stop it from being regularly prescribed by physicians. And amidst these intermittent warnings against radioactivity, the American Medical Association's Council on Pharmacy and Chemistry astonishingly set not a maximum, but a *minimum* allowable emanation dosage for curatives containing radium.

It is these contradictions that Lovecraft exploits to dramatic, and even horrifying, effect in "The Colour out of Space." Realistically, any modern chemist given a list of the meteorite's strange properties—its "very marked" self-luminosity, its "affinity for silicon" (CF 2.372) and ability to melt glass containers, its slow evaporation in atmosphere—should be able to identify it as some type of pure radioactive element. The men of science in "Colour" are befuddled by it not out of narrative expediency but precisely because scientists *of Lovecraft's day* were undecided, or at odds, as to what comprised radioactivity. So it is with the Gardner family; their reluctance or refusal to leave the homestead is not out of some maudlin sentimentality or, worse, the horror-story cliché of the conveniently ignorant victims.

They are unaware of the Colour's terrible threat because the common public was also blind to the dangers of radium. Hapless contemporary pastimes included attending "Radium Dance" performances, where glowing radioactive salts were sprinkled in the air; using radium douches, enemas, and intravenous solutions; and indeed consuming "anything with radium on the label [. . .] whether it was Radium healing balm, Radium spot remover or Radium beer" (Frame and Kolb 3). Compared to such absurdly hazardous activities, the Gardner family eating their "meagre meals" and using a "tainted supply" of water seems mild and almost reasonable.

The thematic presence of radiation poisoning also explains another odd point. Lovecraft, usually known for writing his protagonists as stuffy academics or learned explorers, for some reason chooses the agrarian Gardner family as his main characters in "Colour." He opts not to have the meteorite crash down *in* the city of Arkham but outside it, and the "traditional" Lovecraftian characters, the Miskatonic professors, are marginalized to the point of being nameless. The story could have been told from the point of view of the scientists, or perhaps an investigative journalist from Arkham, but instead Lovecraft purposely chooses Ammi Pierce and, by extension, Nahum Gardner himself, as the mouthpieces of "Colour." Again, this quirk in the story's construction can be tied back to the Radium Girls. In media coverage of that incident, the main focus was firmly on the dial-painters and their injuries, rather than the scientists attempting to trace the radium's route, or the corporation actively trying to avoid responsibility. Claudia Clark points out that although this presentation "won them public sympathy, it confirmed prevailing social sentiments about women's passivity and proper social sphere" (129). Gender issues aside, this is the same treatment that the Gardners receive in "Colour." Their misfortunes are lamented in and around Arkham, but as time passes they become pariahs and, rather than garnering pity, they are viewed as "rustics" who are rightfully ostracized from their neighbors; in their rural solitude, they are reminded only too well of their lower status, as opposed to the "serious men" from Miskatonic University who choose not to investigate the meteorite's strange effects further.

Using these tropes, Lovecraft erects a fictional framework for the Radium Girls scandal, and thus the larger debate about radiation as well, in "Colour." The Gardner family stands in for the innocent, victimized dial-painters; the Arkham scientists clearly correspond to their willfully blinded real-world corollaries; and the Colour itself is the malignant, corruptive force of radium. Although the Colour cannot be said to have motive per se—and thus cannot truly be malignant or benign—it is malicious, at least from the human perspective of prey to its predator, and in that way it mirrors the media portrayal of radium, as one editorial cartoon put it, as a "painful, lingering, but inevitable death" ("Poisoned!"; cited in Clark, frontispiece). This approach explains Lovecraft's atypical composition of "Colour" compared to his other weird stories. Because of its vampiric predations, the Colour is certainly a cosmic threat of the highest order, and a far cry from some of Lovecraft's more innocuous or even beneficent creatures, such as the zoogs or ghouls from *The Dream-Quest of Unknown Kadath*. On these grounds, I must reject Will Murray's contention that the Colour is the "selfsame marauder" as the *Dream-Quest*'s violet gas named S'ngac. There is no thematic link that I can see between the sentient stand-in for radiation poisoning that Lovecraft develops in "Colour" and the knowledge-seeking organism in "Celephaïs" and *Dream-Quest*. Murray's yoking of his argument to the color of S'ngac, and the being's supposed synonymy with Cygnus, the constellation to which the Colour may or may not blast off, is specious at best.

In writing "The Colour out of Space," Lovecraft demonstrated more than just the masterful ability to portray an eerie New England atmosphere, a truly alien entity, and an early form of body horror. The chemical and biological particulars found in the story point to it also being a deeply researched and highly structured metaphorical satire of radioactive quackery and industrial diseases. After being exposed (as it were) to numerous scientific studies, media advertisements, and journalistic tragedies on the topic, Lovecraft synthesized a portrait of radium and radiation poisoning as it stood in his day. Perhaps even more remarkably, his work of weird fiction was able to accomplish what no other popular source did: it combines in one text the different, and often disparate, fields handling radiation at that time. By addressing medicinal uses (and misuses) of radium, its known and speculated chemical properties, its biological effects that were either unproven or ignored, and the societal implications of the widespread use of this powerful element, Lovecraft was an unrecognized pioneer in the field of radiation studies. Aside from being one of his greatest and most frightening pieces of fiction, "The Colour out of Space" is also a meditation on, and a critique of, the very scientific sources that give the story its power.

Works Cited

"Begin Wide Inquiry into Radium Deaths." *New York Times* (20 June 1925).

Clark, Claudia. *Radium Girls: Women and Industrial Health Reform 1910–1935*. Chapel Hill: University of North Carolina Press, 1997.

Contremoulins, Gaston. "Are Modern X-Rays a Public Danger?" *Popular Science* 99, No. 4 (October 1921): 29.

"Danger in Using Radium." *New York Times* (11 April 1910).

"Eight Said to Have Died in Lead Plant." *Providence Evening Bulletin* (22 June 1925).

"Five Deaths Laid to Radium Poison." *Providence Evening Bulletin* (22 June 1925).

Frame, Paul, and William Kolb. *Living with Radiation: The First Hundred Years*. 4th ed. Edgewater, MD: Syntec, 2005.

Harvie, David I. *Deadly Sunshine: The History and Fatal Legacy of Radium*. Stroud, UK: Tempus Publishing, 2005.

Joshi, S. T. *I Am Providence: The Life and Times of H. P. Lovecraft*. New York: Hippocampus Press, 2010.

Lovecraft, H. P. *The Best of H. P. Lovecraft: Bloodcurdling Tales of Horror and the Macabre*. New York: Ballantine Books, 1982.

Mariconda, Steven J. "The Subversion of Sense in 'The Colour out of Space.'" *Lovecraft Studies* Nos. 19-20 (Fall 1989): 20-22; rpt. in Mariconda, *H. P. Lovecraft: Art, Artifact, and Reality* (New York: Hippocampus Press, 2013): 184-89.

Murray, Will. "Sources for 'The Colour out of Space.'" *Crypt of Cthulhu* No. 28 (Yuletide 1984): 3-5.

"New Radium Disease Found; Has Killed 5." *New York Times* (30 May 1925).

"Plans to Safeguard Radium Handlers." *New York Times* (23 June 1925).

"Poisoned!—As They Chatted Merrily at Their Work." Cartoon. *American Weekly* (28 February 1926).

"Radium and Gas as Death Cause Open New Issue." *New York Times* (5 July 1925).

"Radium Is Expected to Turn on Thieves." *Providence Evening Bulletin* (31 May 31 1925).

Wilson, Edmund. "Tales of the Marvelous and the Ridiculous." *New Yorker* (24 November 1945). Rpt. in *H. P. Lovecraft: Four Decades of Criticism*, ed. S. T. Joshi. Athens: Ohio University Press, 1980. 46-49.

Dead Lies Dreaming: H. P. Lovecraft and the Other Side of Modernity

Andrew Lenoir
Columbia University

For all the horror his work inspires, the most difficult space in which to deal with H. P. Lovecraft remains not with the author but the man—specifically, his attitudes toward race. Problems of writing style aside, this endures as the author's most apparent fault. In chapter three, "The Undead, a Haunted Whiteness," of *Pretend We're Dead*, Annalee Newitz dedicates a scant ten pages to her analysis of Lovecraft's work. Reading the various alien species within the Mythos as stand-ins for non-European races and seeing the real horror of Lovecraft to be the illusion of whiteness, she sees little redeeming quality in his prose. Taking the perspective that pulp fiction publications like *Weird Tales* are microcosms of the larger American capitalist society, Newitz writes, "Ongoing absorption with Lovecraft's writing in the United States is testimony to its continued relevance in the allegedly more enlightened eras of melting pots and multiculturalism" (92). While Lovecraft was an undeniably abhorrent racist, to paint the body of work (and indeed its appreciation) with the same brush as the artist is a broad stroke, one that ignores the subtleties and complications that arise when one examines the effect captured in Lovecraft's texts separate from the mentality that may have inspired them. Behind Lovecraft's prejudices lies something else just as disturbing: a deep-seated anxiety about the nature of humanity and the modern condition.

Two indisputable aspects of Lovecraft's bigotries are that they changed upon his arrival in Brooklyn in the 1920s and that they did not apply to his wife—a Ukrainian-born Jewish single mother, Sonia Greene. Lovecraft's own anti-Semitism was justified in his mind, according to his biographer L. Sprague de Camp, because Judaism had given rise to Christianity, and Christianity had destroyed the classical paganism he so admired. As de Camp writes:

> When Lovecraft called Jewish culture (about which he knew practically nothing) "repulsive," he was not making a factual statement about Jews. He was only expressing his emotions towards what, in his ignorance, he imagined Jewish culture to be. It seems not to have occurred to him that some features of this culture, such as sobriety, sexual puritanism, bookishness, and a wry, self-mocking sense of humor, were precisely his own qualities. (111)

Lovecraft met Sonia Greene in 1921, shortly after the death of his mother, through his work with the amateur journalism movement. The fact that Lovecraft's short dating career took off at the moment of his mother's death points to a possible Freudian interpretation of his attraction to Sonia Greene, one that isn't allayed by his comments in letters that their marriage might have lasted "with a wife of the same temperament as my mother and aunts" (*SL* 3.8). Greene, who experimented as a writer on top of her day job as a milliner, was seven years Lovecraft's senior and hardly the type one would have expected him to end up with. Lovecraft refers to her in his letters with the teasing appellations "Greenevsky" and "Greeneva," but seems to have felt a genuine affection for her despite his prejudices. According to Lovecraft,

> The volatility incidental to a continental and non-Aryan heritage should not blind the analytical observer to the solid work and genuine cultivation which underlie it . . . Strange to say, my aunt likes her immensely despite a racial and social chasm which she doesn't often bridge. Gawd! Even the dowagers are getting democratic in these decadent days! But damme if Mme. Greene ain't a good sort, after all. (*SL* 1.189)

Lovecraft's words and actions reveal a lot about his racial beliefs. His sense that the characteristics of heritage can be remedied with hard work suggests an understanding of their illusory nature. He was, at least, willing to overlook them. For instance, Lovecraft did not deny the attraction he felt toward Sonia's money when they first met. In the same letter describing her first visit to Providence, Lovecraft wrote, "For friendliness and generosity she sure beats hell . . . I decline as many times as courtesy permitted—but if she is determined to blow de coin, it ain't no business of mine to stop her" (*SL* 1.189)). He left Providence and his family, the two most important things in his life, to live with her in Flatbush, Brooklyn, when they married in 1924, but his letters home to announce the union are less than romantic, going so far as to call marriage a "soldering process" (SL 1.331).

The marriage's collapse in 1926 had nothing to do with the "racial and social chasm" between them, but with Lovecraft's refusal to sell himself and his work in the pulp market. The popular view that his inability to hold a job was the chief display of Lovecraft's selfishness and determination to avoid reality is equally valid. By his own assessment, the reason for their marriage's collapse was "98% financial" (SL 3.262). After Sonia's hat shop failed, she moved to Cleveland with her daughter to find work, while Lovecraft remained alone in Red Hook.

Lovecraft's literary pursuits did not pay well for a number of reasons, but the chief cause of his abject failure is perhaps best summed up in his attitude. When submitting his stories for publication, he could not restrain himself from taking a crack at the system that would require him to tailor his art for popular taste and consumption. In his first submission to the magazine *Weird Tales* in 1923, he wrote:

> I have no idea that these things will be found suitable for I pay no attention to the demands of commercial writing. My object is such pleasure as I can obtain from the creation of certain bizarre pictures, situations, or atmospheric effects; and the only reader I hold in my mind is myself.
>
> My models are invariably the older writers, especially Poe, who has been my favourite literary figure since early childhood. Should any miracle impel you to consider the publication of my tales, I have but one condition to offer and that is that no excisions be made. If the tale cannot be printed as written, down to the very last semicolon and comma, it must gracefully accept rejection. Excision by others is probably one reason why no living American author has a real prose style. . . . But I am probably safe for my MSS are not likely to win your consideration. "Dagon" has been rejected by *Black Mask* to which I sent it under external compulsion- much as I am sending you the enclosed. (*Miscellaneous Writings* 506)

The tone of this letter—and the fact he not so subtly insults the venue he is soliciting—aside, Lovecraft he took no time to review the format of submissions, sending in single-spaced typewritten pages and using British spellings while refusing to accept editing. This should have been a death sentence. The fact this letter was not thrown away (manuscripts and all), and that *Weird Tales* editor Edwin Baird actually offered to buy the story "Dagon," provided Lovecraft retype it double-spaced, says more about the editor's patience and benevolence than the quality of the story. The fact that Lovecraft nearly refused says much more about him.

By this time Lovecraft was a man of thirty-three who had never held a job. He applied to address envelopes, write advertising copy, and be a salesman for a collection agency, but was repeatedly turned away due to lack of experience. Time and repeated failures grew into greater bitterness, and his original notions of racial prejudice turned into full-scale paranoia. Envisioning a cultural war between "our British Empire that founded this system of colonies" and the invading forces of "organized Jewry," "loathsome Asiatic hordes," etc., Lovecraft posited that "the real problem may be said to exist nowhere but in New York, for only there is the displacement of regular people so hellishly marked. It is not good for a proud, light-skinned Nordic to be cast away alone amongst squat, squint-eyed jabberers with coarse ways and alien emotions" (*Lord of a Visible World* 180-81). Lovecraft's belief in his own talent and his superior status as an Anglo-Saxon could not survive the failure he was faced with, engendering in him what Michel Houellebecq describes as "the brutal hatred of a trapped animal forced to share his cage with other different and frightening animals" (106).

Lovecraft's most notoriously racist story, "The Horror at Red Hook" (1925), seems a direct response to what he termed as "the first idealists [who] opened the gates to scum" (*Lord of a Visible World* 181). He described its themes to Clark Ashton Smith with the words, "The idea that black magic exists in secret today, or that hellish antique rites still exist in obscurity, is one that I have used and shall use again. When you see my new tale 'The Horror at Red Hook', you will see what use I make of the idea in connexion with the gangs of young loafers & herds of evil-looking foreigners that one sees everywhere in New York" (*SL* 2.27). By his own admission, the story wasn't very good.

The only specific villain in Lovecraft's story is the elderly recluse Robert Suydam, the last descendant of a prominent Dutch family who has used his wealth and local clout to turn his real estate holdings into a breeding ground for Kurdish immigrants engaged in building a magical order and human trafficking operation. Suydam, as a representative of the non-English founders of New York, is a stand-in for the white power structure that has given over America to an influx of foreign contagion. Lovecraft sums it up by saying, "it would not have been too much to say that the old scholar's particular circle coincided almost perfectly with the worst of the organised cliques which smuggled ashore certain nameless and unclassified Asian dregs wisely turned back by Ellis Island" (CF 1.488). The group, sacrificing young children to Hecate or perhaps Lilith, eventually turns on Suydam, killing him just when he had successfully turned his life around, and using his body as part of an elaborate magical ritual.

The most characteristic aspect of Lovecraft's racism as seen in "The Horror at Red Hook" is that he never describes any of the immigrants individually. He deals with them en masse:

> Age-old horror is a hydra with a thousand heads, and the cults of darkness are rooted in blasphemies deeper than the well of Democritus. The soul of the beast is omnipresent and triumphant, and Red Hook's legions of bleareyed, pockmarked youths still chant and curse and howl as they file from abyss to abyss, none knows whence or whither, pushed on by blind laws of biology which they may never understand. (CF 1.504)

Upon analysis, it seems clear Lovecraft is not dealing with people, but rather with an internal fear projected outward onto the "hordes" he does not (and makes no attempt to) understand.

A large part of the inspiration behind this story seems to stem from the Immigration Act of 1924, passed the year before "The Horror at Red Hook" was published. Under the new laws, the annual number of immigrants from any one country was limited to 2% of the number of individuals from that country already living in the United States. Specifically designed to limit the number of "undesirable" immigrants into the United States, the act's further prohibition of immigrants from a nationality ineligible to be naturalized completely barred the entrance of immigrants from Japan, China, the Philippines, Thailand, Vietnam, Laos, Singapore, Indonesia, India, Malaysia, Burma, and Korea. In an attempt to preserve a mostly white homogeneity, government limits were lessened for immigrants from Germany, Britain, and Ireland, while they were tightened so harshly for Eastern Europeans, Italians, and Asians that more left the United States in 1924 than entered it. Lovecraft mentions the Immigration Act specifically in one letter during the period of his admiration for Adolf Hitler, citing it as a point of hypocrisy in American anti-Nazi rhetoric:

> As for this flabby talk about "Americanism" which opposes all racial discrimination—that is simply god damned bull-shit! . . . It is what superficial Americans proclaim from their lips while lynching niggers and selling select real-estate on a restrictive basis to keep Jews and Dagoes out. . . . Ever since

1924 American immigration legislation has, under the very thinnest of veils, discouraged the immigration of racial elements radically alien to the original American people; and I do not believe this sound policy will ever be rescinded. We had this much of "Hitlerism" before we had ever heard of Handsome Adolf! (SL 4.250)

While Lovecraft in the same letter rejects the actual biological superiority of any group to any other, he remarks on his preference for people of his own ethnic background and stresses his belief that the influx of formerly foreign peoples can only sway the institutions of the nation away from the interests of those that founded them. In the same letter, Lovecraft writes, "I believe just as strongly that Japan ought to be kept predominantly Japanese; and would resent a wholesale influx of Aryans into Japan as keenly as I would resent a wholesale influx of Japanese into an Aryan nation" (SL 4.249). While Lovecraft's apparent invocation of a "live and let live" philosophy, advocating the preservation of uniquely Japanese art, the experiences of the twentieth century century (many of which Lovecraft did not live to see), including the progress of the Civil Rights movement and the horrors of World War II's European and Pacific fronts, expose the shallow and disingenuous nature of such a position. In fact, it is the current line of reasoning used by the modern Klu Klux Klan.

It would have been interesting to see the development of Lovecraft's ideas had he lived to see the Second World War, but his opinions on the Revolutionary War alone reveal an undiscussed element of his critique. Lovecraft's anti-American position stems from the nation's very beginning, not merely because of the rebellion against his beloved British empire, but due to the motivations he saw behind it. While visiting Canada in 1933, Lovecraft wrote about his joy at seeing the Union Jack flying overhead, "which greed and selfishness pulled down from the flagstaffs of the more southerly colonies" (*Lord of a Visible World* 293). In Lovecraft's estimation, greed and selfishness are at the heart of "the American lie," evidenced from the country's origins in what was—in his estimation—essentially a tax revolt (the Boston Tea Party) and exhibited all around in the business and emigration practices of the early twentieth century. The 1920s were a period of Red Scares and a serious crackdown on organized labor in the United States, allowing the stock market to rise deceptively while the conditions of the average worker fell. Lovecraft's position that America had its own homegrown "Hitlerism" stems from his belief that the contemporary influx of immigrants was in fact a symptom of the removal of the slave class in American society and the need felt by American industries to set up a servile underclass of maltreated migrants coaxed to United States by the false promises of freedom and opportunity.

In his book *H. P. Lovecraft: Against the World, Against Life,* French writer Michel Houellebecq cites a long passage from one of Lovecraft's letters about New York's Lower East Side:

> The organic things—Italo-Semitico-Mongoloid—inhabiting that awful cesspool could not by any stretch of the imagination be call'd human. They were monstrous and nebulous adumbrations of the pithecanthropoid and amoebal; vaguely moulded from some stinking viscous slime of earth's corruption, and slithering and oozing in and on the filthy streets or in and out of windows and doorways in a fashion suggestive of nothing but infesting worms or deep-sea unnamabilities. They—or the degenerate gelatinous fermentation of which they were composed—seem'd to ooze, seep and trickle thro' the gaping cracks in the houses . . . (SL 1.333-34; cited in Houellebecq 106)

Houellebecq follows the quote with his assessment, "Indisputably great Lovecraftian prose. But what race could possibly have provoked this outburst? He himself no longer knew . . . Racial hatred provokes in Lovecraft the trancelike poetic state in which he outdoes himself by the mad rhythmic pulse of curse sentences, this is the source of the hideous and cataclysmic light that illuminates his final works" (107). Houellebecq is close. It is not "racial hatred" in itself that provokes the poetic trance in Lovecraft but the raw, unbridled, overwhelming fear that he experiences when around other races.

Lovecraft's racism, intense and uncomfortable as it is, feels defensive rather than offensive, and calls to mind the oft-repeated anecdote from Sonia Greene's memories of her life with Lovecraft. Supposedly, if while walking the streets of New York together the pair passed any members of another race, Lovecraft's teeth and fists would clench and he would start sweating. He never went so far as a lash out in anger or actually voice his hatred by calling out at the person or persons whose race he despised, and was remembered by most who knew him for his gentile manner and courtesy. His anger seems to be a displacement of a deeper problem: Lovecraft's deeply ingrained anxiety. It was both his greatest literary gift and his personal curse, for while it limited him in his day-to-day living, the sublime, otherworldly character of the prose he was able to channel through that paralyzing terror is precisely what has made him a modern horror icon.

In psychoanalyst Slavoj Žižek's discussion of psychoanalysis and detective fiction, he draws a connection between the way a detective reads a crime scene and the way an analyst interprets a dream:

> We must absolutely avoid the search for the so-called "symbolic meaning" of [the dream's] totality or its constituent parts ... In a dream, "things" themselves are already "structured like a language," their disposition is regulated by the signifying chain in which they stand ... If we look for the "deeper, hidden meaning" of the figures appearing in the dream, we *blind* ourselves to the latent "dream-thought" articulated in it. The link between immediate "dream-contents" and the latent "dream-thought" exists only on the level of word play, i.e., of nonsensical signifying material. (51)

For Žižek, the way to avoid the problem of blinding oneself in the process of dream interpretation is to analyze the meaning of dreams on the formal level; literally reading the form the dream takes. With regards to Lovecraft's opinion of race, this consideration takes on added weight when one considers China Miéville's assessment of "The Horror at Red Hook": it is Lovecraft's "fever dream," symptomatic of his underlying condition and containing hints to the source of Lovecraft's actual distress that he has attempted to sublimate through racial hatred. With this in mind, it is possible to reexamine the features and phrases of the story to find previously untapped contents of Lovecraft's psyche.

According to Freud, "Anxiety has an unmistakable relation to expectation: it is anxiety about something. It has a quality of indefiniteness and lack of object. In precise speech we use the word 'fear' rather than 'anxiety' if it has found an object" (165). It can be said; therefore, that anxiety is a generalized discomfort that precedes fear, and lacks a definite impetus behind the emotions it solicits. Fear, on the other hand, is a more manageable force, because as it is linked to an object. Its effects are bound to a defined source and therefore rendered conditional.

Anxiety can hereby be broken down into two equally valid understandings: as the fear of an indefinite object (an unknown, lurking threat that can be overcome by defining it) and the fear of indefiniteness itself (the sense that something is unmanageable, simply too much to process, which is more unsettling due to its generality and threatens the ego by calling into question its own definition—derived from comparison to the imposed definition of "other"; this variety is overcome through definition of the experience). Anxious persons wish to sublimate and alleviate their anxiety through fear, because a specific phobia can be defined and defeated either by working through why the object of fear scares the individual or simply avoiding the perceived source altogether.

Freud touches on this in his twenty-fifth lecture, "Anxiety and Instinctual Life," by discussing the phobia formation of a hypothetical agoraphobic. The man did not begin as an agoraphobic, but rather suffered repeated anxiety attacks while on the street. The agoraphobia itself is a symptom of the underlying anxiety, a rationalization and inhibition put in place by the ego to spare the subject from his own anxiety. As Freud said:

> Let us suppose that the agoraphobic patient is invariably afraid of feelings of temptation that are aroused in him by meeting people in the street. In his phobia, he brings about a displacement and henceforward is afraid of an external situation. What he gains by this is obviously that he thinks he will be able to protect himself better in that way. One can save oneself from an external danger by flight; fleeing from an internal danger is a difficult enterprise. (776)

Fear, therefore, can be seen as a means of coping with unmanageable anxiety through the choice of an external object on which to project the danger one senses brewing inside them. The creation of phobias is a means by which to externalize one's anxiety and provide and escape from paralyzing discomfort.

Reading the story formally as Žižek suggests, Lovecraft's issue with the youths of Red Hook seems to be a displacement and projection of his own feelings about himself. He too is an unemployed "good-for-nothing," of the same neighborhood, and does not contribute to society in any easily recognizable way. In the "other" of Red Hook he sees the worst parts of himself reflected, the parts of himself he cannot allow himself to see without destroying his sense of identity: his failures, his shortcomings, and his unavoidable animalism. The blind biological impulses that he sees at work in the hordes of Red Hook are the driving forces behind him as well, but projecting this anxiety about his own basic human condition onto another source serves the same purpose of fear as related to anxiety. It provides a way around the deeper issue. In the end, Lovecraft's maladaptive racial opinions are an escape from the paralyzing self-hatred he would otherwise have to deal with directly. This parallax of racial ideology allows Lovecraft to keep living and working, driven onward by his belief that the enemy is at the gate, while not directly facing the fact that his real enemy is internal.

Lovecraft's relationship toward other races reminds one of the attitude of Captain Ahab to Moby Dick: "He heaves me." Just as Ahab sees not a whale, but the end-all be-all, the thing that must be chased, and constructs from the whale a limit of himself, Lovecraft does not see people on the streets of New York, but the outward bounds of himself as delineated by the life and culture he knows and understands. He embodies all "other" as the thousand-headed hydra. As Houellebecq writes, "the ethnic realities at play had long been wiped out; what is certain is that he hated them all and was incapable of any greater specificity" (107). What is important is to understand the function this view served for Lovecraft, one that is best understood by directly engaging his writing. Lovecraft's alien antagonists and their like are expressions of his own masochism—a continuation of the same self-effacing, suicidal streak that caused him at one point to carry a vial of cyanide on him at all times. His protagonists, especially Randolph Carter, are shallow doubles of himself: old-fashioned, antiquarian, academics—the perfect victims of a cruel and uncaring world that worships progress, races toward the future, and leaves the past and all it stood for behind. Beyond issues of race and industry, Lovecraft's biggest fear was an imposing sense of humanity's insignificance, tied to an inherent malignity that taints all existence, marking life itself as evil. To be alive is to be a complicit component in an uncaring cycle, driven onward by unknowable biological drives. When Lovecraft tapped into this sensation of blind panic and anxiety, the prose Houellebecq praised would come to the surface—driven not by the racial object of fear (which acts as a displacement of the more general condition Lovecraft sought to describe) but from a sense of the impossible trauma of reality behind the imaginary enemies of his race-based ideology.

In *Pretend We're Dead*, Annalee Newitz takes a close look at Lovecraft's 1931 story "The Shadow over Innsmouth," paying particular attention to the racial undertones. In her interpretation, the story is a warning against blurring the color-line, and a discussion of a new generation of hybrids rising up after the Civil War with the end of slavery and the acceptance of black citizenship in the United States. In her assessment, the narrator's decision to accept his position as hybrid

> refuses to preserve the sanctity of whiteness and white privilege. Instead, he embraces a racial heritage—and an "eternal" racial future—which is flagrantly hybrid. It is also a future without death. This kind of white person, who dreams of escaping white America to live among "others," is what Lovecraft implies is the true outcome of the Civil War. It is an outcome both terrifying

and hopeful—the future belongs to semi-dead monsters, but once viewed from the monsters' point of view, this really isn't so bad. (98)

Strangely, "this really isn't so bad" is all the space Newitz spends discussing the ending of "The Shadow over Innsmouth," which depending on one's view may be one of the only happy endings in Lovecraft's fiction. The last lines of Olmstead's narration read:

> Stupendous and unheard-of splendours await me below, and I shall seek them soon. Iä-R'lyeh! Cthulhu fhtagn! Iä! Iä! No, I shall not shoot myself—I cannot be made to shoot myself!
>
> I shall plan my cousin's escape from that Canton madhouse, and together we shall go to marvel-shadowed Innsmouth. We shall swim out to that brooding reef in the sea and dive down through black abysses to Cyclopean and many-columned Y'ha-nthlei, and in that lair of the Deep Ones we shall dwell amidst wonder and glory for ever. (CF 3.230)

One cannot read the ending of this passage without deriving a vaguely religious sense from the wording, "amidst wonder and glory forever." This promise of eternal life, and the dreams Olmstead has in which his "dead" grandmother tells him they will be together in their kingdom, are essentially perversions of the Christian heaven, where one lives in the "kingdom, power and glory" of God alongside deceased relatives "forever and ever." This in addition to his statement that "I cannot be made to shoot myself," especially when compared with the fiery suicide of the protagonist in "Facts concerning the Late Arthur Jermyn and His Family" upon discovering his own similarly inhuman heritage, provides a sense that something has changed, that something is different about this story that leaves such clear-cut racial readings inadequate. There seem to be two possibilities: either Lovecraft was so racist that the character's reversal is the source of horror, an example of the brainwashing taking place within those whites that mix with other groups; or Lovecraft had something larger in mind.

Given Zadok Allen's assessment that "they're like us," enough that the Deep Ones and humans can interbreed, it seems likely that the Deep Ones are some sort of parallel to human beings and are probably very humanlike, just having evolved to live underwater. Repeatedly, it is mentioned that the Deep Ones could destroy mankind at any time, and it is only out of laziness or ulterior motives that humanity continues to survive. For unknown reasons, the Deep Ones have brought shoggoths to the surface. It is never questioned why they would want to destroy mankind, just as it is never explained why an immortal race wants to breed at all, let alone breed with human beings. Unlike Lovecraft's other monsters, the Deep Ones can be fathomed by viewing them from a human perspective: they exhibit behavior that appears in human history, and they seem to keep mankind around for the same reasons the Spanish did not exterminate all the Native Americans upon arriving in the New World.

Consider the initial trade-based relationship of the Deep Ones and the people of Innsmouth. The promises of gold and fish keep the humans interested in maintaining contact until the Deep Ones can kill off the humans that don't want them there, and then through interbreeding create subsequent generations already on their side through genetics. This is not unlike the imposition of white Western culture on colonial outposts throughout the age of exploration. Like British colonists, the Deep Ones are a conquering people content with coercion and intimidation until force is necessary. Though this can be viewed as a racial commentary—that the civilization of "White America" is being undermined and infiltrated from the inside—on the flip side, the narrator's realization of his own heritage suggests that the notion of a "White America" was always illusory due to generations of interbreeding and the loosely defined and ever changing status of "whiteness."

Interestingly, the gold treasure of the Deep Ones is also one of the few references to money in all Lovecraft, seen here as luring people toward their destruction—becoming part of the mechanism by which their way of life is destroyed. Is it possible that in Lovecraft's view, the force that threatens mankind is not just racial mixing, but the attitude that permits the sacrifice of one's own people for gold? Lovecraft's earliest experiences with money were directly linked to the deaths of family members, perhaps best exemplified by the recurrence of the $10,000 that Lovecraft's protagonist received in "The Secret Cave" as a treasure not worth the life it has cost. Lovecraft's distaste for money goes beyond a mere abhorrence of avarice to self-sabotage and a refusal to participate in the marketplace. Behind all his positions—anti-immigrant, anti-Semitic, pro-Confederate (in opposition to the Yankee factory system)—there is a consistent theme: a frustration with modern market relations, where one's name and breeding no longer guarantee a place in life, and the intelligent and the idiot are both expected to find the same meaningless, menial jobs to pay their way. To return to "The Horror at Red Hook," the protagonist Thomas Malone isn't haunted by an overwhelming fear of immigrants; more tellingly, he faints at any sign of urban development.

That Lovecraft has been such a successful writer of the pulp fiction genre is fascinating, because he had no intention to be. A refusal to accept editing combined with a preference for British-style spelling might as well have been his undoing and shows a denial of need when one is spiraling into poverty. In fact, one could argue that by writing in a segment of the market so often overlooked, he may have been able to get away with more at a time when many authors would have had to go abroad to print controversial material. What is it embedded within Lovecraft's prose that has endeared him to the modern reader, his readership now higher than ever, despite his character flaws and tangible prejudices? While Annalee Newitz seems to suggest it is precisely because of these prejudices that Lovecraft's popularity has survived, there is another way of viewing it. Lovecraft's critique of the modern condition as it was beginning has remained poignant and valid, despite the racial qualities he himself infused into the critique. Lovecraft's analysis of the problem was so poignant that despite the ethnic beliefs that muddled his vision, his horror has remained terrifying because it reveals a truth.

Repeatedly in his letters, Lovecraft writes about his misgivings with the climate of modern capitalism, writing: "Granted, the machine-victim has leisure. What is he going to do with it? We shall hear of all sorts of futile reforms and reformers—standardized culture-outlines, synthetic sports & spectacles, professional play leaders & study guides & kindred examples of machine-made up life & brotherly spirit... Meanwhile the tension of boredom and unsatisfied imagination will increase" (*SL* 2.308-9). Remembering that Lovecraft worked briefly as a copywriter in New York, participating in the advertising industry as it first grew into itself, the status of created dreams takes on a new significance. The god Cthulhu speaks to mankind in his dreams and tries to sway his behavior, just as the dreams of an attainable "heaven" attract Robert Olmstead to accept a life he otherwise would have killed himself over. Perhaps the key to understanding "The Shadow over Innsmouth" can be found in the shadowy interior of the local Masonic hall, converted into the meeting place for the new religious body, the Esoteric Order of Dagon. While there is no evidence to suggest that Lovecraft was a Freemason, his grandfather was a very active initiate and Lovecraft was certainly exposed to it in his youth. The Esoteric Order of Dagon, a new ideology that has taken root in the seat of his fathers, seems to be a stand-in for the new ideology of the twentieth century, concerning material culture and "bourgeois capitalism."

To extend the metaphor further, just as all Lovecraft's protagonists are victims, so too are all citizen-consumers of Capitalist State-Sponsored Art: the promises of pleasure and ease which erase the past with a prepackaged image, providing an illusion of human control by which a choice of limits and limitation (*Coca-Cola or Pepsi?*) is the greatest exercise of free will.

This is equally true of racially designated identity, which can provide no objective definition of individual subjectivity. For those that lack the confidence to individuate themselves adequately, the imposition of an outward definition like racial categorization is a comfort that secures the belief they are there and that they are worthy (even if no one else seems to acknowledge it). How can Lovecraft recognize this power of dreams and mythology without applying it to his own ideological identification with a vision of Anglo-Saxon Englishness that exists only in his mind? The answer would seem to fall between delusion and willful ignorance. This also seems to explain how he could marry a Jewish woman without violating his own views on race mixing and anti-Semitism. It is perhaps out of this unconscious understanding of his own illusions that the recurrent crime of his heroes is digging too deeply into one's own foundations and seeking to know more than one should. The price is always insanity or death. Already suicidal, it is unclear if Lovecraft could have taken this additional insult. If he had to face the fact that he had failed at everything he'd tried and could not pride himself on any inborn privilege—that he was not a gentleman, whiteness did not exist, and the America he loved was fading into a pre-modern past—could Lovecraft have found the will to live? Is it perhaps the greatest revelation of Lovecraft's hybrids that all people are the summation of their self-deceptions?

Examining the 1923 story "The Rats in the Walls" for issues of race, the first thing that must be discussed is the narrator's black cat named "Nigger-Man." While often cited as one of Lovecraft's most puerile moments of inflammatory language, a biographical point to be established is that "Nigger-Man" was the name of the beloved family cat from his childhood that ran away when he was fourteen. Similarly, apart from the "howling of Negroes" mentioned at the burning of the family plantation in Virginia, a clear representation of the positive myth of slavery popular among supporters of the Confederacy, and the brief mention of "my cousin, young Randolph Delapore of Carfax, who went among the negroes and became a voodoo priest after he returned from the Mexican War" (CF 1.379), this is really a story about white English people. Even in the second example, it is the voodoo rather than the Negroes that is intended to be shocking, as it represents a return to form in the de la Poer family.

Of particular import to understanding this story is the narrator's break from reality as he kills and eats Capt. Norrys:

> Something bumped into me—something soft and plump. It must have been the rats; the viscous, gelatinous, ravenous army that feast on the dead and the living.... Why shouldn't rats eat a de la Poer as a de la Poer eats forbidden things? ... The war ate my boy, damn them all ... and the Yanks ate Carfax with flames and burnt Grandsire Delapore and the secret ... No, no, I tell you, I am *not* that daemon swineherd in the twilit grotto! It was not Edward Norrys' fat face on that flabby, fungous thing! Who says I am a de la Poer? He lived, but my boy died! ... Shall a Norrys hold the lands of a de la Poer? ... It's voodoo, I tell you ... that spotted snake ... Curse you, Thornton, I'll teach you to faint at what my family do! ... 'Sblood, thou stinkard, I'll learn ye how to gust ... wolde ye swynke me thilke wys? ... *Magna Mater! Magna Mater!* ... *Atys* ... *Dia ad aghaidh 's ad aodann ... agus bas dunach ort! Dhonas 's dholas ort, agus leat-sa!* ... Ungl ... ungl ... rrrlh ... chchch ... (CF 1.396)

"The Rats in the Walls" has been viewed by some readers as an homage to Edgar Allan Poe's "The Fall of the House of Usher," as both stories show the interconnection of dying families and their crumbling homes and psychic phenomena no one but the house's heir can hear. In this scene, the history of the house speaks through the narrator, repeating the invocation of the "Magna Mater," the Phrygian goddess Cybele, previously only appearing in the fragmentary Latin found on the Roman ruins that constitute the Priory's foundation. Some commentators, like the scholar S. T. Joshi, have discussed the overlap between this story and Carl Jung's dream inspiration for the Collective Unconscious—walking down unending cellar stairs and passing ancient skeletons—the remnants of the dead past still living inside the human mind. Most notable, however, is this passage's relation to Irvin S. Cobb's story "The Unbroken Chain," in which a Frenchman hit by a car calls out the same phrase as his African ancestor who was struck by a rhino. The sense provided by both these stories is the weight of history and heritage on identity: the narrator, known only as Delapore or de la Poer, moves to the family seat when he discovers it and resumes the family customs once he becomes aware of them. It is interesting to note that while the climax of Cobb's story is directly racial, "The Rats in the Walls" is beyond race, delving instead into the nature of humanity.

The interpretation that can be suggested by the story's last lines—"they must know that I did not do it. They must know it was the rats; the slithering, scurrying rats whose scampering will never let me sleep; the daemon rats that race behind the padding in this room and beckon me down to greater horrors than I have ever known; the rats they can never hear; the rats, the rats in the walls" (CF 1.396)—is that the titular rats are the restless spirits of the past. History is not dead simply because it has already happened, but plays itself out in present action, as what Žižek calls the thing that is in us more than ourselves. The rats are the walls, the imposition of structure that takes the horror of reality—that de la Poers eat forbidden things—and makes it manageable. This can be related to Lovecraft's own feelings about modernity and capitalism, as well as his feelings toward the function of horror. In his own assessment, "only a cynic can create horror—for behind every masterpiece of the sort must reside a driving daemonic force that despises the human race and its illusions, and longs to pull them to pieces and mock them" (letter to Edwin Baird, [early November 1923]; *Miscellaneous Writings* 509).

While Lovecraft's treatment of non-whites and immigrants is never flattering, because it was something he took for granted, the status of such people was only a secondary point within his prose. His first point was to condemn the social and economic system at play that would prize whites and non-whites alike as labor, commodified and processed for consumption, in the same way "the war ate my boy." Moving through the underground chamber full of bones, the protagonist and his party are struck by the variable states of evolution among them: some are highly primitive, not advanced much farther than the Piltdown Man, while others, due to generations of being farmed for food, have become quadrupedal. In one scene, Capt. Norrys is overcome with horror, not due to the evidence of cannibalism, but after discovering in one room the familiar features of an English butcher shop juxtaposed with this new context. It is not so much the act of raising men for slaughter, but the scale and industry of the act that is disturbing. In the absence of any monster or villain in "The Rats in the Walls," the ongoing history of cannibalism and the implication that man eating man is the destiny of mankind itself is the source of the horror. "The Rats in the Walls" is in essence an allegorical representation of the essential truth of the human condition, phrased in the same terms by thinkers as diverse as Hobbes, Freud, Seneca and Schopenhauer, *Homo homini lupus est*: "Man is the wolf of man."

Several years before writing "The Rats in the Walls," Lovecraft wrote, "I sincerely trust you will read Schopenhauer and Nietzsche . . . To emerge from the artificial fog of empty, resonant, mystical words without a single real idea behind them, into the clear light of minds with actual conceptions, is a tonic to the intellect" (*Lord of a Visible World* 115). Indeed, Arthur Schopenhauer's essay, "On the Suffering of the World" from *The World as Will and Representation*, begins with a very Lovecraftian sentiment that seems to almost parallel the openings of "The Call of Cthulhu" and "Arthur Jermyn": "If suffering is not the first and immediate object of our life, then our existence is the most inexpedient and inappropriate thing in the world. For it is absurd to assume that the infinite pain, which everywhere abounds in the world and springs from the want and misery essential to life, could be purposeless and purely accidental." In Schopenhauer's estimation, it seems human beings are unconscious of their contentment and only rallied to attention by displeasure, "just as we do not feel the health of our whole body, but only the small spot where the shoe pinches" (1). Interestingly, this is the same metaphor Lovecraft used to discuss his indignation over New York's multi-ethnic immigrants.

For Schopenhauer, all consciousness is an expression of the will-to-live, and it is only through the illusory *principium individuationis* that people develop their belief in their own unique identity. This important step prefigures the psychoanalytic notion of the "Mirror Phase," wherein exile from oneself is the cost of entering human society, and seems to be at the core of Lovecraft's horror. As Schopenhauer phrased it, "The last secret of life has revealed itself to them in the excess of pain, the secret, namely, that evil and wickedness, suffering and hatred, the tormented and the tormentor, different as they may appear to knowledge that follows the principle of sufficient reason, are in themselves one, phenomenon of the one will-to-live that objectifies its conflict with itself by means of the *principium individuationis*" (252). This "last secret of life" is the recurring maddening truth within Lovecraft's stories, the confrontation with an underlying reality beneath human narratives of history and ideology, that mocks and eats away at the subject's sanity. This element of mockery is best demonstrated by "The Shadow over Innsmouth." The narrator assumes a shambling gait to blend in with the Innsmouth-folk and escape, only to discover he has always-already been one of them. The revelation is a slap in the face, a further insult to all one's efforts to escape his individual suffering and fear. Like the narrator in "The Rats in the Walls," who cannot escape his lineage, or the narrator of "The Call of Cthulhu," all things are complicit in the horror of reality as it is and as it has always been, summed up in the line: "Life is a hideous thing" (CF 1.171).

In his other story from 1931, *At the Mountains of Madness*, Lovecraft provides the creation story of his myth cycle, holding more in common with the work of the early Gnostics than with the biblical genesis. Millions of years ago, the Great Old Ones—or the Elder Things—came to this planet and established their own civilization. The Elder Things are repeatedly referred to in terms of vegetables, another Schopenhauer reference, reflecting the philosopher's belief (echoed by Lovecraft in his letters) that vegetables are the life-forms most at peace, because they are (in their growing) the raw embodiment of unknowing, blind will, which simply absorbs light, "the purest and most perfect kind of knowledge from perception" (Schopenhauer 143). By mixing together elements of animal and plant life, the Elder Things become the perfect organism: the aesthetic invitation of the plant world as a symbol of unity between the one will and the "foreign intelligent individual [the plants need] in order to come from the world of blind willing into representation" (Schopenhauer 140).

As for life originating on earth, everything present today is the result of Darwinian evolution acting upon the leftovers of the Old Ones' original engineering. All life forms that the Old Ones saw as potentially threatening were destroyed, so those that survived until today were either left alone or kept alive for food or entertainment. Most significantly, Prof. Dyer observes, "It interested us to see in some of the very last and most decadent sculptures a shambling primitive mammal, used sometimes for food and sometimes as an amusing buffoon by the land dwellers, whose vaguely simian and human foreshadowings were unmistakable" (CF 3.100). Humanity, in Lovecraft's estimation, is a mistake that higher intelligence saw fit to allow to survive, not due to any particular merit, but the opposite. Mankind was so lacking, it was left alone except to be eaten or laughed at.

Under Lovecraft's formulation, any feeling of one group's objective superiority to another is baseless, as in one letter where he denounces the idea of the biological superiority or inferiority of any racial group as compared to another: "It doesn't matter whether a race is our equal—or even our superior (as, in all probability, the ancient Greek race . . . was)" (SL 4.249). He chose to keep up such distinctions (as that the Elder Things chose to keep humans around) because it amused him to have some semblance of his superiority over someone, anyone, when all other barometers indicated his failings.

In the end, it is this sort of amusement, the artful crafting both of one's outlook, life, and artistic efforts that comes across as both Lovecraft and Schopenhauer's "solution" for the horrors of the world. Two Lovecraft stories deal directly with artists—"The Music of Erich Zann" and "Pickman's Model." Zann is able to hold back the darkness for a while with his art, but Pickman is ultimately more successful, because he stops trying to fight it. He accepts his complicity in that darkness—similar to the narrator of "The Outsider"—and finds freedom in the abandonment and betrayal of humanity.

Pickman, the creator of fantastical paintings containing truths the world cannot abide, calls to mind a strange parallel. Lines like "The only saving grace of the present is that it's too damned stupid to question the past very closely" make it seem like Pickman is the clearer representation of Lovecraft himself (CF 2.61). In his autobiography, "Some Notes on a Nonentity," Lovecraft explains that the name Abdul Alhazred was a name he gave himself in childhood. If one takes this gesture literally, then the *Necronomicon* is the mythos itself—literally, "an account of the Old Ones and their history."

If this is true, then the mythos is more than just a series of stories; it has a specific purpose. Like the *Necronomicon*, which drives men mad with its contents, the mythos is meant to leave a distinct impression upon the reader: that something about this world and the way it has been fashioned is profoundly wrong. The way people, in their desire for money and power, have made this world is horrible—built upon abusive labor practices and a small elite that feeds upon the efforts of the rest of society.

As Lovecraft wrote in "The Shadow over Innsmouth," "After all, even the strangest and maddest of myths are often merely symbols or allegories based upon truth" (CF 3.184).

Works Cited

de Camp, L. Sprague. *Lovecraft: A Biography*. Garden City, NY: Doubleday, 1975.

Freud, Sigmund. *The Freud Reader*. Ed. Peter Gay. New York: W. W. Norton, 1995.

Houellebecq, Michel. *H. P. Lovecraft: Against the Wall, Against Life*. Tr. Dorna Khazeni. San Francisco: McSweeney's, 2005.

Lovecraft, H. P. *Lord of a Visible World: An Autobiography in Letters*. Ed. S. T. Joshi and David E. Schultz. Athens: Ohio University Press, 2000.

———. *Miscellaneous Writings*. Ed. S. T. Joshi. Sauk City, WI: Arkham House, 1995.

Newitz, Annalee. *Pretend We're Dead*. Durham, NC: Duke University Press, 2006.

Schopenhauer, Arthur. *The World as Will and Representation*. Tr. E. F. J. Payne. New York: Dover, 1966.

Žižek, Slavoj. *Looking Awry*. Cambridge, MA: MIT Press, 1991.

Lovecraftian Milton: Prophetic Certainties, Romantic Rebellions, and Horrific Imaginings in the Weird Worlds of Milton and Lovecraft

Marcello C. Ricciardi
St. Joseph's College

Premise: There are three Miltons for Lovecraft: 1) the **Prophetic Milton**, which can be broken down into two subdivisions, a) a young visionary like Lovecraft, idealistic and exilic, seeking a purer, more hallowed world, and b) a seasoned harbinger of doom, heralding an oncoming apocalypse and chastisement; 2) the **Romantic Milton**, a dark, brooding Byronic presence who is, as Blake maintained, unconsciously "of the devil's party" with his sympathetic, dynamic, and rebellious portrayal of Satan; and 3) the **Weird Milton**, with Satan as a prototypical Cthulhu monster, an extraterrestrial, cosmic terrorist ravaging worlds in his path, accompanied by a grotesque menagerie of devilish minions.

Both Milton and Lovecraft were anachronisms, Milton writing the last epic in Western literature, and Lovecraft, the last, according to E. F. Bleiler, and "most important American supernaturalist since Poe" (iii), pushing the boundaries, even for weird fiction. Milton employed antiquated syntax, with his peculiar spellings and Latinate diction, always looking backwards in time, unlike the forward-thinking Shakespeare, and in total opposition to the satirical wit and secularism of Restoration drama then on the rise. Even Samuel Johnson, Milton's greatest biographer, observes: "Through all his greater works there prevails an uniform peculiarity of diction, a mode and cast of expression which bears little resemblance to that of any former writer and which is so far removed from common use that an unlearned reader when he first opens the book finds himself surprised by a new language" (442). And we learn from Peter Cannon that Lovecraft preferred British to American spellings, "including such archaisms as *shew* for the verb *show*," Lovecraft also trying to evoke a nobler and older world (2). Both men were in self-imposed exile from their current cultural and literary milieus and both were theophanists, which I will explore later on.

Despite Lovecraft's attraction to the eighteenth century, he, much like Gerard Manly Hopkins and T. S Eliot, has a seventeenth-century frame of mind, or metaphysical sensibility, in the tradition of Donne, Vaughan, Herbert, Crashaw, and Milton. Of course, the obvious difference that would make such an observation absurd is Lovecraft's atheism, but although I am not disputing such a claim in its historical and biographical context, I would like to suggest that from an imaginative and mythic perspective his writings do convey what I would call a Dark Theodicy or Dark Theophany and that Milton and Lovecraft occupy opposite ends of the same spectrum, one embodying cosmos, the other chaos—much like George Lucas's mythic Jedi and Sith dichotomy. Both writers are authentically engaged in chaoskampf, but Milton's God and man always have the upper hand, while the human inhabitants of Lovecraft's universe are hopelessly outgunned and overmatched. Nonetheless, Lovecraft, like Milton, is always seeking to *evoke* and *invoke* a Presence, a *Someone* in Milton's case, a *Something* in Lovecraft's: "Nothing has ever seemed to fascinate me so much," explains Lovecraft, "as the thought of some curious interruption in the prosaic laws of Nature, or some monstrous intrusion on our familiar world by unknown things from the limitless abysses outside" (*Lord of a Visible World* 345). Reading Lovecraft, at times, feels like watching the film *Cloverfield*, waiting for an epic hero who never arrives to save the day, or like reading Wordsworth's *Prelude*, re-imagining an Eden minus its first inhabitants. First, I realize that noting Miltonic allusions in Lovecraft is not new and I am indebted to essays by Thomas Quale as well as James Egan, both assisting me in defining the Milton-Lovecraft duality.

First, let us look at some immediate resemblances—each artist an inversion or doppelgänger of the other. Milton was virulently anti-Catholic but had Catholic friends and married a Catholic royalist, while Lovecraft was a racial purist but took a Jewish bride. Both had secluded youths spent in constant study and steady ruminations but took up traveling later on in life, Lovecraft more so than Milton, Milton touring Europe, Lovecraft America. Milton was called the Lady of Christ's College and had a reputation for personal attractiveness, while Lovecraft loathed his appearance and was reared to think of himself as an ugly child. Both men had an attraction to astronomy, Lovecraft gazing at the stars in lonely isolation with his telescope, and a youthful Milton touring the Continent and meeting Galileo under house arrest. Interestingly enough, Lovecraft's early astronomical writings questioning whether there is life on the Moon and Mars (Joshi 38-39) parallels passages in *Paradise Lost* where Milton ponders whether there is life on other planets (7.621-22) while ruminating upon the mechanics of the cosmos. Each of them was fascinated by the infinity of space and time, Milton designated "the poet of space" (666) by William Riley Parker, and Lovecraft shrugging off thoughts of suicide because he was too curious about "the vast gulfs of space outside all familiar lands" (Joshi 31).

Both men had difficulties at school, feeling superior to their instructors, with Milton, like Lovecraft, guilty of sporadic attendance and long sabbaticals. Both had youthful forays into heroic self-posturing, Lovecraft with his Providence Detective Agency, equipped with a pistol-toting Lovecraft (*Lord of a Visible World* 17) and Milton with his Platonian Republican scheme of establishing a religio-military academy (Milton, "Of Education" 633-34), replete with a broadsword-wielding Milton (Milton, "Second Defense of the English People" 824). Lovecraft could be generous and supportive to friends but scalding and scathing in his epistolary pronouncements on civilization and culture, much like Milton's terms of endearment to his closest associates but merciless assaults in his political invectives against his foes. Both were advocates of companionate marriage and condoned divorce based on temperamental incompatibility.

Milton and Lovecraft were vocational artists, neither one of them feeling completely justified unless writing; Lovecraft grumbling about his matrimonial responsibilities and Milton complaining about his meddlesome in-laws who prevented him from finding a moments peace so he can write. Each was, by temperament, an aristocrat, Lovecraft aesthetically and Milton morally. Milton spent most of his life investing all his talents into writing political treatises in defense of liberty, sacrificing his eyes and his youthful epic ambitions for what he believed to be his civic duty. Fame came late and was tarnished by his political involvements. Lovecraft saw all his work published in low-grade magazines, never living to see his work applauded or legitimized by the mainstream literary community.

Both were cosmologists and metaphysical thinkers, Milton of course subscribing to a Christian theodicy and Lovecraft not, but both sharing the commitment to a sustained treatment of the nature and order or disorder of the universe in their works. Milton, from his earliest translation of the Psalms at age eighteen to his last heroic work, *Samson Agonistes* at sixty-two, was committed to writing Christophanies. From the onset of his youth he felt a sense of high destiny and intense gravitas. Lovecraft's entire corpus, even his juvenilia, is a herculean attempt to evade, avoid, and escape normalcy, domesticity, and the quotidian, exploring the inner, the outer, and the underworlds that defy space and time.

Like but unlike Milton, Lovecraft was committed to forging hierophanies, a term coined by Mircea Eliade (11), which he defined as encounters with either extraterrestrial or interdimensional beings that are not sacred but sublime, awe-inspiring, and always self-destructive. Lovecraft's claim to have had a "half-sincere belief in the old gods and Nature-spirits" (CE 5.146) is more of a testimonial to his paganistic poetics than to his atheistic sensibilities. In a letter to Edwin Baird in February 1924, Lovecraft cautiously confesses to having a vision of "dryads and satyrs in the woods at dusk":

> Once I firmly thought I beheld some of these sylvan creatures dancing under autumnal oaks; a kind of "religious experience" as true in its way as the subjective ecstasies of any Christian ... whose unimaginative emotionalism and my unemotional imaginativeness are of equal valuelessness from an intellectual point of view. If such a Christian tell me he has *felt* the reality of Jesus or Jahveh, I can reply that I have *seen* the hoofed Pan and his sisters of the Hesperian Phaëthusa. (SL 1.300; cf. CE 5.146)

Lovecraft's dual response, one of ambiguity and reluctant admission, reinforces that incongruity of temperament so indicative of the man, in which he both avows and disavows the possibility of a paranormal experience, bifurcating the affective from the cognitive experience and relegating the entire episode to the cusp of an inconsequential imagining.

Such an approach to experience, normal or supernal, leads Lovecraft to the brink of psychic disengagement, both from himself and from the world around him, admitting that the

> tales of ordinary characters would appeal to a larger class, but I have no wish to make such an appeal. The opinions of the masses are of no interest to me.... There are probably seven persons, in all, who really like my work; and they are enough.... I could not write about 'ordinary people' because I am not in the least interested in them.... Man's relations to man do not captivate my fancy. It is man's relationship to the cosmos—to the unknown—which alone arouses in me the spark of creative imagination. (CE 5.53)

This conception is no different from Milton's admission in *Paradise Lost* that "fit audience find, though few" (7.30) "unless an age too late, or cold climate, or years damp my intended wing deprest" (9.45). Samuel Johnson, both resistant to and embracive of Milton, intuitively knew what constituted Milton's greatness and remoteness. He could be easily speaking about Lovecraft here:

> The appearance of nature and the occurrences of life did not satiate his appetite of greatness. To paint things as they are requires a minute attention and employs the memory rather than the fancy. Milton's delight was not to sport in the wide regions of possibility; reality was a scene too narrow for his mind. He sent his faculties out upon discovery into worlds where only imagination can travel and delighted to form new modes of existence and furnish sentiment and action to superior beings. (Johnson 435)

Neither Milton's nor Lovecraft's protagonists are content with the quotidian. Perhaps this is what Johnson meant when he said that the "want of human interest is always felt" (439) when reading Milton. When Lovecraft in his poem "Background" says he can "never be tied to raw, new things" but must journey "Across the changeless walls of earth and heaven . . . To stand alone before eternity" (AT 92), he follows in the same footsteps as Milton the poet-hero who "with no middle flight intends to soar above the Aonian Mount, while [he] pursues / Things unattempted yet in prose or Rhyme" (1.15). Peter Cannon comments on Lovecraft's "adventurous expectancy" as a sentiment whereby "the speaker feels a kind of cosmic rapture before the unknown" (14). From a theological perspective, that cosmic rapture, as previously noted by Lovecraft, is called ecstasy, a type of mystical experience, and both Milton and Lovecraft know how to recognize and convey it but in diametrically opposite terms. Joyce Carol Oates observes the inherent paradox contained within Lovecraft: "Despite Lovecraft's expressed contempt for mysticism, clearly he was a kind of mystic, drawing intuitively upon a cosmology of images that came to him unbidden, from the 'underside' of his life: all that was repressed, denied, 'defeated'" (xv). Such a claim is not a leap of the imagination, especially when Lovecraft himself admits in "Some Notes on a Nonentity" of how "subtly out of place" he feels in "the modern period," leading him "to think of time as a mystical portentous thing in which all sorts of unexpected wonders might be discovered" (CE 5.208). Once again, this is the language of religious ecstasy, albeit in a religiously anonymous and unselfconscious way. Both men claimed night visitations, the Holy Spirit in *Paradise Lost* "visiting Milton's slumbers Nightly" and "governing his song"

(7.30–33), and Lovecraft plagued by night terrors, or dreams of night-gaunts, whirling him about and impaling him upon their tridents, which he imputed to Doré's illustrations to *Paradise Lost*. "That was my one prayer back in '96—each night—to keep awake and ward off the night gaunts!" (*Lord of a Visible World* 11), so "obviously related," according to Barton Levi St. Armand, "to the nightmare archetypes of Bogeyman, Devil, Vampire, and Incubus" (92).

Like Milton, Lovecraft admitted that he worked best under the mantle of night when inspired, spontaneous, and experiencing a dreamscape: "Some of my tales involve actual dreams I have experienced. My speed and manner of writing vary widely in different cases, but I always work best at night" (CE 5.210). Lovecraft even acknowledged some form of automatic writing when composing, in many ways reminiscent of some of W. B. Yeats's and James Merrill's poetry: "'Nyarlathotep' is a nightmare—an actual phantasm of my own, with the first paragraph written *before I fully awaked*" (SL 1.160). Milton and Lovecraft both transformed and transfigured their experiences and themselves into art, Milton as poet-prophet, Lovecraft as apocalyptic- soothsayer. Joyce Carol Oates asks if there "is a poignant triumph of a kind in the way in which the aggrieved, terrorized child [in Lovecraft] refashions himself, through countless nocturnal-insomniac sessions of writing into a purely cerebral being?" (x). The question then remains: Did Lovecraft deliberately seek to reinvent himself as a Hobbesian materialist in an attempt to repudiate, repress, and restrain any mystical proclivities stirring within him? In other words, was he a closet mystic? According to Rudolf Otto in *The Idea of the Holy*, "there has never been in the West a mysticism of horror, such as we find in certain kinds of Indian mysticism, both Buddhist and Hindu—in the Bhagavad-Gita . . . in some forms of the Shiva and Durga worship, and in the horrible forms of Tantrism" (quoted in St. Armand 84). "It was just this kind of horror mysticism," observes St. Armand, that "Lovecraft was seeking, and that he partially constructed by means of his Cthulhu Mythos, with its Oriental plethora of gods, emanations, and metamorphic demons" (84). The "central experience" that Otto is explicitly referring to is "the numinous (Latin *numen*, 'spirit') in which the Other (i.e., the transcendent) appears as a *mysterium tremendum et fascinans*—that is, a mystery before which man both trembles and is fascinated, is both repelled and attracted" (*Encyclopaedia Britannica*). It is this *tremendous mystery* that both repels and attracts Lovecraft, fostering a certain cognitive dissonance between his rational and non-rational powers of perception (Ganson 194).

It is here that I would like to take a close look at the Miltonic elements intrinsic to Lovecraft. Lovecraft, in "Supernatural Horror in Literature," readily admits that it is in "poetry that we first encounter the permanent entry of the weird into standard literature" (CE 2.86). He rightly alludes to the fantastical in *Beowulf* and Malory, but it is when he comes to "Elizabethan drama, with its *Dr. Faustus*, the witches in *Macbeth*, the ghost in *Hamlet*, and the horrible gruesomeness of Webster that we may easily discern the strong hold of the demonic on the public mind" (CE 2.86). Curiously enough though, Milton is excluded. That Lovecraft read Milton is documented through the Doré allusions, Joshi's *Lovecraft's Library*, and also in a letter Lovecraft wrote to J. Vernon Shea: "As for Milton—I don't see how you . . . can argue away the distinctive charm of a large part of his work. He has the power of evoking unlimited images for persons of active imagination and no amount of academic theory can explain that away" (SL 4.158). Lovecraft is speaking of the then modern antipathy in academia that was prevailing against Milton in the early part of the twentieth century, with T. S. Eliot leading the critical charge against Milton's poetical relevance. Although Milton was displaced for a time by Donne and the metaphysical poets, Lovecraft realized that Milton, like his Samson, was a force too great to be restrained and eventually must be reckoned with. Perhaps this is what Johnson had in mind when he says, "But such is the power of [Milton's] poetry, that his call is obeyed without resistance, the reader feels himself in captivity to a higher and nobler mind, and criticism sinks into admiration" (442).

Although there is no verifiable documentation, as a student of the eighteenth century Lovecraft may have read Edmund Burke's *Essay on the Sublime and Beautiful*, the seminal text on the supernal, influenced extensively by Milton's dark sublime in *Paradise Lost*. Burke seems to have assimilated Milton into his writings, especially in his *Reflections on the French Revolution*, as he presents the French conflict as another War in Heaven, "heaping mountains upon mountains" and wag[ing] war with heaven itself" (92), a variation of the defeated rebel angels buried deep beneath the mountains in Book VI of *Paradise Lost* (6.652). But most provocatively is Burke's masterful study of "Obscurity" in Section III of the *Sublime and Beautiful*:

> To make anything terrible, obscurity seems in general to be necessary. When we know the full extent of any danger, when we can accustom our eyes to it, a great deal of the apprehension vanishes. Everyone will be sensible of this who considers how greatly night adds to our dread, in all cases of danger, and how much the notions of ghosts and goblins, of which none can form clear ideas, affect minds, which give credit to the popular tales concerning such beings.... No person seems better to have understood the secret of heightening, or of setting terrible things, if I may use the expression, in their strongest light by the force of judicious obscurity, than Milton. (59)

Lovecraft, once again, in "Supernatural Horror in Literature," almost perfectly mirrors Burke:

> The oldest and strongest emotion of mankind is fear, and the oldest and strongest kind of fear is fear of the unknown.... The one test of the really weird is simply this—whether or not there excited in the reader a profound sense of dread, and of contact with unknown spheres and powers; a subtle attitude of awed listening, as if for the beating of black wings or the scratching of outside shapes and entities on the known universe's utmost rim. (CE 2.82, 84)

Milton and Lovecraft are both adept at dramatizing entities whose beating black wings scrape against the underbelly of cavernous abodes, be it Satan or Cthulhu, scratching at the peripheries of the visible world, be it Eden or Providence, and lurking there, waiting to infest and infiltrate the slender membrane separating the known from the unknown universe. To sum up, Lovecraft's and Milton's genius lies in the distinctiveness of their indistinctive vision, in other words, in their mastery of the sublime in all its elusiveness.

The Evidence: Prophetic Milton:

"The Tomb" (1917): Lovecraft as anti-empiricist, inverse mystic is evident here:

> It is an unfortunate fact that the bulk of humanity is too limited in its mental vision to weigh with patience and intelligence those isolated phenomena, seen and felt only by a psychologically sensitive few, which lie outside its common experience. Men of broader intellect know that there is no sharp distinction betwixt the real and the unreal; [...] but the prosaic materialism of the majority condemns as madness the flashes of super-sight which penetrate the common veil of obvious empiricism. (CF 1.38-39)

Milton would undoubtedly concur. Milton, too, speak of things "invisible to mortal sight" in Book VII of *Paradise Lost* and of a "fit audience find, though few" (7.30). For Lovecraft: "All day I have been wandering through the mystic groves of the hollow; thinking thoughts I need not discuss, and conversing with things I need not name. In years a child of ten, I had seen and heard many wonders unknown to the throng; and was oddly aged in certain respects" (CF 1.41). Milton in the opening Prologue of Book III in *Paradise Lost*, lines 27-29, also speaks of wandering "where the muses haunt/ Clear Spring, or shady Grove, or Sunny Hill, / Smit with the love of sacred Song."

"Celephaïs" (1920): Lovecraft introduces a certain degree of mythic self-fashioning in this passage:

> There are not many persons who know what wonders are opened to them in the stories and visions of their youth; [. . .] But some of us awake in the night with strange phantasms of enchanted hills and gardens, of fountains that sing in the sun, of golden cliffs overhanging murmuring seas, and of plains that stretch down to sleeping cities of bronze and stone, and of shadowy companies of heroes that ride caparisoned white horses along the edges of thick forests [. . .] (CF 1.185).

As cited above, this is another variation of the opening theme in Book III of *Paradise Lost*, of Milton wandering where the Muses haunt, but Lovecraft's youthful Miltonian precociousness comes into play here also as in Milton's own *Apology for Smectymnus*, where he celebrates the chivalric ideal of becoming a knight: "Next (for hear me out now, readers), that I may tell ye whether my younger feet wandered: I betook me among those lofty fables and romances, which recount in solemn cantos the deeds of knighthood founded by our victorious kings. . . . Only this my mind gave me, that every free and gentle spirit . . . ought to be born a knight" (694). Both men, like Shakespeare's Coriolanus, dreamed of a world elsewhere, and both forged a hard-wrought interior sense of self-worth independent of any objective evaluations.

"The Quest of Iranon" (1921): Iranon, like Milton, seems "Smit with the love of sacred Song" (*Paradise Lost* 3.29) in a world that devalues the higher life, as Milton reminds his audience repeatedly. Lovecraft's poetic visionary shares the same sentiments: "Ye toil to live, but is not life made of beauty and song? And if ye suffer no singers among you, where shall be the fruits of your toil?" (CF 1.250). Milton's "fit audience find though few" (7.31), once again, reverberates here, the vision-filled minority surrounded by the visionless majority. And if we compare the ending of "The Quest of Iranon" with the ending of Milton's *Lycidas*, the similarities are even more striking.

First Milton:

> Thus sang the uncouth Swain to th'Oaks and rills
> While the still morn went out with Sandals gray; . . .
> And now the Sun had stretch't out all the hills,
> And now was dropt into the Western bay;
> At last he rose, and twitch't his Mantle blue:
> Tomorrow to fresh Woods, and Pastures new. (186-93)

Now Lovecraft:

> Into the sunset wandered Iranon, seeking still for his native land and for men who would understand and cherish his songs and dreams. In all the cities of Cydathria and in the lands beyond the Bnazic desert gay-faced children laughed at his olden songs and tattered robe of purple; but Iranon stayed ever young, and wore wreaths upon his golden head whilst he sang of Aira, delight of the past and hope of the future. (CF 1.254)

A forlornness haunts these two passages, Milton singing to oaks and streams and Lovecraft seeking better men in better lands, even though both poet-prophets are filled with hope as they are about to commence upon their high vocation, committed to their aesthetic vision despite the opinion of popular consensus.

"The Colour out of Space" (1927): Here, most graphically, is Lovecraft's dark theophany, where he appropriates religious terminology concerning demonic infiltration and possession and the stages leading up to it within a pseudo-scientific, extraterrestrial framework. This can be seen as well in "The Call of Cthulhu" with aliens as interdimensional beings who assume "shape" but are "not made of matter" (CF 2.39), a vague allusion to Milton's good and evil angels who are ethereal in nature, but of a spiritual substance (*Paradise Lost* 6.330), which is neither solid or liquid, and like the Great Old Ones, can "plunge from world to world through the sky" ("The Call of Cthulhu" [CF 2.39]). The Angel Raphael, in Book V of *Paradise Lost*, possessing both form and formlessness, is described when leaving God the Father's court: "up springing light / Flew through the midst of Heav'n" (5.250), but when descending to earth "his proper shape returns / A Seraph wing'd" (5.276-77). Milton and Lovecraft always negotiate a healthy dialogue between body and bodylessness with their divine or demonic entities. As in "The Colour out of Space," the entity is described as "jest a cloud of colour like that light out thar now, that ye can hardly see an' can't tell what it is" (CF 2.391). As mentioned previously, indistinctiveness fulfills both Burke's and Lovecraft's prerequisites for horror. This is nowhere more dramatically visualized than in the first appearance of Death in Book II line 666 of *Paradise Lost*:

> The other shape,
> If shape it might be call'd that shape had none
> Distinguishable in member, joint, or limb,
> Or substance might be call'd that shadow seem'd
> For each seem'd either; black it stood as night. (2.266-70)

The sense of presence and absence, form and formlessness, is reminiscent of the creature from "The Color out of Space," described as a "column of unknown color" with "fiendish contours" (CF 2.395) but also of some of Lovecraft's most amorphous monsters, gliding, sliding, and shapeshifting their way across the landscape. Milton's repetitive use of "might be called" and "seemed" conveys a state of indeterminacy and therefore of authentic horror because of the interior eyes' murky perception of what is transpiring.

J. R. R. Tolkien uses this same technique in his description of the Balrog in *The Fellowship of the Rings*. The description is brief and succinct, and quite at odds with Peter Jackson's more corporeal and literal rendition in his cinematic adaptation:

> Something was coming up behind them. What it was could not be seen: it was like a great shadow, in the middle of which was a dark form, of man-shape *maybe*, yet greater; and a power and terror *seemed* to be in it and to go before it. . . . The dark figure streaming with fire raced towards them. His enemy halted again, facing him, and the shadow about it reached out like two vast wings. (344)

Tolkien's Balrog is never clearly conceptualized as having wings, unlike Jackson's version. Readers are left with somewhat conflicting images and are left to imaginatively fend for themselves. And that exactly is what exacerbates the fear—an impending sense of urgency accompanied by an increasing sense of impotence in the face of the growing unnamable. Algernon Blackwood is more than adept at this, especially in "The Willows," a precursor in many ways to the film *The Blair Witch Project*.

Despite Tolkien's personal antipathy to Milton, his Balrog and Milton's Death are close cousins.

Lovecraft's allusions to the Celestial Cloud over Mount Sinai from the Book of Exodus mirrors Milton's description of the cloud concealing God the Father in Book III, lines 376–80, of *Paradise Lost*, both heralding and intimating the presence of concealed power, an extraterrestrial for Lovecraft, Yahweh for Milton. Although James Egan in "Dark Apocalypse" would consider this a parodic account, I would disagree, seeing that terror and awe in the face of the unknowable seem to be the end result: "Not a man breathed for several seconds. Then a cloud of darker depth passed over the moon [. . .] At this there was a general cry, muffled with awe, but husky and almost identical from every throat" ("The Colour out of Space" [CF 2.392-93]). Lovecraft continues this theophanic or hierophanic analogy as he then alludes to the burning bush on Mt. Sinai when he speaks of "a thousand points of faint and unhallowed radiance, tipping each bough like the fire of St. Elmo or the flames that came down on the apostles heads at Pentecost" (CF 2.393). Interestingly enough, it is this same fire that lights upon Ahab's harpoon in the Quarterdeck scene of *Moby-Dick*, and one in which he impudently and blasphemously puts out (Melville 497). Lovecraft employs the symbolism of religious discourse without the substance or traditional intent, but he is conveying a hierophanic encounter, one even more terrifying because of the Gnosticism behind it. For Lovecraft, the extraterrestrial dimension, regardless of its intent, is always superior to the terrestrial, since it essentially frees man from himself, frees him from the complacency of smug self-delusion and self-satisfaction. Lovecraft himself readily admits to his "longing for cosmic liberation" (*Lord of a Visible World* 269). Through transference, the alien other becomes a God surrogate, similar to, but radically dissimilar from, the Spielbergian cosmos where a type of covenantal contract is re-enacted on a holy mountain between benevolent space gods and humanity, best exemplified at the end of *Close Encounters of the Third Kind*. "Column of unknown color" and "tongues of foul flame" ("The Colour out of Space" [CF 2.394, 395])—a parodic approach to religion or a re-appropriation of it, a replacement of the divine with the ominous ontological Other or a negation of it? Lovecraft writes to Clark Ashton Smith:

> My conception of phantasy, as a genuine art-form, is *an extension rather than a negation of reality*. . . . The true function of phantasy is to give the imagination

a ground for limitless expansion, and to satisfy aesthetically the sincere and burning curiosity and sense of awe which a sensitive minority of mankind feel toward the alluring and provocative abysses of unplumbed space and unguessed entity which press in upon the known world from unknown infinities and in unknown relationships of time, space, matter, force, dimensionality, and consciousness. (*Lord of a Visible World* 213)

And elsewhere, Lovecraft once again speaks of the unknowability of "unthinkable galaxies and unplumbed dimensions" (*Lord of a Visible World* 258), differentiating between extraterrestrial and interdimensional life. Whether elder or older gods, Lovecraft seems to be saying that man needs his deities, for better or for worse. Lovecraft as atheistic theist is no more absurd than Milton as Christian traditionalist, evident in his poetry if not always in his prose. But Milton readily admits to writing poetry with his right hand and prose with his left, prose being "a mortal thing . . . of no empyreal conceit" ("The Reason of Church Government" 667). Ultimately, "The Colour out of Space" is a dark theodicy, as noted earlier, an unholy *Paradise Lost*. The Colour's emanations over the countryside, as it touches everything in its path, is an unholy Pentecostal image, as the boughs of the trees "were all straining skyward, tipped with tongues of foul flame, and lambent tricklings of the same monstrous fire were creeping about the ridgepoles of the house, barn, and sheds. [. . .] and over all the rest reigned that riot of luminous amorphousness, that alien and undiminished rainbow of cryptic poison [. . .] in its cosmic and unrecognisable chromaticism" (CF 2.395-96). Biblically, fire is an image of either purification or punitiveness, and is associated either with the divine or the demonic. Lovecraft purposely seems to coalesce and confuse the two here, in which a scene of great toxic beauty is being conveyed, akin in many ways to a theophanic encounter. Fiery manifestations in trees is, of course, an allusion to Moses witnessing the Burning Bush on Mt. Sinai, which Milton adapts to Adam's first encounter with God in *Paradise Lost*: "Here had new begun / My wand'ring, had not hee who was my Guide / Up hither, from among the Trees appear'd, / Presence Divine" (7.311-14).

Romantic Milton

"Dagon" (1917): This is one of the first instances of Byronic Satanism introduced into the Lovecraftian cosmos, overcoming arduous ordeals in the face of overwhelming odds—a hallmark of the Romantic hero: "I felt myself on the edge of the world; peering over the rim into a fathomless chaos of eternal night. Through my terror ran curious reminiscences of 'Paradise Lost', and of Satan's hideous climb through the unfashioned realms of darkness" (CF 1.55). This is a strong feature in Lovecraft, especially when he speaks of the exclusivity of the man of character in one of his letter: "but nothing in heaven or earth is so important to the man of spirit and imagination as the inviolate integrity of his cerebral life—his sense of utter integration and defiant independence as a proud, lone entity face to face with the illimitable cosmos" (*Lord of a Visible World* 195). Milton's Satan's cry, "Better to reign in Hell, than serve in Heav'n" (1.263), and the Nietzschean überman's fist shaking at the cosmos seem just a stone's throw away in this instance.

"Beyond the Wall of Sleep" (1919): This seems to be Lovecraft's rendition of *Moby-Dick*, although he first refers to the book only in 1929 (*SL* 3.13). Just as Ahab has been read as Milton's Satan on a whaling ship waging war against a Leviathan god, Joe Slater bears considerable affinities to his two predecessors, pursuing his own cosmic hunt. Like Ahab-Satan, he rages against "some mysterious blazing entity that shook and laughed and mocked at him. This vast, vague personality seemed to have done him a terrible wrong, and to kill it in a triumphant revenge was his paramount desire. In order to reach it, he said, he would soar through abysses of emptiness, burning every obstacle that stood in his way" (CF 1.76). Satan and Ahab's sense of "injured merit" (*Paradise Lost* 1.98) is transfigured into:

> This *thing* had done Slater some hideous but unnamed wrong, which the maniac (if maniac he were) yearned to avenge. From the manner in which Slater alluded to their dealings, I judged that he and the luminous *thing* had met on equal terms; that in his dream existence the man was himself a luminous *thing* of the same race as his enemy. This impression was sustained by frequent references to *flying through space* and *burning* all that impeded his progress. (CF 1.78)

Slater, Ahab, and Satan as monomaniacs is evident here. Ahab, speaks of himself as a "worshiper of fire" (Melville 496) and Satan is compared innumerable times to a blazing comet—"and like a Comet burn'd" (*Paradise Lost* 2.708). Ahab defiantly declares "Who's over me?" (Melville 164) and Satan constantly speaks of his equality with God—"Whom reason hath equall'd, force hath made supreme / Above his equals" (*Paradise Lost* 1.248-49). Here, Lovecraft's Satan is, of course, the Romantic Satan, victimized victimizer of an unjust deity, which was appropriated by Melville in Ahab. It should be noted that Melville, a deep reader or misreader of Milton, deeply interiorized Milton's Satan, so much so that he had a print of John Martin's *Satan Presiding at the Infernal Council* hanging over his bed. Of special significance is that Melville was a married man at the time.

"Facts concerning the Late Arthur Jermyn and His Family" (1920): The opening lines are reminiscent of Ahab's "All visible objects, man, are but as pasteboard masks . . . If man will strike, strike through the mask! . . . I see in him outrageous strength, with an inscrutable malice sinewing it" (Melville 164). Lovecraft begins with: "Life is a hideous thing, and from the background behind what we know of it peer daemonical hints of truth which makes it sometimes a thousandfold more hideous" (CF 1.171).

"The Moon-Bog" (1921): The ending of this story is similar to the ending of Milton's *On the Morning of Christ's Nativity*, where the denizens of hell leave the world upon the arrival of the Christ Child. Milton conveys both repulsion and poetic fascination:

> So when the Sun in bed,
> Curtain'd with cloudy red,
> Pillows his chin upon an orient wave,
> The flocking shadows pale
> Troop to th'infernal jail:
> Each fetter'd Ghost slips to his several grave,
> And the yellow-skirted fays
> Fly after the Night-steeds, leaving their Moon-lov'd maze. (229-36)

Lovecraft conveys the same sense of horrific splendor as these elusive phantasms sink back into their primal ooze:

> There my eyes dilated again with a wild wonder as great as if I had not just turned from a scene beyond the pale of Nature, for on the ghastly red-litten plain was moving a procession of beings in such a manner as none ever saw before save in nightmares.
> Half gliding, half floating in the air, the white-clad bog-wraiths were slowly retreating toward the still waters and the island ruin in fantastic formations suggesting some ancient and solemn ceremonial dance. (CF 1.262-63)

A variation of this occurs again in "The Horror at Red Hook," where a "ceremonial procession" of a "nightmare hoard"—"goat, satyr, and Ægipan, incubus, succuba, and lemur [. . .] skip and leap with Dionysiac fury" (CF 1.500), but now not in flight but to take hold of their ancient abodes.

Milton's catalogue includes: Apollo, Nymphs, Lars, Lemurs, Peor, Baalim, Moloch, Isis, Orus, Anubis, Osiris, Fays, and Typhon (Milton, *Nativity* XIX-XXV). And in "The Shadow over Innsmouth," Lovecraft continues these Miltonic litanies when he has Zadok admit: "I was a mighty little critter, but I heerd what I heerd an' seen what I seen—Dagon an' Ashtoreth—Belial an' Beëlzebub—Golden Caff an' the idols o' Canaan an' the Philistines—Babylonish abominations" (CF 3.193), all referenced in Milton's catalogue of devils in the opening of Book II of *Paradise Lost* (2.43-389). Both Lovecraft and Milton Homerically revel in their lists.

"Hypnos" (1922): In many ways, this remarkable tale reads like a microcosmic hybrid of Books I and II of *Paradise Lost*. Just as Milton speaks of how "with no middle flight" he intends to soar "above th' Aonian Mount" (1.14-15), the Lovecraftian narrator speaks of his own *"plungings"* and *"soarings"* on his cosmic flight (CF 1.396). What is most striking is the narrator's description of his fellow journeyer, described as "golden" with a "strange light and frightful with its weird beauty [. . .] youthful cheeks [. . .] burning eyes [. . .] Olympian brow and shadowing hair" (CF 1.328), the very embodiment of a flaming seraphim and a perfect counterpart to Milton's Satan. "I will hint—only hint—" the narrator continues, "that he had designs which involved the rulership of the visible universe and more; designs whereby the earth and stars would move at his command, and the destinies of all living things be his" (CF 1.328). Lovecraft, assuming the role of bardic witness, also makes brief allusion to Satan's aspiration to wage War in Heaven when he speaks of the "unmentionable warfare in unmentionable spheres by which alone one might achieve success" (CF 1.328), soon admitting afterwards that he himself is "no man of strength to risk" (CF 1.328) such an undertaking. Following this is an allusion to Satan's encounter with Chaos before the gates of hell in Book II of *Paradise Lost*, a "hoary deep, a dark / Illimitable Ocean without bound, / Without dimension" (2.890-93) of confusion, "for hot, cold, moist and dry . . . / Strive here for Maistry" (2.898). Just as Satan must make his away across such an abyss of density and contrariety, so too does Lovecraft describe his companion's trek into that "limitless vacua beyond all thought and entity," an "awesome ocean of virgin aether . . . a sticky, clammy, mass, if such terms can be applied to analogous qualities in a non-material sphere" (CF 1.328-29). This brief, imaginative reworking of Satan's diabolical journey, with Lovecraft as both witness and limited participant, corresponds in many ways to Milton's role in the poem, with Satan serving as Milton's doppelgänger, thereby allowing the poet to exorcise his own evil inclinations and project them upon his dark representative. Melville does the same with his Ishmael-Ahab dichotomy, allowing him to admit that he has written "a wicked book, and feel[s] spotless as the Lamb" (letter to Nathaniel Hawthorne, in *Moby Dick* 566).

Weird Milton

"Polaris" (1918): "In my shame and despair I sometimes scream frantically," cries Lovecraft's narrator, "begging the dream creatures around me to waken me ere the Inutos steal up the pass behind the peak Noton and take the citadel by surprise; but these creatures are daemons, for they laugh at me and tell me I am not dreaming. They mock me whilst I sleep, and whilst the squat yellow foe may be creeping silently upon us" (CF 1.69). Lovecraft presents a double allusion here. One is to Milton's *Paradise Regain'd* when Christ, asleep in the wilderness, is assaulted by his own night-gaunts:

> But shelter'd slept in vain, for at his head
> The Tempter watch'd, and soon with ugly dreams
> Disturb'd his sleep . . . nor yet stay'd the terror there.
> Infernal Ghosts, and Hellish Furies, round
> Environ'd thee, some howl'd, some yell'd, some shriek'd,
> Some bent at thee thir fiery darts." (4.407-22)

The "squat yellow foe" Lovecraft alludes to is a direct reference to Satan in Book III of *Paradise Lost*:

> Squat like a Toad, close at the ear of Eve;
> Assaying by his Devilish art to reach
> The organs of her fancy, and with them forge
> Illusions as he list, Phantasms and Dreams. (3.800-803)

According to Joshi's *Lovecraft's Library*, Lovecraft did own a copy of *The Poetical Works of Milton, Young, Gray, Beattie, and Collins* (#704). Whether he read *Paradise Regain'd* or whether the poem was included in his edition is unknown to me. However, in a letter to his aunt about his anticipated return home, an end to Miltonic exile is not far from his mind: "But Providence would always be at the back of my head as a goal to be worked toward—an ultimate Paradise to be regain'd at last" (*Lord of a Visible World* 188).

"Pickman's Model" (1926): Here is Lovecraft's Milton-Doré-Fuseli analogy, conflating the three when Milton as Prophetical Weird precursor comes into play. "That's because," observes Lovecraft-Pickman, "only a real artist knows the actual anatomy of the terrible or the physiology of fear—the exact sort of lines and proportions that connect up with latent instincts or hereditary memories of fright, and the proper colour contrasts and lighting effects to stir the dormant sense of strangeness" (CF 2.57). Lovecraft then proceeds to reference Fuseli and Doré, both renowned interpretative illustrators of Milton's *Paradise Lost*, and both particularly adept at dark, brooding depictions of the demonic, especially of Milton's Hell. Lovecraft's definition of the weird artist seems to capture Milton's unearthly visitations. "Well," continues Lovecraft, "I should say that the really weird artist has a kind of vision which makes models, or summons up what amounts to actual scenes from the spectral world he lives in" (CF 2.58). Both Lovecraft and Milton delve into the realm of the diabolical, but both counterbalance that dark sojourn—Lovecraft through his dream quests into other worlds and alternate interdimensional realities and Milton through imaginative, Ignatian meditation, wandering through undefined locales where the Muses haunt, a geographical hybrid between England and Israel. Both, as weird artists, achieve relief and release from their dark internal and external pressures that threaten to consume them by engaging in these self-contained and parallel universes.

"The Dunwich Horror" (1928): This is another example of the Prophetical Weird: "The Old Ones were, the Old Ones are, and the Old Ones shall be. Not in the spaces we know, but *between* them" (CF 2.434). This is an inversion and perversion of the confession of faith in Christ as He "who is and who was and who is to come" (Revelation 1:8). Christ who is "the gate" (John 10:7) of life is replaced with "*Yog-Sothoth* [who] knows the gate. *Yog-Sothoth* [who] is the gate" (CF 2.434), Old Ones who have begotten on their elect their own image an inversion of the power of the Holy Spirit to beget within humanity the image of Christ and an allusion to the Nicene Creed where The Son is begotten from or consubstantial with the Father, not made (*Catechism* 56). Lovecraft's own Alpha and Omega is a cosmological infiltration and transfiguration of humanity, and once again, for better or for worse, it will be different. When the monstrous Whateley is found dead, his appearance below the waist is inhuman, but especially his abdominal region where "a score of long greenish-grey tentacles with red sucking mouths protruded limply" (CF 2.439); the snaky configurations emanating from his midsection echo Milton's description of Sin in Book II of *Paradise Lost*, where "Hell Hounds" are described "about her middle round" which "never ceasing bark'd. . . . A hideous Peal" (2.654-56)—the bitter fruit of her incestuous rape by her son, Death. Both Whateley and Sin are semi-anthropomorphic beings, shadowy vestiges of the humanly inhuman, the product of grotesque mating—Whateley's mother with Yog-Sothoth, and Sin with her father Satan. Lovecraft and Milton never let us forget that the radically Other may disguise itself as something else, but Leviathan is always lurking underneath.

Milton initially introduces Satan through epic similes as a floating island, an abode of apparent safety, but in reality a treacherous reef for sail and sailor alike. Milton, like Lovecraft, shares the same preoccupation with serpentine beings who undergo Ovidian metamorphoses such as in Book I of *Paradise Lost,* where Satan is described as a Typhonic creature of "monstrous size" with "head up-lift above the wave, and Eyes / That sparkling blaz'd" (1.193-97). Nothing but death awaits the wayfarer who seeks "With fixed Anchor[age] in his scaly rind" to "Moor by his side under the Lee, while Night / Invests the Sea" (1.206-8). First contact will always lead to final corruption. In Lovecraft's world, as well as in Milton's, the senses may discern the appearance of normalcy, but in the end mind and eye are misaligned, perception falls betrayed, and the human gives way to the humanoid. A talking Snake in Eden gives proof of that. Even at the end of *Paradise Lost,* Satan's true form is finally revealed in Hell, as he becomes the image of the thing he always was, transformed into the primeval chaos monster, arms clinging to his ribs, legs entwining, forked tongue issuing forth a "dismal universal hiss" . . . "till supplanted down he fell / A monstrous Serpent on his belly prone" (10.507-13). And Milton concludes with his usual litany of devilish names as well, but somehow divested of the romantic aura and wonder that haunted his earlier poetry. Instead, we are left with a grizzly "thick swarming" assortment of

> complicated monsters, head and tail,
> Scorpion and Asp, and Amphisbaena dire,
> Cerastes horn'd, Hydrus, and Ellops drear,
> And Dipsas . . .
> but still greatest [Satan in] the midst,
> Now Dragon grown. (10.521-29)

And in a way, being Satan's final exit from the poem, this is appropriate, since Lovecraft's alien entities also become more progressively alienated from us and from each other as well—extraterrestrial in the most horrific sense of the word.

Milton and Lovecraft are ostensibly outsiders, Milton reminding us in Book VII of *Paradise Lost* that he has "fallen on evil days and evil tongues," "in darkness and with dangers compast round, and solitude" (7.26-28), and Lovecraft, at the end of his semi-autobiographical work "The Outsider," unable to penetrate beyond a cold and unyielding surface of polished glass, to escape from and beyond himself into the world around him, resignedly concluding: "I know always that I am an outsider; a stranger in this century and among those who are still men" (CF 1.272). So, too, does Milton also know what it is like to be the stranger and wonders if his "higher Argument" will ever be "sufficient" for the world around him "unless an age too late, or cold . . . damp [his] intended wing / Deprest" (*Paradise Lost* 9.42-46). And what Lovecraft says of himself is ultimately applicable to Milton as well: "It is now clear to me that any actual literary merit I have is confined to tales of dream-life, strange shadow, and cosmic 'outsideness', notwithstanding a keen interest in many other departments of life" (*Lord of a Visible World* 349). In the end, however, Lovecraft yearned for a communion with something more, something greater than the totality of himself. Despite his cosmicism, his philosophy of indifferentism, he sought some type of psychic integration, to belong to and lose himself in a continuum of being—past, present, and future, a cultural apotheosis of sorts that also, simultaneously and paradoxically, denied and defied religious connotations. "Religious people," observes Lovecraft,

> seek a mystical identification with a system of hereditary myths; whereas I, who am non-religious, seek a corresponding mystical identification with the only immediate tangible external reality which my perceptions acknowledge—i.e., the continuous stream of folkways around me. I achieve this mystical identification simply by a symbolic acceptance of the minor externals whose synthesis constitutes the surrounding stream. I follow this acceptance purely for my own personal pleasure—*because I would feel lost in a limitless and impersonal cosmos if I had no way of thinking of myself but as a dissociated and independent point.* (*Lord of a Visible World* 233-34; my emphasis)

Both Lovecraft and Milton struggled against this feeling of lostness, and both strove to reclaim and recover themselves from the abyss of anonymity. Brothers in the supernatural, although on two opposite ends of the spectrum, Lovecraft and Milton, like Set and Osiris, Hades and Zeus, ultimately spring from the same cosmic womb.

Works Cited

Bleiler, E. F. "Introduction to the Dover Edition." In Lovecraft's *Supernatural Horror in Literature*. New York: Dover, 1973. iii–viii.

Burke, Edmund. *A Philosophical Enquiry into the Origin of Our Ideas of the Sublime and Beautiful*. Ed. James T. Boulton. Notre Dame, IN: University of Notre Dame Press, 1986.

——. *Reflections on the Revolution in France*. New York: Penguin, 1984.

Cannon, Peter. *H. P. Lovecraft*. Boston: Twayne, 1989.

Catechism of the Catholic Church. New York: Doubleday, 1997.

Egan, James. "Dark Apocalyptic: Lovecraft's Cthulhu Mythos as a Parody of Traditional Christianity." *Extrapolation* 23 (Spring 1983): 362–76.

Eliade, Mircea. *The Sacred and the Profane*. New York: Harcourt, 1959.

Ganson, Todd Stuart. "The Rational/Non-Rational Distinction in Plato's *Republic*." http://www.academia.edu/7832466/The_rational_non-rational_distinction_in_Plato_s_Republic Accessed August 17, 2013. Web.

Johnson, Samuel. *Selected Poetry and Prose*. Ed. Frank Brady and W. K. Wimsatt. Berkeley: University of California Press, 1977.

Joshi, S. T. *H. P. Lovecraft: Nightmare Countries*. New York: Metro Books, 2012.

——. *Lovecraft's Library: A Catalogue*. New York: Hippocampus Press, 2002.

Lovecraft, H.P. *Lord of a Visible World: An Autobiography in Letters*. Ed. S. T. Joshi and David E. Schultz. Athens: Ohio University Press, 2000.

Melville, Herman. *Moby Dick*. Ed. Harrison Hayford and Hershel Parker. New York: Norton, 1967 (rev. ed. 1976).

Milton, John. *Complete Poems and Major Prose*. Ed. Merritt Y. Hughes. Englewood Cliffs, NJ: Prentice-Hall, 1957.

Oates, Joyce Carol. "H. P. Lovecraft: An Introduction." In *Tales of H. P. Lovecraft*. Hopewell, NJ: Ecco Press, 1997. vii–xvi.

Parker, William Riley. *John Milton: A Biography*. New York: Oxford University Press, 1954.

Quale, Thomas. "The Blind Idiot God: Miltonic Echoes in the Cthulhu Mythos." *Crypt of Cthulhu* No. 49 (Lammas 1987): 24–28.

St. Armand, Barton Levi. *The Roots of Horror in the Fiction of H. P. Lovecraft*. Elizabethtown, NY: Dragon Press, 1977.

Tolkien, J. R. R. *The Lord of the Rings*. New York: Harper, 1999.

The Failed Promises of Rationality: Sam J. Lundwall on the Individual Lost in an Uncaring and Soulless World

Lars G. E. Backstrom
Independent Scholar

"However [said the Central Brain], the nature of the universe being what it is—"

"Rotten," said Bernhard, "to the core.... Just let me out of here," Bernhard suggested. He looked around at the drooling plants that surrounded him.

"What's behind those monsters?"

"More monsters."

—Sam J. Lundwall, *Bernhard the Conqueror* (146)

The aim of this paper is to analyze the Lovecraftian influences on Sam J. Lundwall's earlier works, and to introduce this remarkable Swedish SF author to the readers of today. Lundwall is credited with introducing H. P. Lovecraft to a wider Swedish readership in 1973. Since then he has translated Lovecraft's more important stories into Swedish and published them in several anthologies and collections; therefore, his name is closely linked to Lovecraft's.

Lundwall's relation to Lovecraft works on three levels: there is a direct influence; there is an influence from the same writers who influenced Lovecraft; and there is parallelism in both authors' writing. Common themes in Lundwall's novels are humanity's insignificance to the universe, humanity being trapped by forces we just cannot understand, a strong feeling of alienation and hopelessness, and characters who are not heroes and do not influence the unfolding of events.

Born in Stockholm in 1941, Sam J. Lundwall (Figure 1) is perhaps the most respected and influential Swedish SF author, both nationally and internationally. Apart from writing several popular novels and short stories, he has been a driving force in Swedish and international fandom since the

1960s while also working as a troubadour, photographer, publisher, editor, translator, and broadcaster. Lundwall has been chairman of World SF and a board member of the Science Fiction Writers of America. While he is still very active in fandom, he does not do interviews nor answer questions about his relation to Lovecraft for personal reasons (Lundwall, personal communication, 2013). As far as I know, a scholarly study of Lundwall's fiction has never before been done; and since I assume that most readers will not be familiar with Lundwall's oeuvre, I will begin with a short biography and a partial bibliography where only the works relevant to this study will be included.

Figure 1. Sam J. Lundwall at Eurocon 2011 in Stockholm, Sweden. Photo: commons.wikimedia.org.

Lundwall's first major publication was the nonfiction book *Science fiction: från Begynnelsen till våra Dagar* (1969; Science Fiction: From the Beginning to the Present Day), later translated into English as *Science Fiction: An Illustrated History*. This book is still a valuable reference work.

Originally written in English and then translated into Swedish by himself, Lundwall's first professional fiction publication was the 1971 Ace Double *No Time for Heroes* and *Alice's World*. In the novels humans are confronted with their ancient dreams and myths, who, after millennia of neglect, have become independent sentients. The antihero in *No Time for Heroes*, Bernhard Rordin, returns in the 1973 stand-alone sequel *Bernhard the Conqueror*.

Table 1. Selected Bibliography (*Indicates publication in Swedish)

Title	Year
Nonfiction	
Science fiction: från Begynnelsen till våra Dagar*	1969
Science Fiction: An Illustrated History	1977
Novels	
Alice's World	1971
No Time for Heroes	1971
Bernhard the Conqueror	1973
2018 A.D. or the King Kong Blues	1975
Bernards Magiska Sommar*	1975
Fängelsestaden*	1978
Flickan i Fönstret vid Världens Kant*	1980
Novella	
Gäst i Frankensteins Hus*	1976
Anthologies and Collections	
Skräckens Labyrinter, 1st ed.*	1973
Den Fantastiska Romanen 2: Gotisk Skräckromantik från Horace Walpole till H. P. Lovecraft*	1973
Cthulhu 1*	1988
Cthulhu 2*	1988
Första Stora Monsterboken*	1991
Skräckens Hus och Andra Noveller*	1991
Andra Stora Monsterboken*	1992
Midnattsgästerna och Andra Noveller*	1992
Dagon och Andra Noveller*	1992
Skräckens Labyrinter, 2nd ed.*	1993
Necronomicon: de Döda Namnens Bok*	1995
Cthulhus Arv*	1996
Stora Necronomicon*	1998

In 1974 Lundwall published *King Kong Blues*, which was translated by himself into English as *2018 A.D. or the King Kong Blues*. It is set in a world frighteningly similar to our own, where failed political experiments and mega-corporate greed have created a society in which the only goal for the individual is instant gratification as an escape from the horrors of daily life. The novel is a scathing satire on his times and especially of the so-called Swedish System, which was then a socialist-capitalist mixed economy with a state obsessed with controlling and surveying its citizens. Lundwall writes in the preface to the US edition that "I envisaged there would be no one to revolt against, no one to turn your Kalashnikov against, no one a Mr. Winston [sic] could be forced to love in the end, because there would be no Big Brother as such, and he couldn't care less if you loved him or not anyway, if he existed" (6). The book was a huge success and was translated into several languages, including Mandarin, and circulated as illegal *samizdat* copies in the Soviet Union (*2018 A.D.* 7). *King Kong Blues* still feels relevant, since the societal problems depicted are still with us and the dehumanizing effects they have on the main characters would be the same if it was written today. In some respects I think it is even more daring than most mainstream SF would care to be in the present day.

In 1976 Lundwall wrote the Gothic pastiche *Gäst i Frankensteins hus* (*Guest in Frankenstein's House*), a poststructuralist novella that blends black humor with a homage to old monster movies. The novel 1978 *Fängelsestaden* (*The Prison City*) is set in the earth's distant past in the era when the supercontinent Pangea is starting to fragmentate. Humanity huddles in a vast, labyrinthine, nameless city on the coast of the Thetys Sea. The unnamed city is built by an alien race and has a distorted architecture. It consists of vast blocks carved out of the living rock, each block split into 'houses,' and each block and house is itself a labyrinth so complex that it can never be explored. Exact dating is difficult, but a date around 250 million years ago in the Permian Triassic boundary is likely (see Nield 179; Ogg et al. 95).

In 1980 Lundwall again changed style and wrote the romance *Flickan i fönstret vid världens kant* (*The Girl in the Window at the Edge of the World*). It is set on a flat earth where time endlessly repeats itself. Lundwall continued to write fiction until 1997, in the same setting as *Flickan i fönstret vid världens kant*, when he officially announced his retirement as an author.

It might be that Lovecraft's influence on Lundwall can be traced all the way back to his own youth. On 11 February 1954, "The Outsider," and then on April 1, "The Picture in the House," were broadcast on Swedish Public Radio in a late night radio show (Andersson, quoted in Lovecraft, *Skräcknoveller* 575). Lundwall was around thirteen then, so he would probably not have willingly missed these broadcasts. I read both my first Lovecraft and Lundwall stories at about that age myself, and I can vouch for the enormous impact such powerful stories can have on a young impressionable mind.

In 1973 Lundwall translated several of Lovecraft's stories into Swedish, in the collection *Skräckens labyrinter* (Labyrinths of Fear). In the anthology *Den fantastiska romanen 2: Gotisk skräckromantik från Horace Walpole to H. P. Lovecraft* (The Fantastic Novel 2: Gothic Romances from Horace Walpole to H. P. Lovecraft), intended for undergraduate studies in literature, Lundwall includes "The Rats in the Walls." Ever since then, their two names have been closely linked in Sweden (see Fyhr 114). In addition, Lundwall has edited several volumes, either partly or completely containing works by Lovecraft (see table 1).

Lundwall himself does not seem to be able to decide what he thinks about Lovecraft. In *Skräckens labyrinter*, he writes that Lovecraft's fiction "surpasses everything in gothic literature, including his more famous compatriot Edgar Allan Poe's works" (quoted in Fyhr 114). In the same year, in the anthology *Den fantastiska romanen 2*, his introduction to "The Rats in the Walls" claims that Lovecraft can be repetitive although occasionally very effective (291). However, in *Science Fiction: An Illustrated History* he claims that Lovecraft's writings end "up as mere sounds, terrors without substance . . . and his enormous popularity is a constant surprise to me." Yet he gives Lovecraft more than double the space he gives Poe, and no fewer than three illustrations (33). It seems as if Lundwall freely admits the influence Lovecraft has had on the genre, but he is hesitant to acknowledge the quality of Lovecraft's writing, perhaps because he does not want to admit the influence Lovecraft has had on his own writing.

Lundwall himself lists as his literary influences Edgar Allan Poe, Lord Dunsany, Clark Ashton Smith, and Jack Vance (*Bernards Magiska Summar* 110, 114). Lundwall has also admitted to being influenced by *Mad* magazine illustrator Will Elder (*An Illustrated History* 161). Strangely enough, nowhere does Lundwall claim inspiration from Lovecraft. Even so, the literary influence of Lovecraft on Lundwall is undeniable.

The literary friendship and mutual influence between Lovecraft and Clark Ashton Smith is well known, and Jack Vance was in his turn influenced by Smith. There is also some parallelism in that they have shared influences: Lovecraft was also influenced by Poe and Lord Dunsany, and one of the main inspirations for *Fängelsestaden* (The Prison City) is *Le carceri d'invenzione* (The Imaginary Prisons), a suite of sixteen prints by Italian artist Giovanni Battista Piranesi (1720–1778) (Figure 2). It is very possible that Lovecraft with his interest in both architecture and the eighteenth century was familiar with these prints. The novel also contains themes such as self-referral, infinity, libraries, and labyrinths that show influence from the Argentinian author Jorge Luis Borges, who was himself influenced by Lovecraft.

The novella *Gäst i Frankensteins hus* possibly contains the only direct reference to Lovecraft's writings: "With deft hands the beautiful Zenta now prepared an excellent Sole Menuiére, which we had together with a few bottles of Chateau d'Arkham of a good vintage" (11). In a similar tribute, the castle in the romance *Flickan i fönstret vid världens kant*, where the two incestuous siblings spent their youth and where the now grown-up brother resides alone remembering his runaway sister, shows an uncanny similarity to Exham Priory in "The Rats in the Walls," complete with an ancient altar in a hidden crypt beneath. There are also several passages in Lundwall's works that show clear Lovecraftian influences. Take this passage from *Bernhard the Conqueror*, for instance:

> ... for a moment the heavens split, giving Bernhard a fleeting glimpse of a horrifying darkness deeper than space, devoid of stars and filled with sluggishly moving shadows that fought to get out through the gash ...
>
> "That was something from outside our space-time continuum [said the God machine] and I am not sure we even saw whatever it was there. You only saw something that your small brain wrought together as it tried to relate to something totally alien to your own pitiable notions of the universe ... Tell me, what did you see?" Bernhard told the machine. "Interesting," it muttered. "I thought I saw ..." (129)

Compare that with this passage from "The Haunter of the Dark": "And beyond all else he glimpsed an infinite gulf of sheer darkness, where solid and semi-solid forms were known only by their windy stirrings, and cloudy patterns of force seemed to superimpose order on chaos and hold forth a key to all the paradoxes and arcana of the worlds we know" (CF 3.465). Or with this passage from "The Music of Erich Zann": "I saw no city spread below, and no friendly lights gleaming from remembered streets, but only the blackness of space illimitable; unimagined space alive with motion and music, and having no semblance to anything on earth" (CF 1.289).

Figure 2. Print XIV, The Gothic Arch, from Giovanni Battista Piranesi's Le Carceri d'Invenzione suite. Source: http://arthistoryblogger.blogspot.co.uk/2011/08/imaginary-prisons-of-piranesi.html

Lundwall uses a writing technique extensively used by Lovecraft called 'unwriting,' which means that the author writes in an elusive way, essentially just providing hints and leaving the reader to fill in the blanks. This technique captures the gap between what the protagonist experiences and what he comprehends. In addition, the technique lets the reader share the protagonist's confusion over what is going on, resulting in the reader feeling as alienated and uncomprehending as the protagonist (Harman 3, 27f.). Perhaps the best-known example of this in Lovecraft's work is the description of Wilcox's base-relief in "The Call of Cthulhu":

> Above these apparent hieroglyphics was a figure of evidently pictorial intent, though its impressionistic execution forbade a very clear idea of its nature. It seemed to be a sort of monster, or symbol representing a monster, of a form which only a diseased fancy could conceive. If I say that my somewhat extravagant imagination yielded simultaneous pictures of an octopus, a dragon, and a human caricature, I shall not be unfaithful to the spirit of the thing. A pulpy, tentacled head surmounted a grotesque and scaly body with rudimentary wings; but it was the *general outline* of the whole which made it most shockingly frightful. (CF 2.23-24)

As Timo Airaksinen points out, in Lovecraft "everything remains, externalized, reified, projected, and ultimately empty" (35) and "everything is mystery, unknowable, and even unnamable" (54). And "When logic and physics fail, so, too, the writing of the story must be replaced by unwriting" (177).

The passage from *Bernhard the Conqueror* above is an example of where Lundwall uses this technique and so is the following passage from *Fängelsestaden*:

> At least four religious sects among the subordinates had chosen halls in the House and now unashamedly used them as stages for weird and repulsive rites. And so on. The House was in a deplorable condition, and all the effort to introduce some element of order in this chaos went through Guielo. Why did the House support six pale men whose only task appeared to consist of every morning in a certain order unlocking the six doors to a hexagonal dreary hall and then in the evening locking them again? Why was a bricked up cellar door guarded around the clock with surprising eagerness by three toothless old hags who either did not know or did not want to tell why they had received this pointless chore. (162)

It is not the actual description of the object that is the message: it is what cannot be described that is the message to the reader. The reader ends up feeling the same inability to understand as Guielo or the late Francis Wayland Thurston.

Perhaps even more important is that there are also thematic similarities between the two authors. As in the title of this paper, one is the individual lost in an uncaring and soulless universe. Lovecraft believed in a strictly mechanistic view of the universe governed by natural laws with no room for a God (Houellebecq 32). His universe is so impersonal that even being becomes unimportant ("all human life is weary, incomplete, unsatisfying, and sardonically purposeless": cited in St. Armand 53), and as a consequence all human relations become meaningless. Lovecraft's protagonists are all the time "getting lost and thus losing themselves" (Airaksinen 31). They want, above everything else, to escape from their role as powerless observers, but they cannot. They cannot control or even change events, much less their fate (Houellebecq 69; Airaksinen 24).

Similar ideas permeate Lundwall's writings. The novels *No Time for Heroes* and *Bernhard the Conqueror* are set in a distant post-Foundation future. The protagonist is Bernhard Rordin, ex-navy scout and escaped convict from the Emperor's Prison Planet No. 1224, affectionately known as Ol' Slow Death by the inmates. Bernhard is a stupid, uneducated coward whose goals in life are to flee from any situation he is presently finds himself in, or find an ancient, still-functioning imperial robot-brothel and lock himself in there until he dies, or failing in the above, just getting revenge on his prison guard, Old Ironjaw. In the novels, too many galactic empires have come and gone, each being a little more degenerate than the last. Now millions of empirelets scavenge what they can from the wreckage left by the ancient civilizations. All that is left is to grab what you can, when and where you can find it, no matter from who or how. Nobody even asks why anymore. Principles that regulate relations between humans are forgotten or their meaning lost:

> "Look what that gangster did," [Bernhard] grumbled. "Stole my new uniform, he did. Is that justice?"
>
> "Justice," asked the robot. "What's that?" Bernhard thought about it . . . it was one of those words that everybody used but nobody knew much about . . . He frowned helplessly, then brightened.
>
> "Justice," he said triumphantly, "is when an officer doesn't take your new fancy uniform away from you even though he is bigger than you and has a gun."

"Never heard of it," the robot said. "Besides . . . why shouldn't he take it away from you if he's bigger than you and has a gun too? Stupidity is what I would call it." (*Bernhard the Conqueror* 24)

2018 A.D. or The King Kong Blues is set in our own near future and depicts the dehumanizing processes in a society that does not care whether the inhabitants live or die. The world is surprisingly similar to our own, with offensive and intrusive reality shows, war on terror, pollution, water shortages, 24/7 government and corporate surveillance, mega-corporate greed, and rampant mob and gang criminality. Combined, they all work to numb the citizens, isolating them from one another and from their own reflective selves. In the novel, a junior executive assistant, Erik Lenning, is sent to retrieve Anniki Norjin, the first born of the new century, to star in an inane advertising campaign. The problem is that Ms. Norjin does not exist: after her computer records were erased in a terrorist raid, she chose to disappear and live beyond and beneath government control and care. Lenning is forced to leave his protected life in a suburban gated community and confront the brutal reality of the Stockholm underworld, where the value of a person is fleeting and purely dependent on momentary satisfaction:

> Lenning rose. "You mean he would charge me for talking to her? Just like she was a piece of meat?"
> "You couldn't afford her if she was a piece of meat," Jonson said over his glass. "Let's say a recycled soy fruit dessert; artificially flavored, to be returned after use." Lenning fled, ears burning, followed by Jonson's rolling laugh. (124)

In *Fängelstaden*, local crime lord Anastas Bogor holds captive a deformed and diseased lunatic, Ygor, who lives in an eternal now, experiencing everything that is happening, has happened, and will ever happen to him at the same time. When Ygor escapes from his prison, Bogor recruits one of his clients, the actress Melicent—whose special training in empathy enables her to reach into other humans' minds and reflect back their innermost emotions—to help him find the refugee. Their quest entangles them with the howling, frenzied, murderous, fanatical cultists who swarm to Ygor in their millions, and together with a sadistic priesthood follow him in his apparently aimless odyssey. In the end Melicent accepts that as an individual she has no raison d'être, something she in any case understood as an actress, and joins the multitudes, leaving Bogor, who cannot accept his insignificance, to his unknown fate.

The reader can sympathize with the loneliness and vulnerability of Bernhard, Lenning, and Bogor, and their status of outsiders forces them to observe and to some extent reflect upon the state of the world around them:

> Bernhard said, "It's funny, but everywhere I go things seem to be much the same as back home. Names are different and customs might appear strange, but just scratch a bit on the surface and you're back on Ol' Slow Death again."
> "This is the only true Utopian society," Heenlyn said.
> "Sure. And back home is the only true democracy." (*Bernhard the Conqueror* 141)

The hopelessness in Lundwall's novels is related to Lovecraft's rejection of any future for mankind. Partly this stems from Lovecraft's rejection of all human values and relations, and partly from his belief that evolution, or something worse, will replace us with something else (Airaksinen 40-43; St. Armand 5f., 79). In Lovecraft's fiction it is postulated that, even though there is no God beyond our senses and understanding, there are beings unimaginably more intelligent and powerful than us (Houellebec1 33; St. Armand 35). Most of them ignore us, but others observe or even manipulate us for their own ends. For some, we are vermin to be cleared away.

For instance, in *Fängelsestaden* it is never explained how humans came to live hundreds of millions of years in the earth's past. Two possible explanations for the city are given in the book: either it was purposely built for humans to serve as a prison; or, like hermit crabs, the humans occupy the abandoned shell, or skeletal remains, left behind by some vast and fantastic creature. That the humans are manipulated by some outside force for unknown purposes is hinted at. For a reader of Lovecraft, the thought of something to do with the Great Race does occur. The dating of the novel, interestingly enough, corresponds almost exactly with the time Professor Peaslee, in "The Shadow out of Time," spent with the Great Race (if one considers that Lovecraft is wrong with his chronology but correct with his geological era and period information).

This idea that there are unseen forces manipulating humanity also occurs in *2018 A.D. or the King Kong Blues*, where an Arabian oil sheik owns the entire Western world, and in the books with Bernhard Rordin, where supercomputers with godlike powers sometimes choose to manipulate humans just to ease their own boredom. However, humanity is quickly becoming irrelevant, or perhaps has never even been relevant: "'It's a good universe,' the God machine said; 'or it will be as soon as you humans are out of the way, which probably won't be long, judging by the way you're going on. I won't miss you, that's for sure'" (*Bernhard the Conqueror* 133).

There is also a case of parallelism in Lundwall's and Lovecraft's writings. This is not exactly a Lovecraftian influence, but it might explain the literary appeal Lovecraft held for Lundwall. Both were to some extent disillusioned with their times: Lovecraft felt displaced in the 1920s, especially the thoroughly "modern" New York with its machines, which he saw as a way to control the citizens, greed and crowds of ungentlemanly *strange* people.

Lundwall's writings during the 1970s show a clear dissatisfaction with the various forms of utopias that were then both at their peak and showing advanced signs of breaking down (e.g., the Cultural Revolution in the People's Republic of China, the Khmer Rouge killing fields in Kampuchea, the Mexico City Olympics, the Prague Spring, the Vietnam War, and even the Swedish 'Third-Way' socialist mixed-economy system). In his writing Lundwall is clearly anti-authoritarian and skeptical of any kind of utopias. Instead of falling into the trap of preaching alternative utopias, he chose to write about the negative effect they had on human society.

Lovecraft managed to let the reader feel his own alienation toward his own times in particular and to human society in general (Fyhr 167), while Lundwall's intention seems to have been to instill in the reader a healthy disrespect and distrust of utopian dreams and political and commercial promises.

Similar to Lovecraft, Lundwall has been given short shrift by literary critics, not for what he actually wrote but for the genre he chose to write in, even when according to critical theory "the quality of the response to life that we discover enshrined in the works" (Roberts 69) is more important than the genre that authors choose to use. Rather, they have been victims of individuals with their own prejudices, claiming their opinion has universal validity (Roberts 91).

The texts of H. P. Lovecraft had a pronounced influence on the stories Lundwall wrote in the 1970s. It is possible that he was exposed to the works of Lovecraft in his early teens, but what is certain is that Lundwall was influenced by authors who influenced Lovecraft and authors who were influenced by Lovecraft. Like Lovecraft, Lundwall uses a narrative technique called 'unwriting' to let the reader experience the same feelings of alienation and incomprehension as the protagonists in the texts. In addition, Lundwall's texts show a strong thematic influence from Lovecraft. For instance, Lovecraft's literary universe is mechanistic and impersonal, where all human relations and strivings become moot and pointless. Lovecraft's protagonistss are confronted by their own isolation, insignificance and helplessness and similarly, protagonists in Lundwall's stories are alone and vulnerable in a world where all human relations have been blunted by commercialism and political ideologies. Even though there is no God in the literary universe of both authors, there exist powerful entities in them. Most of the time these entities are indifferent to humanity, but some might occasionally use or manipulate humans for their own purposes. Society has also collapsed, corrupting all human interactions with a twisted survival-of-the-fittest logic. With these novels Lundwall can be seen as a precursor to the French author Michel Houellebecq, himself influenced by Lovecraft.

The scope of Lundwall's writings is more limited than Lovecraft's—Lundwall wrote about the human predicament and not cosmicism, and he wrote social satire rather than cosmic horror—but his stories are similarly powerful. Similar to Lovecraft his themes are timeless, even though he chose satire over horror to present them to the reader. Lundwall's humor and storytelling still touches.

Works Cited

Airaksinen, Timo. *The Philosophy of H. P. Lovecraft: The Route to Horror.* New York: Peter Lang, 1999.

Fyhr, Mattias. *Död med Drömmande: H. P. Lovecraft och den Magiska Modernismen.* Lund, Sweden: Ellerströms Förlag, 2006.

Harman, Graham. *Weird Realism: Lovecraft and Philosophy.* Winchester, UK: Zero Books, 2011.

Houellebecq, Michel. *H. P. Lovecraft: Against the World, Against Life.* Tr. Dorna Khazeni. San Francisco: Believer Books, 2005.

Lovecraft, H. P. *Skräcknoveller.* Ed. Martin Andersson. Stockholm: Vertigo Förlag, 2011.

——. *Miscellaneous Writings.* Ed. S. T. Joshi. Sauk City, WI: Arkham House, 1995.

Lundwall, Sam J. *Fängelsestaden*. Stockholm: P. A. Norstedt & Söners Förlag, 1978.

———. *Science Fiction: An Illustrated History*. New York: Grosset & Dunlap, 1977.

———. *Gäst i Frankensteins Hus*. Stockholm: Delta Förlags AB, 1976.

———. *2018 A.D. or The King Kong Blues*. New York: DAW, 1975.

———. *Bernards Magiska Sommar*. Stockholm: Lindquist Förlag, 1975.

———. *Bernhard the Conqueror*. New York: DAW, 1973.

———. Introduction to "Råttorna i Muren." In *Den Fantastiska Romanen 2: Gotisk Skräckromantik från Horace Walpole till H. P. Lovecraft*, ed. Sam J. Lundwall. Stockholm: Gummesons Grafiska Grupp, 1973. 288–91.

Nield, Ted. *Supercontinent: Ten Billion Years in the Life of Our Planet*. London: Granta Books, 2007.

Ogg, James G.; Ogg, Gabi; and Gradstein, Felix M. *The Concise Geologic Time Scale*. Cambridge: Cambridge University Press, 2008.

Roberts, Mark. *The Fundamentals of Literary Criticism*. Oxford: Basil Blackwell, 1974.

St. Armand, Barton Levi. *The Roots of Horror in the Fiction of H. P. Lovecraft*. Elizabethtown, NY: Dragon Press, 1977.

New England's Curator: Colonial Revival in the Travelogue and Fiction of H. P. Lovecraft

Kenneth W. Lai
University of California, Irvine

A veritable mix of facts and fictions emerge from H. P. Lovecraft's life and writing. His correspondences as often put on the persona and archaic style of an "eighteenth-century English Tory," as his stories refurbished history to better serve the ends of his horrific imagination (de Camp 4).[1] Between epistle and short story, his travelogues, which scholarship has not yet sufficiently explored, seem to develop a third ground between fact and fiction, an experimental interstice that I will argue is crucial to understanding the factual-fictive space that Lovecraft's stories occupy, a space that enables Lovecraft to act as a curator for New England.

While scholars have looked at similarities between Lovecraft's travelogues and his fiction, there is yet a lack of understanding as to his motivation in employing the conventions deployed in and developed through his antiquarian writing, what precisely those conventions are, and to what extent New England history, architecture, and atmosphere becomes subjected to the weird aesthetic. Timothy H. Evans has come the closest to developing a satisfying explanation for the first of these three problems in "Tradition and Illusion" and "A Last Defense Against the Dark." While his travel writings supply an independent search for one tourist's account of colonial New England, Evans argues, Lovecraft's fiction draws on these sightseeing experiences to produce an atmosphere simultaneously "authentic and threatening" ("Tradition and Illusion: 187–89). The primary

---

1. In *The Philosophy of H. P. Lovecraft*, especially pp. 18–19, Airaksinen makes the claim that Lovecraft's letters ought to be read as a "fictional autobiography," but his premises—developing an epistolary epistemology, as it were—are questionable: "most people fictionalize themselves."

force of this argument is to locate Lovecraft in an emerging movement of heritage tourism, an increasingly popular commercial outlet for early twentieth-century leisure culture, and thus to interrogate the relationship of Lovecraft's works to tradition and horror.[2] Once habituated, sightseeing becomes ritualized, culminating in the individual's arrival at the presence of sights and monuments, vessels for historicity and transmitters of "authentic" experience; antiquarianism and consequently weird fiction become the only viable response to the alienation of work from culture, which has condemned "modern man ... to look elsewhere, everywhere, for his authenticity, to see if he can catch a glimpse of it reflected in the simplicity, poverty, chastity or purity of others" (MacCannell 41).

While this approach, in employing elements of cultural materialism, boasts the advantage of locating Lovecraft's antimodernist pursuit of antiquity in a broad, historical timeline, its disadvantage lies in its inability to determine specific components reflected across Lovecraft's works that contribute to his particular vision of the weird. How, for instance, do the structure and logic of the travelogue form find their way into Lovecraft's fiction? To what extent does such a conflation contribute to the aesthetic of cosmic horror? If Lovecraft's fiction is read in light of his travelogues, can the reverse also be done? The answers to these questions are much wanting in Lovecraftian scholarship, which has only begun to deal with the travelogues. Rather than interrogating Lovecraft's travels within an increasingly travel-minded culture, my goal is to understand, more specifical-

---

2. Tourism, from its commercial boom in late nineteenth-century America, represents a key dialectical awakening of the modern consciousness over against alienation from one's cultural roots as immigration patterns vastly increasing in the late nineteenth century. In response, the tourist yearned for authenticity, problematizing the true American experience and heritage. Tourism thus arrived at a point in time that "connected ... the desire to see and know the real America. Touring offered a way to learn about America, and in seeing America to become an American" (Shaffer 227). Furthermore, sightseeing quickly evolved into a democratizing project, by which tourists "embraced the values of official culture expressed by prescriptive literature in their search to discover America, and they simultaneously challenged the official ideal of national unity with their own concerns, ideals and anxieties" (241). This broad analysis of tourism provides a compelling explanation for the diffusion of Lovecraft's travel interests into his larger corpus works, but fails to explain their relationship with Lovecraft's fiction, which is not directly interested in national identity.

ly, Lovecraft's travel *writings* and their relationship with his fiction. More important than the travel itself, and indeed the starting point from which those travels can in the first place be extrapolated, are the *records* of his journeys that Lovecraft himself wrote down, the minute details that are distilled from the vast, ripe ferment of the American lands and refined into the detailed observations and recurring patterns of his travelogues, details that would later re-emerge in his fictional works as an authentication and revival of colonial New England.

While my contention is that this cross-genre study of Lovecraft can be applied to Lovecraft's short stories, especially those written after 1921,[3] my analysis of Lovecraft's fiction will deal primarily with two texts. The first is *The Case of Charles Dexter Ward* (1927), which is his fullest fictional treatment of his hometown, Providence, Rhode Island.[4] As Providence was the city in which Lovecraft spent most of his life, *Charles Dexter Ward* can be read as one of Lovecraft's most heartfelt attempts to preserve the city he most loves.[5] The second fictional work I will examine is "The Shadow over

---

3. This date is more convenient that it is descriptive. See Lovecraft's letter to E. Hoffmann Price of 31 August 1934: "When I depart from reality I have to turn to some form of unreality which is vivid and authentic to me. . . . Set the calendar back a century and bring in some event involving Old Nantucket or Providence of Charleston Life, and my interest grows. . . . but even there my knowledge and technique are insufficient . . . I know, after repeated experiments dating 1921, that I can't [write authentically]" (ms., John Hay Library, Brown University). On the other hand, S. T. Joshi marks 1919 as an equally important year for when Lovecraft begins traveling outside Rhode Island, Massachusetts, and Connecticut and 1922 as the year Lovecraft began using his diaries and letters to Lillian D. Clark, one of his aunts, as records for his travels (introduction, *CE* 4.7).

4. While Evans discerns "The Shadow over Innsmouth" (1931) as the "ultimate transformation of travelogue into horror story," supplying its autobiographical nature and uncanny preservation of the colonial landscape as chief evidence of this phase in Lovecraft's career, curiously enough he fails to mention *Charles Dexter Ward*, which shares much of the same characteristics as "Innsmouth," in his list of "Antiquarian Explorations in Lovecraft's Fiction" ("Last Defense" 113–15).

5. See, for instance, his letter to R. H. Barlow on [24 May 1935]: "Bad news in tonight's paper—although it's something I knew was coming. Colonial houses on lower slope of College St. to be replaced by new building of the R.I. School of Design. . . . Silver lining to cloud—the bottom building . . . will be saved, restored, and incorporated into the new building. . . . The new edifice will be in the best colonial architecture. . . . Old Prov-

Innsmouth" (1931), which is written after his travel-writing reaches a pinnacle with "An Account of Charleston" (1930) and *A Description of the Town of Quebeck* (1930-31). Linked together with the starting date of Lovecraft's travel interests (see note 3), "Innsmouth" rounds off Lovecraft's travelogue-fiction experimentation between the years 1919 and 1931, a range not unsurprisingly close to what is conventionally referred to as the Dream Cycle phase in Lovecraft's writing career: 1918-32.[6] While this temporal coincidence does not alone prove the necessary connection between the Dream Cycle and Lovecraft's antiquarian travel writings, and indeed additionally provokes the inclusion of "Innsmouth" in the Dream Cycle, it does create an incentive to reevaluate the Dream Cycle and read this set of texts as part and parcel of the curatorial aesthetic I discuss in this paper.

As *Charles Dexter Ward* antedates Lovecraft's most prolific period of travel-writings and "Innsmouth" postdates them, changes from the former to the latter will form an important part of my analysis in developing the way Lovecraft's weird method evolves. Common to his travelogues and this period of fiction, at any rate, is Lovecraft's employment of the tripartite structure of historical summary, atmospheric survey, and walking itinerary. Lovecraft's works thus do much more than develop an atmosphere of profound terror: in his facts, he assimilates imaginative observations; in his fiction, historical truths and real settings.

This commingling of historicity and horror is an anomaly that many Lovecraft scholars have wrestled with.[7] I will argue that this factional-fictive space is motivated by an aesthetic that I will call "weird curation."

---

idence will never go modernistic. We remain true to the style in which the town first crystallized after the rise to supremacy about 1760" (*O Fortunate Floridian* 276-77).

6. Further work will be required to defend even the range I have supplied for Lovecraft's experimentation into travelogue-fiction. Instead of when Lovecraft's experimentation took place, this essay is concerned with addressing how the experiment unfolded. Namely, this paper will provide a vocabulary by which to approach the study of Lovecraft's travelogue-fiction writings and an inquiry into the governing aesthetic behind the implicit authentication of the weird through antiquarian writings.

7. The most recent book-length example is Graham Harman's *Weird Realism: Lovecraft and Philosophy*, a fascinating discussion of Lovecraft's writing as a noumenal vision of the "gap" between objects of inexhaustible qualities (2-6). In this reading, historicity is discarded entirely; the enigmatic ontology of weird fiction is, instead, both the primary component of terror and a profound challenge to historicity in any sense.

Such an aesthetic employs the weird as a method of preservation, achieving the link between fiction and reality through "the turn of cosmic horror": the key switch from the play between dreaming, madness, and the supernatural,[8] a convention of Lovecraft's weird style, to historicity affixes the horror onto the curatorial object. In this moment, the subject is engulfed by a threatening cosmos suddenly but momentarily revealed through the hitherto innocent object; space and time collapse into this moment of utter objectification and produces an epiphany of profound terror and pleasure that can only have emerged through the intersection of history and object.[9]

As a productive method, weird curation responds to and to a certain extent aligns with Colonial Revival, a prominent contemporary traditionalist movement in support of preserving or otherwise returning to New England roots, by uniquely acknowledging the transience of one's material cultural heritage.[10] Performing similar work as a tour guide, weird curation supplies all necessary contexts for and during the tour, but provides a fictionalized account of the itinerary rather than recommending one. By electing to *perform* the itinerary through prose composition, Lovecraft in effect preserves the decaying façade of New England before its inevitable annihilation by either the artificial and ahistorical method of physical preservation or the slow, all-vanquishing decay of time.

The Structure of the Travelogues

The divisive tripartite focus of history, atmosphere, and itinerary, is drawn up most clearly in the table of contents of both "An Account of

---

8. Its best formulation is perhaps in "The Outsider": "I neither knew nor cared whether my experience was insanity, dreaming, or magic" (CF 1.269). For Lovecraft's own discussion of the role psychology, dreaming, and magic plays in his aesthetic, see *The Annotated Supernatural Horror in Literature* 25–28.

9. While this sounds close to the Burkean or Kantian sublime, the aesthetic of cosmic horror, as Vivian Ralickas's "'Cosmic Horror' and the Question of the Sublime in Lovecraft" rightly points out, the aesthetic of cosmic horror is not linked to a positive subjective reconstitution that both Kant and Burke prescribe to the sublime experience.

10. For an excellent collection of essays on Colonial Revival, see Axelrod. For a set of analyses more contemporary to Lovecraft's time, including discussions of Norman Morrison Ishman, one of Lovecraft's favorite antiquarian architects, see Lindgren.

Charleston" and *A Description of the Town of Quebeck*, and proceed chronologically in the respective accounts. In Lovecraft's other travelogues, perhaps because they are much shorter, the history-atmosphere-itinerary divisions flow freely together, but each component seamlessly evokes the next: history dazzles the reader as the traveler journeys down cobblestone roads and beneath incandescent lights that peer through Palladian windows, architectural features such as the gabled houses of Benefit Street betray their colonial roots, and the modern sightseer discovers herself thrown into the folds of time, into the antiquated architectural landscape of the modern town. In fact, the itinerary is part and parcel of parcel of the images it valorizes.[11] One vanishes and the other becomes instantly meaningless. When itinerary is brought together with the antiquarian image, however, building and history coalesce into a single landscape in the wake of the tourist; from the ashes of the dying present, the past is born anew. There are, however, several issues with this idealization, problematic for historical inquiry, on the one hand, inspiring to the writer, on the other.

Particularly in Lovecraft's historical introductions to "Charleston" and *Quebeck*, it soon becomes evident that Lovecraft's historiography accounts not for the change of man over time, but for the change of objects. While the narrativization of historical events ought, properly speaking, to weave together so many threads of history to various unities and patterns, effecting "a symbolic representation of the processes by which human life is endowed with symbolic meaning," Lovecraft's historical method instead endows architecture, landscape, and atmosphere with meaning (White 178). Implicit in Lovecraft's philosophy of history is the immense value placed on what tatters and ruins have held up against the weathering of time and the destruction of industrial modernity.[12] The dilapidated figures preserved triumphantly through the ages are simultaneously the signifiers of historicity and the mute witnesses of those bygone days; their scars boast a truth now lost in time. Not the subjectivity of a people fostered

---

11. This complete certitude in authenticity quickly develops into touristic rhetoric: "this is a typical native house; this is the very place the leader fell; this is the actual pen used to sign the law; this is the original manuscript; this is an authentic Tlingit fish club; this is a real piece of the true Crown of Thorns" (MacCannell 14; his emphasis).

12. For the "historical survey" section I designate for "Charleston" and *Quebeck*, see respectively CE 4.70-84 and 108-75.

through time and won through war, but the still-resounding echoes of street cries (White 178),[13] those siren-like tunes of street-side hawkers, attest to the greatness of the immaculately preserved New England city; similarly, the gambrel roofs (CE 4.29, 37, 178, 180, 186, 200, 222-23, 255, 272) and wrought-ironwork (CE 4.68, 74-75, 78, 87, 89, 96-97, 99, 101-4, 262-63, 265, 269-77) that characterize a city signifies its resistance to the "the mechanized desert of decadence call'd North-America" (CE 4.74). As the world around them turns, the objects stagnate in cobwebbed antiquity. These remnants of pre-modern, pre-industrial society in turn evidence "the sound taste of the eighteenth century in architecture . . . [that] has come down unbroken to this day" (CE 4.79).

The historiography of object over against that of humans is most evidently found in Lovecraft's interruptions from the primary historical narrative. Rather than pausing in a moment of time to discuss the biography of a fearless governor or a stalwart general, Lovecraft spends most of his digressions on architectural annotations and racial diatribes, establishing the atmosphere that characterizes the city. More than once, Lovecraft stops to provide an entire list of "notable" buildings that emerge from a certain time period—significantly, under the demarcated sections of *Quebeck* and "Charleston," these abbreviations fall under the "history" rather than the "atmosphere" category (CE 4.43, 54, 78, and 128 are just a few examples); this categorical distinction signifies that buildings listed in such a manner do not demonstrate the *feeling* of the colonial atmosphere, but the *perseverance* of heritage and history. What is typically relegated to a footnote in a historical study is brought to the foreground in Lovecraft's historiography, most importantly noting the name of the building, its date of construction, and its location, most accurately represented by an intersection. Particularly in representing the intersection nearest the building, Lovecraft's historical survey charts the points of interest to be later covered in full in the walking itinerary, thus unifying history, atmosphere, and itinerary from the outset. The addition of architectural personalities is icing on the cake: the introduction of "roof-tiling" and "wrought-iron" at certain points in time becomes an important marker for colonial architecture. The atmospheric tangents upon which Lovecraft embarks attest to

---

13. See CE 4.69, 83-84, 265. Even in these instances, the subject is completely alienated from the disembodied "street cry."

his belief in the permanence of architecture, by which buildings become portals that transport the subject through time.

This same permanence, not surprisingly, characterizes also Lovecraft's infamous socio-racial attitude. Although I will not attempt to make an apology for Lovecraft, it is interesting to note that the rhetorical claims of ineffaceability are consistent between architecture, race, and social class (i.e., atmosphere). Charleston and Quebec fascinate Lovecraft because they not only foster an undying connection with their roots, but the "*completeness* of their antiquity" even extends to and is authenticated by genealogical and structural features alike (Joshi, in CE 4.9). Put more bluntly, race and architecture become equally objectified in order to serve as visible and tangible historical landmarks that in turn take on the role of unbreakable links between present and past. Just as Lovecraft draws on the consistent style of "stone and succo cover'd brick" to denote a "highly dramatick, unique and unalterable character" and symbolize the historical stability of the city across the centuries, Lovecraft, for the same reason, takes note of which "surnames [persist] to this day because of Charleston's happy immunity from value-destroying change," valorizes the "sturdy persistence of French blood" over against the "general mongrelisation" of New England, marks out Piermont's "vast negro settlement" as a "sinister study in decadence," and ennobles the purebred gentility of the "original families" of Charleston that "still hold sway—Rhetts, Izards, Pringles, Bulls, Hugers, Ravenels, Manigaults, Draytons, Stoneys, Rutledges, and so on" (CE 4.126, 73, 123, 18, 82).[14] Good blood flourishes and cultivates; bad blood festers and infects. Whether surname or skin color, building material or structure, each object—or otherwise objectified individual—serves as a crucial barometer of change, for which constancy reigns supreme according to Lovecraft's historiography.

From a brief overview of Lovecraft's historical method, two themes thus become apparent. First, history carves out objects, which in turn at-

---

14. Although the first quotation specifically addresses the "unalterable character" of a town due to its "landscape setting" (126), for Lovecraft, landscape is here nothing more than a blueprint for architecture. A "flat town," he writes, can change, but a town "set amidst permanent geographick features" is built such that the architecture must conform to the rolling of the land, to the effect that the buildings and their functions must never change.

test to their own historicity. This applies in a broad range, from the features of a building to the collective purity of family lines. Second, Lovecraft notes the observable for easy handling by the tourist. The significance of historical permanence is one that, for the purposes of Lovecraft studies, cannot be overstated. For the fiercely subjective emotional force of history, his contemplation of Providence is worth quoting at length:

> Home—amongst the unnumber'd influences and sights and sounds which, operating through a full half of my heredity for three hundred years and through all my life from infant memories onward, has little by little moulded my germ-plasm and my spirit. . . . For what is any man but the impress of his home and lineage? What is in us, that our pasts have not placed there? Truly, no man is himself save among the scenes that have shaped him and his father; nor cou'd I ever hope to find a lasting peace save close to the ancient monuments of green-leaved, hill-crowning Providence—Providence is I, and I am Providence. One and inseparable! (CE 4.30)

History, in other words, becomes determinate and can furthermore be traced by none other than its own constituent objects: the buildings, blood, and landscape, all of which survive the passage of time. By marking out surnames and intersections, families and architecture become observable units for the sightseer, the latter of which is immediately utilized in the atmospheric survey, which demonstrates just how true a city has stayed to its roots.

It becomes increasingly important, however, to note that atmosphere and architecture, at least for Lovecraft, seem at times almost interchangeable. While architecture is always either a form of atmosphere or history, however, the opposite is not true. Atmosphere, rather, denotes a very specific metric in Lovecraft's aesthetic: "Atmosphere is the all-important thing, for the final criterion of authenticity is . . . the creation of a given sensation. . . . Therefore we must judge a weird tale not by the author's intent, or by the mere mechanics of the plot; but by the emotional level which it attains at its least mundane point" (CE 2.84). Thus, architecture is only atmosphere when it provokes an emotional state; when it authenticates, it serves as history. Whereas architecture *qua* history demonstrates the period at which a certain "culture crystallised and their mode of thought, their institutions, and their very pronunciation keep the flavor of the age," architecture *qua* atmosphere evokes "a miraculously crystallis'd fragment of one of those vague, elusive dreams, where all our memories of art and literature and experience fuse tantalizingly into some momentary panorama of luminous ultimate wonder and beauty corresponding to nothing in objective existence" (CE 4.78, 82). Whereas history produces stasis, atmosphere conveys transcendence. Thus, the reader who has carefully watched the buildings razed to the ground by sword and fire is invariably awakened, reading through the atmospheric survey, to the unflagging nature of antique architecture erected back up by blood and sweat. Lovecraft's mastery in producing a study of atmosphere is not to destabilize architecture from its historical roots, but rather to demonstrate a city's historicity by alternately romanticizing and dissecting it.[15]

Through a romantic study of atmosphere, the mundane becomes beautiful. Through the atmospheric survey, the city develops personality and aesthetic, both of which produce emotional responses. Wrought-iron work, no longer just a marker of time, becomes "opulent and exquisite"; the falls of the Montmorency River, which as parts of historical study quite matter-of-factly "thunder'd as they do today down a cliff of no more than 250 feet into the St. Lawrence," as elements of the atmosphere are elevated another twenty feet: "Over the cliff-line, from a height of 270 feet ... there thunders the rushing bulk of the Montmorency River–plunging from its pine-grown plateau to the flats of the St. Lawrence level in a mass of tumultuous foam" (CE 4.89, 127, 181). Although the atmospheric study of Charleston and Quebeck is given comparatively much less space, this more dramatic, more emotionally charged language is rather what characterizes most of his other travelogues: these are the wild fantasies of his imaginations unleashed by the grand landscapes and cities of antiquity, the side of his narrative language that is perhaps superficially nearest his fiction.[16] Where suggestions exceed description, we find in Lovecraft's

---

15. For the "atmospheric survey" section I designate for "Charleston" and *Quebeck*, see respectively CE 4.85–90 and 176–92.

16. See *In Defence of Dagon* for Lovecraft's aesthetics in this regard: "since imagination is so much less widely diffused than are emotion and analytical reason, it follows that such literary type must be relatively rare, and decidedly restricted in its appeal... The imaginative writer devotes himself to art in its most essential sense. He is a painter of moods and mind-pictures ... a voyager into those unheard-of lands which are glimpsed through the veil of actuality but rarely, and only by the most sensitive. He is one who not only sees objects, but follows up all the bizarre trails of associated ideas which encompass and lead away from them" (CE 5.47; my emphasis).

travelogues some of best prose: "I need say nothing in detail about the marvelous caves [the Endless Caverns in Virginia's Shenandoah Valley] themselves.... Buried areas—submerged civilisations—subterraneous universes and unsuspected orders of beings and influences that haunt the sightless depths—all these flitted thro' an imagination confronted by the actual presence of soundless and eternal night" (CE 4.29).

On the other hand, Lovecraft's atmospheric study also attempts to be scientific, dissecting architecture and city noises into their component parts. In this regard, Lovecraft boasts an incredible wealth of knowledge. The analysis itself moves from suggestive romanticism to comparative study: the "rural cottages, with curving eaves" of the Hugenots are strikingly like those of the New England settlers in Charleston, though the brickwork of the latter, due to the French predilection towards stone, signifies that Charleston is "distinctly more *Dutch* than *French*" (CE 4.184, 86). This comparative study then drifts into a catalogue of sights and sounds characteristic of the city: "Clatter of horses' hooves—sweet bells from silver steeples—repose and courtesy—civilised, easy-going ways—symbols of His Maj$^{ty's}$ glorious and unbroken rule in the form of flags, the royal arms on post boxes, red-painted mail-collecting gigs, government shops, and shops in general—signs of sacerdotal supremacy": the list goes on (CE 4.190). Whereas the emotional atmosphere offers stimulus, the scientific atmosphere allows assimilation. By comparing and contrasting architectural structures, one with the other, the subject can adjust to the areas of similarity and difference; by analyzing the characteristic scene of the city, and performing it through catalogue, the reader is already present in the city. With this acquired familiarity of the history and atmosphere, the reader has only naturally next to see the city.

The walking itinerary merely connects what is already familiar.[17] History and atmosphere have set the city in place, and the pedestrian has only to come upon it through the contingencies of established roads and careful steps. As opposed to a list of sights to visit and recommended routes that optimize intersection with the city's great monuments, however, Lovecraft's walking itineraries, at least in "Charleston" and *Quebeck*, are long, blocky stream-of-consciousness style excurses on city-wide adventures.

---

17. For the "walking itinerary" section I designate for "Charleston" and *Quebeck*, see respectively CE 4.91–105 and 193–227.

Rather than recommending the itinerary, Lovecraft thus *performs* it. Together with him, we are constantly crossing streets, seeing sights, turning back, and emerging upon new avenues. Lovecraft's style is frantic and hasty, yet manages to bring the history and atmosphere of the city together with the pedestrian in masterful settings. As we pass down Champlain St., we recall from the historical account that "Montgomery, Cheesman, and Macpherson, along with ten others, fell dead," and look for "the interminable flight of rickety steps leads up from the crumbling Champlain St. slum ... to a board walk on the plateau which stretches across the still wild cove fields" that we recall from the atmospheric survey, but find instead "something spectral in this disjoin'd and half-forgotten district ... we come to weave disquieting dreams wherein we connect some hideous palaeogean rock-sentience and evil purposiveness with the slaying of the 66 so many years ago" (CE 4.161, 192, 213). And it is not until we look beyond the bend in the road that we see those "interminable flight of rickety steps" ascend to the Cove Fields. This moment on Champlain St., however brief, unifies time and place with the horror of historicity. The ghosts of history and the familiarity of place become defamiliarized in that moment where the two evoke weird imagination.

Altogether, this brief examination of Lovecraft's travelogues reveals patterns that will prove useful in examining their crossings-over into fictional territory. The static historiography, the alternately romanticizing and scientific atmospheric survey, and their meeting place in the walking itinerary, for instance, are profoundly similar to the structure of *Charles Dexter Ward* and "Innsmouth." Already in the dusty road of Champlain St. and in the dank caves of Virginia, Lovecraft's imagination achieves the pangs of horror. By the direct application of the history-atmosphere-itinerary structure to fiction, Lovecraft thus produces a factual-fictive space that allows the curation of colonial New England.

Travelogue, Fiction, and the Turn of Cosmic Horror

While "Innsmouth" and *Charles Dexter Ward* imagine largely fictional plots, interspersed with real historical facts, that their settings are strikingly real has been well known and studied in Lovecraftian scholarship.[18]

---

18. See Shreffler 46-50 and 88-92 for a brief discussion of the sources and historicity of *Charles Dexter Ward* and "Innsmouth."

Comparing and contrasting the key conventions of travelogue discussed above, these two stories demonstrate maturing fictionalizations of Lovecraft's travelogue. By turning real, innocent objects into menacing, fictionalized sources of horror—what I refer to as the "turn of cosmic horror"—fiction and travelogue genres cross over. Fact and fiction mixed together, real objects simultaneously achieve the weird aesthetic as fictional plots become grounded in real settings.

While the travelogue conventions employed in *Charles Dexter Ward* are cruder, "Innsmouth" is much clearly delineated. *Ward* jumps back and forth through the categories. The most prominent identifiable categories include the walking itinerary of the young Ward (494-96), the atmospheric catalogue of alley names (496), and Curwen's history (498-503), though afterwards the categories are very mixed. Curwen's house in Olney Court is of particular fascination for the young Ward and becomes an archaeological obsession that quickly leads to his own destruction. "Innsmouth," on the other hand, begins with a historical study of Innsmouth (809-13), an atmospheric study of the tall tiara (813-14) and Innsmouth (816-22), and a walking itinerary (823-25), followed by another set of a historical account (827-37), atmospheric changes (837-47), and the final itineraries (847-52).

Contained within the travelogue-style fictions, the turn of cosmic horror truly problematizes the space of fact and fiction. In *Charles Dexter Ward*, that crucial turn is not, I believe, to be found in the group of vigilantes that Shreffler points to as a source of confusion (49-50), but is to be found rather in Curwen's house, the dreaded house in Olney Court. It is this house that the young Ward has passed by so many times in innocence and does not realize the significance of until his genealogical research, after which he discovers the house to be the essential link to his fragmented genealogy, and the portal to a world of unspeakable horror, primordial magic, and phlegmatic chants. In "The Shadow over Innsmouth," on the other hand, the turn of cosmic horror is supplied by the tall tiara sported by the fish-frog cultists of Dagon. This tiara, which languishes in absolute obscurity in the display room of the Newburyport Historical Society and the vaulted collection of the narrative's deceased uncle. Both horrific realizations, in either story, are a throwback to the history that precedes the respective turns and the self-contained survey of the city's atmosphere that is simultaneously unwholesome and colonial. There is furthermore evidence of maturation in the "Innsmouth" story. Whereas the house in Olney Court is an imagined, though prototypical, colonial house, the tall tiara of the Deep Ones is a pervasive quagmire of colonial collections and, furthermore, an actual link to a mysterious tiara-decorated statue on display in Newburyport—the Olney Court house, though also real, is not suffused in the same mystery (Shreffler 92).

The power to enchant the unenchanted, to narrativize the unspoken, is not only the primary method of weird curation, it is the primary medium of *all* curation. Thus, there is an essential, inexplicable association of curatorial interest that is necessarily linked with Lovecraft's fiction. Read properly, Lovecraft's weird tales are deep contemplations of the links between the objects of our past and the magical experience of the present. That link is, in fact, not the touristic fetish of authentic experience, but the post-industrial and atemporal memorialization of literary curation.

Works Cited

Airaksinen, Timo. *The Philosophy of H. P. Lovecraft: The Route to Horror*. New York: Peter Lang, 1990.

Axelrod, Alan, ed. *The Colonial Revival in America*. New York: W. W. Norton, 1985.

de Camp, L. Sprague. *Lovecraft: A Biography*. Garden City, NY: Doubleday, 1975.

Evans, Timothy H. "A Last Defense against the Dark: Folklore, Horror, and the Uses of Tradition in the Works of H. P. Lovecraft." *Journal of Folklore Research* 42, No. 1 (January–April 2005): 99–135.

———. "Tradition and Illusion: Antiquarianism, Tourism, and Horror in H. P. Lovecraft." *Extrapolation* 45, No. 2 (Summer 2004): 176–95.

Harman, Graham. *Weird Realism: Lovecraft and Philosophy*. Alresford, UK: Zero Books, 2012.

Lindgren, James M., ed. *Preserving Historic New England: Preservation, Progressivism, and the Remaking of Memory*. New York: Oxford University Press, 1995.

Lovecraft, H. P. *O Fortunate Floridian: H. P. Lovecraft's Letters to R. H. Barlow*. Ed. S. T. Joshi and David E. Schultz. Tampa, FL: University of Tampa Press, 2007.

MacCannell, Dean. *The Tourist: A New Theory of the Leisure Class*. New York: Shocken Books, 1976.

Ralickas, Vivian. "'Cosmic Horror' and the Question of the Sublime in Lovecraft." *Journal of the Fantastic in the Arts* 18, No. 3 (2007): 364–98.

Shaffer, Marguerite. *See America First*. Washington, DC: Smithsonian Institution Press, 2001.

Shreffler, Phillip A. *The H. P. Lovecraft Companion*. Westport, CT: Greenwood Press, 1977.

White, Hayden. *The Content of Form: Narrative Discourse and Historical Representation*. Baltimore: Johns Hopkins University Press, 1987.

Lovecraft, Fear, and the Medieval Body Frame

Perry Neil Harrison
Baylor University

In the opening lines of his 1927 essay "Supernatural Horror in Literature," H. P. Lovecraft famously proclaims: "The oldest and strongest emotion of mankind is fear, and the oldest and strongest kind of fear is fear of the unknown" (CE 2.82). Lovecraft draws upon this manner of unknown, and often unknowable, fear to craft the foundation of his mythos, and this emotion, more than his creatures and locations, works to unify his mythopoeia. However, while Lovecraft is among the most prominent authors to utilize the fear of things outside of human knowledge and understanding during the last century, he was also notably aware of the deep history inherent in the horror genre. Of the origins of the genre, he notes rightly, "As may naturally be expected of a form so closely connected with primal emotion, the horror-tale is as old as human thought and speech themselves" (CE 2.85). Yet, while Lovecraft readily acknowledges the importance of old stories upon the shaping of the horror tale, he cites nineteenth-century practitioners, such as Poe, Arthur Machen, and Robert W. Chambers, as his most important and direct influences. Similarly, the lengthy historical survey of horror in fiction provided within his essay begins in earnest with the examination of the Gothic novel, opting to summarize briefly the general influence of works produced earlier than this milestone. However, if the human desire to draw upon the fear of the unknown to craft fiction truly began with the ability to produce speech, the question remains as to what role the texts that predate the advent of the Gothic novel played in informing and guiding Lovecraft's own works. Perhaps most notably, the monstrous forms that Lovecraft often relies upon to generate the sense of the unknown within his works owes a tremendous debt to the common inhuman bodily images found within the literature of the Middle Ages.

Before an examination of the monstrous body frame can begin in earnest, it is first necessary to clarify what is meant when speaking of monstrosity itself. Over the last two decades, a tremendous surge of scholarly interest has been focused on the significance of monstrous literary bodies, specifically those described during the Middle Ages. In defining and describing the function and depiction of these bodies within works of literature, medievalist and cultural theorist Jeffery Jerome Cohen presents seven "theses" in the opening chapter of his 1996 edited collection *Monster Theory*. While it is outside the scope of this study to examine Lovecraft's own monstrous entities in light of Cohen's "theses" as a whole, two of his assertions are particularly relevant to the creatures frequently represented within the Lovecraft mythos. Cohen's first "thesis," "The Monster Is a Cultural Body," describes the monster as "an embodiment of a certain cultural moment—of a time, a feeling, and a place" (4). Of equal (or perhaps greater, given Lovecraft's propensity for hybrid bodies) importance is Cohen's fourth "thesis," "The Monster Dwells at the Gates of Difference." Quite simply, Cohen explains, "The monster is difference made flesh, come to dwell among us" (7). Yet it is not only his or her flesh that represents the monster's separation from the larger society. Bettina Bildhauer further discusses the nature of this isolation by elaborating on the fundamental nature of the monster suggested by Cohen. She remarks: "It is often not [the monster's] misshapen or hybrid body that makes the monster, but its relation to other bodies, social or individual" (75). The monster, as such, is a being that is both physically and socially representative of distance from the communally accepted norm.

Regarding the Middle Ages and its contribution to the horror story, Lovecraft has surprisingly little to say, although the commentary he does provide is beneficial to unraveling the nature of his corpus of works' connection to the time period. Most notably, he asserts, "The Middle Ages, steeped in fanciful darkness, gave [the horror story] an enormous impulse toward expression" (*CE* 2.85). The medieval period, in Lovecraft's view, represented a time of expansion for the horror tale, allowing it to spread and evolve more swiftly and proliferate mysteries to wider audiences in newfound ways. Among the reactions that came about as a result of the ever-encroaching presence of the unknown was an increased fascination with the monstrous body frame. With the borders of the map and interaction with unfamiliar cultures and customs ever growing, the number of potential sources of apprehension expanded concurrently, and with this came the need to represent these newfound fears in writing as beings of flesh. With this in mind, it seems logical that an interest in monsters would flourish within the literature of the Middle Ages, as their presence worked as a direct reaction to the increased presence of the unknown.

Additionally, the essay also speaks to Lovecraft's awareness of the place of medieval texts within the chronological progression of the horror tale, as well as an acute knowledge of medieval stories and texts themselves. Of particular interest, however, are the works he chooses to discuss within his essay. While the essay cites the importance of many of the canonical writers of the Middle Ages, such as Dante and Sir Thomas Malory, to the shaping of the horror tale, he also pays homage to a number of markedly more obscure texts. Particularly, he directly references the occult writings of Albertus Magnus, Raymond Lully, and Johannes Trithemius.[1]

Yet it is a seemingly innocuous statement that displays the truly wide-reaching nature of the author's medieval readings: "The Scandinavian Eddas and Sagas thunder with cosmic horror, and shake with the stark fear of Ymir and his shapeless spawn; whilst our own Anglo-Saxon *Beowulf* . . . [is] full of eldritch weirdness" (CE 2.86). The influence of the mythology of Northern Europe has already been discussed at length by Jason C. Eckhardt in his essay "Cthulhu's Scald: Lovecraft and the Nordic Tradition," and, likewise, Eckhardt deftly observes that Lovecraft "could not deny his Anglo-Saxon blood" (210). The direct citation of the horrific aspects of the Anglo-Saxon epic poem *Beowulf* runs in direct conflict with the academic trends of the time period. While the reading and study of these aspects of *Beowulf* are commonplace in contemporary education, the reach of the Anglo-Saxon epic in 1927 was mostly limited to the realms of historians and philologists. While modern English translations of the poem had been available since the early nineteenth century (Magennis 48), serious academic analysis of the work, especially of the monstrous and horrific aspects of the work, did not truly begin until nearly a decade later in response to J. R. R. Tolkien's 1936 British Academy Lecture, "Beowulf: The Monsters and the Critics."[2]

---

1. For more information regarding Lovecraft's use of these medieval occultists and mystics, see S. T. Joshi's notes 7, 8, and 11 in Lovecraft, *The Annotated Supernatural Horror in Literature* 104–5.

2. Michael D. C. Drout remarks in "'Beowulf: The Monsters and the Critics' Seventy-Five Years Later" (*Mythlore* 30, Nos. 1/2 [2011]: 6), that Tolkien's lecture "pulled *Beo-*

As such, Lovecraft's knowledge of this work, and his open placement of the epic within the chronology of supernatural horror, display an interest in medieval texts that extended beyond a cursory knowledge and suggest an expansive knowledge not only of the common texts of the Middle Ages, but also of the less widely read and analyzed works of the period.

While Lovecraft both acknowledges and discusses the influence of the Middle Ages upon his tradition of writing, the most notable mention of the medieval period comes in the form of his attribution of medieval influences to Arthur Machen, observing, "He has absorbed the mediaeval mystery of dark woods and ancient customs, and is a champion of the Middle Ages in all things" (CE 2.187). While Lovecraft's view of the Middle Ages as a time of expressive growth provides a more general framework for establishing the larger-scale influence of the period upon his works, his comments regarding Machen provide a much more immediate corollary. Speaking of Machen's direct influence upon Lovecraft's "The Dunwich Horror," Robert M. Price observes, "There is little in Lovecraft's story that does not come directly out of Machen's fiction" (ix). Thus, while the direct influences upon Lovecraft's writing come from the nineteenth century, the roots of some of his works exist within the Middle Ages.

Within Lovecraft's writings, it is important to note that there are, in essence, two different forms of monstrosity. The first category is the deific entities that often serve as the seldom-seen motivators of the tales. These entities possess little homogeneity among their number and, in fact, sometimes vary greatly between representations and descriptions (as is the case of Nyarlathotep in "The Rats in the Walls" and other depictions)—a trend that can be attributed to a conscious choice by Lovecraft to accentuate their core "unknowability." Because of the level of variation, this particular form of Lovecraft's monstrous body is beyond the scope of this paper, although many observations will undoubtedly apply to the Old Ones and Outer Gods. However, the second form of Lovecraftian monster, the hybrid forms that tend to function as servitors to the deific entities, are significantly more reminiscent of the monstrous bodies described by medieval writers such as Sir John Mandeville and Gerald of Wales. As

---

wulf out of the academic ghetto." A complete version of Tolkien's speech can be found in Tolkien's *The Monsters and the Critics and Other Essays*, ed. Christopher Tolkien (Boston: Houghton Mifflin, 1984), 5–48.

such, this study will concentrate on uncovering the significance of the medieval tropes inherent in these lesser body frames.

The monstrous body frames demonstrated within the Middle Ages both inspire and reflect the theories presented by Cohen and Bildhauer, specifically in the utilization of inhuman forms as a representation of cultural outliers and sources of dread. While representations of liminally monstrous figures have existed in English since the earliest Anglo-Saxon texts, specifically in *Beowulf* and "Wonders of the East," perhaps the two medieval texts that demonstrate the greatest correlation to Machen's (and subsequently Lovecraft's) writings are *The Travels of Sir John Mandeville* and the writings of Gerald of Wales, specifically *The Topography of Ireland*. Mandeville's writings represent an intriguing case when analyzing the source culture's relations to its outside world. While the author depicts several outside cultures within his writing, he never, in actuality, traveled to any of these places. As a result of this, Mandeville does not represent the historical realities of the nationalities he encounters, but rather illustrates these peoples as possessing physical traits directly linked to the author's perception of how they *should* be depicted. Of the numerous oddities Mandeville describes over the course of his fabricated travels, one of his recurring images is the representation of unfamiliar peoples, specifically those of different nationalities, as possessing likewise unfamiliar bodies. These monstrous features are not attributed randomly, but rather provide a glimpse into the nature of Mandeville's culture; as Martin Camargo notes, "As Mandeville moves away from Jerusalem (chs. 16-34), he encounters increasingly outlandish creatures" (81). This use of deviant physical forms to conceptualize the unknown aspects of these cultures vividly illustrates Cohen's fourth thesis.

Gerald of Wales' fourteenth-century *Topography of Ireland* provides a more direct commentary on the perception of the monstrous body during the Middle Ages. Much like Mandeville, Gerald presents a fictitious encounter with a creature akin to the merging of an ox and a man (often referred to as the "Ox-man of Wicklow"). In presenting this hybrid figure, the clergyman attributes the creature's bodily form to an Irish appetite for bestiality. In this, Gerald directly links monstrosity with the performance of actions seen to be outside of social acceptability—in the medieval period monstrosity, in effect, was an outward indicator of social deviancy. The utilization of the monstrous body frame to project suspected vices upon an unknown culture is strongly reminiscent of Cohen's first thesis. By assigning animalistic or distorted features to an outside culture, especially a culture that experienced notable friction with the intended readership (as Ireland did with Wales), the physical form and its associated meanings become synonymous with those peoples in the eyes of the audience, rendering the monster as an emblem of the society as a whole.

As the work that is noted to draw most directly upon the works of Machen, both in style and in plot, "The Dunwich Horror" seems the obvious work to begin unearthing the presence of medieval tropes and fears within Lovecraft's own work. While the titular Dunwich Horror (whose invisibility makes examining its own body frame impossible) is perhaps the most evident inhuman entity found within the short story, a second, more visible, monstrous body exists within the work: that of Wilbur Whateley. Upon discovering the true details of Whateley's corpse, the tale's narrator describes his form thus: "It was partly human, beyond a doubt, with very manlike hands and head, and the goatish, chinless face had the stamp of the Whateleys upon it. But the torso and lower parts of the body were teratologically fabulous, so that only generous clothing could ever have enabled it to walk on earth unchallenged or uneradicated" (648).

In this description, Whateley is clearly portrayed as possessing not only exaggerated human features, but also markedly inhuman, animalistic features. It is in this blending of the distorted human form into recognizably "other" shapes, this hybridity, that Lovecraft's tale finds a notable direct analogue to the bodily representations of the Middle Ages. During his travels through the desert of Egypt, Mandeville encountered a monster who is described in a manner notably similar to Whateley (as well as Machen's own monstrous analogue within *The Three Imposters*): "And this monstre that mette with this holy heremyte was as it hadde ben a man that hadde ii. Hornes trenchant on his forehead, and he hadde a body lyk a man vnto the navele, and benethe he hadde the body lych a goot" (33). Like Lovecraft's character, this satyr-like creature is notably human-like in his torso and visage; thus, at first glance, he may appear similar to the human frame, but his form is also starkly and fundamentally distinct. While it is impossible to assert that Lovecraft himself would have been familiar with this creature (or other medieval bodies similar to this image), Machen, as a "champion of the Middle Ages," would have surely been familiar with Mandeville's text, a work that has often been described as enjoying popularity "greater than that of any other prose work of the Middle Ages" (Campbell 122).

The simple acknowledgment of the influence of a body form prevalent during the medieval period upon Lovecraft's writing does little to expose its purpose within his work. By borrowing this monstrous image, Lovecraft also draws upon its social ramifications. While Mandeville's satyr is indicative of the author's apprehension of the unknown peoples of foreign lands, Lovecraft's monsters represent a different kind of "fear of the unknown." Like the creatures seen in Mandeville's book, the monstrous forms in Lovecraft's work represent a movement away from established social norms and the values and beliefs of the author himself. Specifically, Lovecraft notably valued intelligence, materialism, and skepticism (specifically of science and religion) in both his personal life and his writings, and those who possess inhuman bodies are, almost categorically, in opposition to the cognitively detached lifestyle the author espoused. However, he describes the town of Dunwich as almost completely divergent from these beliefs. The story notes that the townsfolk have "come to form a race by themselves, with the well-defined mental and physical stigmata of degeneracy and inbreeding. The average of their intelligence is woefully low, whist their annals reek of overt viciousness" (635). This willful demonization of both place and inhabitants is reflected by a statement made by the author himself in a letter noting the influences that brought about the shaping of his fictional location, wherein he states it to be "a vague echo of the decadent Massachusetts countryside" (*SL* 3.108). In crafting Dunwich, Lovecraft deliberately seeks to engender a location that is perceived to be just as despicable and degenerate as the people he created to inhabit it. Whateley, by demonstrating a physical degeneration and separation to match the outside perception of a town as a whole, is therefore able to serve the function as an outward manifestation of the apprehensions "civilized society" holds for the location itself.

It is worth noting that Wilbur Whateley's physical appearance is not the only marker of his difference from the outside world. Indeed, even before his birth, his family possessed a notable stigma. In introducing his origins, Lovecraft explains explained that "[Wilbur's] mother was one of the decadent Whateley's, a somewhat deformed, unattractive albino woman of 35" while further noting that the family, much like the town itself once had, possessed a reputation for dabbling in wizardry (636). The Whateley line itself is fundamentally an "unknown" entity, and, as an unknown, is an inherent cause of suspicion and fear.

This blending of Whateley's (and, by extension, his bloodline's) body frame with outsiders' feelings surrounding the town itself is reminiscent of both Mandeville's method of painting cultures that were situated away from what he deemed to be the "center of civilization" and, in turn, of Cohen's fourth thesis. On the surface, the details of the author's situations differ tremendously, as the multitude of geographical mysteries that troubled Mandeville so greatly had been largely eliminated by the time of Lovecraft's writing. As a result of this, Lovecraft was forced to look inward and to nearby places of difference, such as rural locations on the fringes of society that are commonly viewed as "backwards" and "uncultured" by those in the center of civilization. Mandeville's satyr represents a desire by medieval readers to dehumanize the citizens of a rival nation and therefore reaffirm themselves through these proposed differences. The exaggeratedly inhuman peoples of Dunwich represent a similar need: a reinforcement of social structures. Through this manner of representation, Lovecraft provides assurance that the occupants of locations akin to Dunwich on the edges of society are deserving of their status as outcasts.

Although Wilbur Whateley's hybrid illustrates the role of monstrosity in gesturing toward the sources of unknown fear, it is the denizens of the town of Innsmouth that, perhaps, most fully employ medieval tropes in order to construct the fear of the unknown seen within the story. Like the ox-man described by Gerald of Wales, the "Innsmouth look" that afflicts the people of the New England town comes as a direct result of their performance of a secret taboo—in this case, their breeding with the amphibious Deep Ones. As the offspring of these unions grow and transform to resemble their inhuman parent more closely, they gradually take on exaggerated features of their human shape. Lovecraft describes Joe Sargent, in particular, as possessing "a narrow head, bulging, watery-blue eyes that seemed never to wink, a flat nose, a receding forehead and chin, and singularly undeveloped ears" as well as discolored hands that described as "large and heavily veined" ("The Shadow over Innsmouth" 815). As in the Middle Ages, the sexual pairing of the human form with a species that is undeniably inhuman evokes a fundamental fear of the unknown. Like Dunwich, the town of Innsmouth is noted as being both mysterious and undesirable to those outside of its borders, a fear that stems in large part from the physiological transformation exhibited by the townspeople. While the outside world is right to be suspicious of the denizens of Innsmouth, it is, as Bildhauer suggests, not the body that sparks the initial apprehension, but rather the fear that resides behind the body and the suspicion that this fear represents a truth that differs fundamentally from what is perceived to be socially acceptable.

Through fear, the mutated residents of Innsmouth mirror Cohen's first thesis in a manner akin the ox-man. Like Gerald's accusations regarding the taboos committed by the Irish, the citizens of nearby New England towns symbolize the transgressions that brought about the origin of their physical blight, attributing the "look" to legends surrounding "Old Captain Marsh driving bargains with the devil and bringing imps out of hell to live in the Innsmouth" and demons that dwell within the reef near the town ("The Shadow over Innsmouth" 809). At their origin, the body frames described in "The Shadow over Innsmouth" are reflections of their cultural significance. Just as the ox-man of Wicklow functioned as a singular embodiment of the vices of all the Irish people, the growing of the citizens' bodies toward uniformity allows them, individually and collectively, to stand for the outward social image of the town. While descriptions of the town's citizens during various stages of transformation are numerous (perhaps even to the point of being the work's primary focus), no image demonstrates the singularity of Innsmouth's cultural body more clearly than Robert Olmstead's own transformation at the climax of the tale. While, prior to the discovery of his heritage, Olmstead had been obviously repulsed by the inhuman forms that he encountered within the town, and was willing to endure great hardship and personal risk to escape the town rather than confront its residents, his attitudes shift completely upon his discovery and the subsequent beginnings of his own transformation; as his body transforms to match the unified cultural body, his mind follows suit, allowing Lovecraft to emphasize the fundamental role of the monstrous frame as representative both individual degeneracy and that of a larger social order.

It should be finally noted that monsters, by nature, are "polysemous entities" capable of taking on numerous layers of meaning (Bildhauer and Mills 1). Thus, just as the inhuman figures found within "The Dunwich Horror" and "The Shadow over Innsmouth" fulfill Cohen's fourth and first theses, respectively, their significance is not limited by their application; it is the purpose of these observations to illuminate, rather than confine, the monstrous. With this in mind, it can just as easily be asserted that those possessing the "Innsmouth look" could be considered as much a "gateway" to the unknown as Wilbur Whateley. Indeed, it is the thoroughness with which Lovecraft interweaves these tropes into the fabric of his tales that lends his work such depth. Lovecraft's drawing upon, whether knowingly or by way of his more direct influences, the monstrous body frames commonly seen within the Middle Ages provides the writer with one of his most valuable tools in constructing the core elements of fear found within his mythos. By harkening back to the writings of a time that routinely experienced and was forced to confront and understand the "fear of the unknown" that he held within such high reverence, Lovecraft was able to tap into the core anxieties inherent in humanity, and therefore create tales that continue to hold significance to contemporary audiences.

Works Cited

Bildhauer, Bettina. "Blood, Jews and Monsters in Medieval Culture." In *The Monstrous Middle Ages*, ed. Bettina Bildhauer and Robert Mills. Toronto: University of Toronto Press, 2001.

Bildhauer, Bettina, and Robert Mills. "Introduction: Concept-ualizing the Monstrous." In *The Monstrous Middle Ages*, ed. Bettina Bildhauer and Robert Mills. Toronto: University of Toronto Press, 2001.

Camargo, Martin. "*The Book of John Mandeville* and The Geography of Identity." In *Monsters, Marvels and Miracles: Studies in the Medieval and Early Modern Imagination*, ed. Timothy S. Jones and David A. Sprunger. Kalamazoo. MI: Medieval Institute Publications, 2002.

Campbell, Mary B. *The Witness and the Other World: Exotic European Travel Writing, 400–1600*. Ithaca, NY: Cornell University Press, 1988.

Cohen, Jeffery Jerome. "Monster Culture (Seven Theses)." In *Monster Theory*, ed. Jeffery Jerome Cohen. Minneapolis: University of Minnesota Press, 1996.

Eckhardt, Jason C. "Cthulhu's Scald: Lovecraft and the Nordic Tradition." In *Dissecting Cthulhu: Essays on the Cthulhu Mythos*, ed. S.T. Joshi. Lakeland, FL: Miskatonic River Press, 2011.

Lovecraft, H. P. "Supernatural Horror in Literature." In *Collected Essays: Volume 2–Literary Criticism*, New York: Hippocampus Press, 2012.

Magennis, Hugh. *Translating Beowulf: Modern Versions in English Verse*. Cambridge, MA: D. S. Brewer, 2011.

Mandeville, Sir John. *Mandeville's Travels*. Ed. M. C. Seymour. Oxford: Clarendon Press, 1967.

Price, Robert M. "Introduction." In *The Dunwich Cycle*, ed. Robert M. Price. Hayward, CA: Chaosium, 1996.

Attempting to "Untangle" the Mind, Body, and Phallus in Lovecraft's "The Thing on the Doorstep"

Zack Rearick
Georgia State University

Questions about the mind and its relationship with the body have been mulled over by centuries of philosophers—indeed, philosophy has an entire field reserved for pursuits along this line: philosophy of mind. This field can be said to begin roughly with the writings of the Greek philosophers Plato and Aristotle, continues on through the centuries in the works of thinkers like Descartes, Hegel, Lacan, Marx, Foucault, and Derrida, and survives more recently in the persons of Rorty, Dennett, Langer, Sagan, and Nagel. But literature too probes these questions, from the "invention of the human" of Shakespeare[1] to the multiplicity of selves of Stevenson and Cixous to the instability of identity of writers like Clare, Joyce, Berryman, and the language poets.

These sorts of questions—of self, mind, body, and identity—may be approached from a variety of theoretical lenses and in a variety of works. They are the focus of H. P. Lovecraft's 1933 short story, "The Thing on the Doorstep." The story, which follows narrator Daniel Upton's retelling of his murder of close friend Edward Derby, raises (and occasionally answers) many compelling questions about the relationship between the mind and the body. I believe that it is most productive to read this story psychoanalytically by addressing the relationship of the mind and body through (and with) the theoretical phalluses of Freud, Lacan, and (to a degree) Judith Butler. The story involves many instances of mind-body switching; by its conclusion, the reader has seen the same mind pass from

---

1. Harold Bloom's term, from his book of the same name.

the body of Ephraim (the father of Edward's wife, Asenath Waite) to Asenath to Edward. Lovecraft's story argues for the preeminence of the mind over the body in determining identity and, in the process, comments on gender and sexuality in ways that are advanced for the time.[2] "The Thing on the Doorstep" unmistakably places Lovecraft as an author of theoretically "aware" fiction, dealing with the complexities of poststructuralist questionings of truth and the self, third wave feminist critiques of the collapsing of sex and gender into one category, and philosophy of mind's investigations into the knowability of the self and the potential for the self's re-constitution and re-creation.

"The Thing on the Doorstep" begins with a telling assertion of the preeminence of the mind over the body in regards to the establishing of identity: "It is true that I have sent six bullets through the head of my best friend, and yet I hope to shew by this statement that I am not his murderer" (CF 3.324). Upton believes that, since an exchange of minds results in the creation of two entirely new entities (Ephraim's-body-with-Asenath's-mind and Asenath's-body-with-Ephraim's-mind), these entities are identifiable through their minds primarily and through their physical bodies secondarily. Upton centers the proof for his opening statement around fact

---

2. I have chosen to use the phrase "Lovecraft's story" for this project in order to make a clearer distinction between the work and its author. To say that "The Thing on the Doorstep" believes one thing about the relationship of the mind and the body is not to say that Lovecraft himself believed it. For whatever reason, Lovecraft seems to be read in this manner more than most authors, so I am employing this somewhat clumsy qualifier in hopes of reinforcing this crucial distinction. Reading Lovecraft *as* a character in his own works does have its merits, particularly in a New Historicist reading, one that enters the story through Lovecraft's biography. There is also a kind of "traditional" psychoanalysis that attempts this sort of work, but I will confine myself strictly to psychoanalysis as a literary critical discourse. For brief readings of the former kind, in which Edward Derby is seen as a fictional representation of Lovecraft, see Cannon 2, 15, 116-19; de Camp 383-86. S. T. Joshi and David E. Schultz consider Derby "a synthesis of [Lovecraft's] various protégés—chiefly Frank Belknap Long and Alfred Galpin—and perhaps Clark Ashton Smith," but they also see his reaction to his mother's death reflected in the beginning of this story and note that "some features of Edward Derby's life supply a twisted version of [Lovecraft's] own childhood" (*An H. P. Lovecraft Encyclopedia* 64, 154, 262). Joshi, the paramount Lovecraft scholar, reiterates this reading his introduction to "The Thing on the Doorstep" in *H. P. Lovecraft: The Fiction* (New York: Barnes & Noble, 2008).

rather than conjecture or opinion: "Later some of my readers will weigh each statement, correlate it with the known facts, and ask themselves how I could have believed otherwise than as I did after facing the evidence of that horror" (CF 3.324). Though Upton feels he may be "mad [himself]," he also laughs at the "weakly" concocted theories of police, who are at "their wits' ends" (CF 3.325). Ultimately, Upton is a philosopher and is in opposition to romantic identity-questioning narrators like Dostoevsky's Underground Man and Nabokov's Charles Kinbote. He takes in evidence via his senses and interprets it based on the most logical (though not always the sanest) interpretation, and he questions any conclusions that don't line up with what he knows to be true. This makes Upton more Cartesian than Shakespearean or Cixousian, more Sherlock Holmes than Leopold Bloom.[3] Because Upton resists the conclusions he is ultimately forced to come to (and, even as he takes part in Edward's murder, admits that a man must sometimes "strike before reckoning the consequences" [CF 3.325]), his approach to the events that unfold in "The Thing on the Doorstep" similarly prepares readers to approach those conclusions from a philosopher's or theoretician's (rather than "artist's") perspective.[4]

Such a move becomes important in interpreting even the first paragraph of the story. Upton takes his stand concerning the separation of mind and body and the preeminence of the former over the latter when he asserts that he is not murderer of his best friend. The entity he shot was not Edward, he says, because it was the mind of the old man Ephraim in Edward's body. This may seem to some to be an obvious conclusion based on the plot of the story, but it has been an area of much disagreement in philosophy of mind, and Edward himself, though frequently in the grips of unimaginable horrors, seems at times not to agree with it, persisting in calling Asenath "she" even after he is aware that her body houses Ephraim's mind (CF 3.349, 350).

Before further arguments are advanced, it is perhaps worthwhile to summarize the plot of "The Thing on the Doorstep." The story is told from the perspective of Daniel Upton, an architect and Harvard graduate

---

3. Peter Cannon argues that "[Upton] plays the a skeptic, he at first seeks rational explanations." Cannon actually assigns Upton the role of the "Dr. Watson to Derby's Sherlock Holmes," but that is a question of perspective, not of methodology (Cannon 118).

4. All these terms are, as Derrida would say, used *sous rature*.

practicing in Lovecraft's beloved Arkham, and principally concerns his relationship with Miskatonic University student Edward Derby. Edward is a scholar of "phantasy and strangeness" (as well as a "Poe-like" poet) (CF 3.327) and the coddled child of well-off parents. He eventually falls in love with (or at least under the influence of) Asenath Waite, the perspicacious daughter of Ephraim Waite, an old man renowned, feared, and avoided on account of his "prodigious" talents in the dark arts. Asenath is also heir to the legend of the Innsmouth Waites, a family rumored to be connected to "horrible bargains" and "a strange element 'not quite human'" (CF 3.329). Edward and Asenath eventually marry, and what follows is a tale of horror only a careful reading can fully unravel. At the story's conclusion, we as readers know the full extent of Ephraim's evil, how he forced Asenath out of her own body, completely conquering her and trapping her in his own frail body, how he (in her guise) seduced Edward in hopes of similarly conquering him and taking his body, how Edward was able to fight him off for a while but not forever, how Edward was forced into the mutilated corpse of Asenath as Ephraim finally gained control of the weaker man's body, and how, steeled by the dying Edward's final pleading note, Upton shot Edward-Ephraim, seemingly killing his best friend but, in his mind, killing the "old wizard" (CF 3.336).

It is readily apparent that Lovecraft's story accepts the familiar Cartesian model of a mind-body dichotomy. The French philosopher famously stated that the only thing he could be certain of was that he was at that moment thinking, a realization that led him to postulate that the mind and body must be different things. In *Meditations on First Philosophy*, Descartes concluded that the mind is an "immaterial thing" and that it was the essence of the man to whom it belonged, which causally interacts with the body, a non-thinking, ontologically separate entity in which the mind is housed: "the soul is understood to be an immaterial substantial form. Recall that the immaterial mind or soul as substantial form is supposed to act on a properly disposed human body in order to result in a full-fledged human being." In Descartes's writings, the mind is given superiority over the body (it is the body that Descartes can "exist without," not the mind; 76), both by the nature of its ontological certainty and by its representation as the quintessence (the importance of the word "soul" within the context of Enlightenment philosophy, and of seventeenth-century thinking in general, is easily evidenced) of its subject.⁵ Though this dichotomy has been challenged by thinkers like Elizabeth of Bohemia, Karl Popper, and John Searle, it remains a highly influential way of conceptualizing the self and its parts.

Following Descartes's model, "The Thing on the Doorstep" takes the mind-over-body approach to personal identity.⁶ Throughout the story, persons are identified by the entity controlling the body (the "mind" or "spirit" of the person) rather than the physical body they occupy, except on those occasions where the speaker is not aware (or willing to accept) that mind-body switches are possible. This position is taken not only in the book's opening, in which Upton denies being Edward's murderer on the basis of Edward's body being under Ephraim's control, but also in passages like, "the caller had vowed that in that instant the sad, muddled eyes of poor Edward were gazing out from [Asenath's body]" (CF 3.335) and the revelation from Edward that Asenath *"isn't Asenath at all, but really old Ephraim himself. . . . I know it now"* (CF 3.347). In this Lovecraftian world of "hideous exchanges of personality" (CF 3.336), such switches of minds to different bodies are a question of willpower; Asenath and Edward are chosen because they are weak and childish (both in will and in constitution), with the former also being a prime candidate due to her gender/sex. Ephraim is able to "crowd" Asenath out of her own body entirely (she never appears in the story properly except as a few muffled sobs beyond closed curtains), and he accomplishes the same task with Edward, though with much greater difficulty. In fact, Upton seems to be steeling himself for an attempt on Ephraim's part on *his* identity when he resolves, "I *will not* be driven out of my body . . . I *will not* change souls with that bullet-

---

5. It is worth noting that Descartes would have rejected mind-body switches of the kind that appear in "The Thing on the Doorstep" on an ontological basis: "I think that this body, which by some special right I called 'mine,' pertains to me more than any other bodies do: for I could not ever be separated from it" (74).

6. Timo Airaksinen argues that Lovecraft is "counter-Cartesian." However, his argument is mostly concerned with Lovecraft's personal philosophy (specifically, how his fictions fail to "create a self"), which, as I have noted, is not being addressed here. I do take issue with Airaksinen's notion that the "Lovecraftian world . . . does not allow anyone to be represented as the immanent 'I,'" particularly in a story like this one, in which the persistent and undissolvable entitaveness of each character's mind is crucial to the story's plot. See Airaksinen 25, 30–35.

ridden lich in the madhouse!" (*CF* 3.354). And this mind-body dichotomy is not a human creation either. Lovecraft's story adds about Asenath (while she is being controlled by Ephraim's mind) that "animals markedly disliked her, and she could make any dog howl by certain motions of her right hand" (*CF* 3.330), taking the conception of the mind as chief determinant of identity outside of the purely philosophical realm and placing it in the realm of the "natural" as well.

But "The Thing on the Doorstep" has even more types of questions to raise. Gender and sex play a pivotal role in the plot and character motivations in Lovecraft's story. Indeed, critical discussions of the story have often made its gender politics their focus (see Wisker). Peter Cannon is not alone in thinking of Asenath as "Lovecraft's most prominent female character" (117). The story seems, at its surface, to take a third wave feminist stance toward sex and gender as identity categories. Among other things, third wave feminism clarifies and solidifies the position that sex and gender are separate from one another, with sex being primarily biological and gender being primarily a function of one's culture and personality. And Lovecraft's story explicitly argues for a clear distinction between the two categories.[7] The "hideous exchange" can occur regardless of the sex or gender of the exchanger/recipient; that is, Ephraim can (at separate times) occupy the bodies of both Asenath and Edward even though he is male in both sex and gender. Furthermore, it is clear that the mind, regardless of the body it is housed in, retains whatever gender-coded characteristics it had previously. Neither Edward nor Ephraim become more feminine in personality while occupying Asenath's body, a contrast between mind/gender and body/sex that is most striking when Ephraim is in control of his daughter's body. Because these switches locate identity in the mind, the sex of the body occupied is of little relevance in making such determinations. Masculinity and femininity are products of the self (and therefore of the mind, since Lovecraft takes the Cartesian position that the mind is where the self is seated) and are thus not determined by the biology of the physical form in which a mind is contained. In this way, Lovecraft follows third wave feminism's distinction between sex and gender very closely.

But this distinction alone is not the telos of third wave feminism, and

---

7. Cannon acknowledges this distinction: Asenath and Edward's marriage "muddles the gender issue, though which sex it is preferable to be is never in doubt" (117).

Lovecraft's conception of gender and sex in "The Thing on the Doorstep" must be distinguished from some of the movement's further explorations on this theme. Most relevantly, Lovecraft's use of sex and gender in this story must be distinguished from the idea of "gender performativity" for which Judith Butler is usually credited. In her books *Gender Trouble* and *Bodies That Matter*, Butler argues that gender is not an inherent thing tied to biological sex nor a solidified state that one is born possessing, but rather that it is a culturally constructed way of understanding one's identity that must be continuously reified by one's action, literally "performed" in the sense that masculinity and femininity are arbitrary markers containing nothing truly "male" or "female" aside from what the individual culture has demarcated as such).[8] The idea of "performativity" greatly informs what Butler calls the "lesbian phallus."

Butler's "lesbian phallus" is a rejection of the immutably masculine and heterosexual phalluses of Jacques Lacan and Sigmund Freud. Both of these highly influential twentieth-century thinkers understood the phallus to be the seat of power in any relational or epistemological dynamic. For Freud, the phallus is mostly related to understandings of human psychosexual development. Freud's phallus is, in its simplest form, the locus of intellectual power and sexual dominion, whether over others or one's own desires. To have the phallus is to have power, even if that phallus is ultimately unattainable, particularly for women.

Lacan's phallus is also unattainable (and also particularly so for women), the psychoanalytic manifestation of the shift from the "structuralist" signification of Saussure to the "poststructuralist" signification of Lacan and Barthes. For Lacan, power (and, consequently, the phallus) exists, as does everything, only in words. The phallus "designates as a whole the effects of signification" (12), and that signification can only occur within language. This "logocentric"[9] approach to the phallus was the result of a

---

8. See Butler, *Gender Trouble*. A common misinterpretation of this concept is that such performativity allows for the individual to construct (via performance) their gender freely. Butler refers to this derogatorily as a "humanist" mistake in her second book, arguing that gender as a category precludes the notion of a "choosing subject," that the subject cannot decide on its gender because it is it "decided *by*" its gender. Butler, *Bodies That Matter* x.

9. Derrida's term for Lacan's take on Freud is "phallologocentric." Derrida's own un-

poststructural understanding of "truth" that separated that which we know from that which we can never know (in Lacan's terms, "the Real"). This second entity is Truth, but since language is a closed circle (a rose is a rose is a rose), we can never get to it. Thus, for Lacan, to have the phallus is to have knowledge, but only knowledge *through* words, which is not true Knowledge at all, but the closest that is possible.[10]

Along with Luce Irigaray and Hélène Cixous, Judith Butler attempts to move away from a conception of the phallus that was, as were Freud's and Lacan's, ultimately ingrained in a culture that "normativized" whiteness, masculinity, and heterosexuality. Butler's "lesbian phallus" is an attempt to move away from those phalluses to a new kind of phallus (and thus, a new kind of power):

> To insist, on the contrary, on the transferability of the phallus, the phallus as transferable or plastic property, is to destabilize the distinction between being and having the phallus, and to suggest that the logic of non-contradiction does not necessarily hold between these two positions. In effect, the "having" is a symbolic position which, for Lacan, institutes the masculine position within a heterosexual matrix, and which presumes an idealized relation of property which is then only partially and vainly approximated by those marked masculine beings who vainly and partially occupy that position within language ... the repression of that denial [of transferability] will constitute the system internally and, therefore, pose as a promising spectre of its destabilization. (*Bodies That Matter* 61)

One can readily see how a Butlerian reading of the mind-body switching in Lovecraft's story might function. If the phallus is power and if knowledge is power, then it makes sense that the transferability of knowledge would indict a re-orienting (or rather, a re-constructing) of the phallus from its initial position within a matrix of white/male/heterosexual normativity into a new matrix, creating a "lesbian phallus," a power that could be held by someone (anyone) else.[11] And it seems only natural to imagine that a story

---

derstanding of language as the only means by which the mind can interact with itself and the world around it is quite similar to Lacan's, though with several crucial differences that are not worth explicating here.

10. This has significant resonances of Foucault's knowledge-power from *Discipline and Punish*.

11. This is somewhat of a misuse of Butler's phallus, which exists primarily as a tool

that includes mind-body switching across biological sex and among three people (not to mention those hinted at in other passages) would be one that lines up with Butler's transferability.

But such a reading of "The Thing on the Doorstep" would ultimately be a misreading. Though it is true that the phallus is centered in knowledge in the story (particularly in a knowledge of the "dark arts" sufficient to engage in mind-body switching),[12] this phallus is not truly "transferable" in Butler's sense. It is here that the lines between Butler's arguments about gender and sex and those in Lovecraft's story must be clearly drawn. For both, gender and sex are discrete entities, but Butler's gender performativity has no parallel in Lovecraft's story. While both Edward and Ephraim do occupy Asenath's body (and she occupies her father's), the genders of the respective occupants are never in flux. Robert H. Waugh asks readers of Lovecraft to "finally accept that [hermaphrodites in Lovecraft's stories, such as Asenath-Ephraim] . . . transcend the divisions of human gender" (141), but there is no evidence for that claim in *this* particular story. Indeed, Matolcsy contends that "Asenath-Ephraim's figure . . . is plainly patriarchal" (177), and for Joel Pace the "gender otherness of Asenath is clear here" (114).[13]

---

to demonstrate the degree to which the way we relate to the material of our bodies (particularly the ways we think about our bodies as biologically male and female) is always already constructed. Though I have taken the concept outside of its original context, I think its power as a tool of deconstruction is equally valuable in the field of philosophy of mind.

12, Kálmán Matolcsy has suggested that "knowledge is always harmful, and both knowledge and harm are closely tied to gender" (172) in Lovecraft. This seems to me further evidence for the phallus as Lovecraft uses it in this story being Lacanian. "Men achieve access to the privileges of the phallus . . . by denying their last link to the Real," which becomes harmful since "the real [sic] continues to erupt whenever we are made to acknowledge the materiality of our existence, an acknowledgement that is usually perceived as traumatic" (Felluga). That this relationship is mapped onto the male body in a different way than the female body reinforces the "close ties" to gender that Matolcsy has noted.

13 See Pace 114. Pace later remarks that Ephraim "becomes a symbol of gender . . . hybridity" (126), which is a claim that is complicated by the multi-valence of "hybridity." I trust that my paper makes clear the ways in which I am in agreement and opposition to this claim.

It is Ephraim in the guise of Asenath who proudly boasts that "she [sic] [is] not a man; since she believed a male brain had certain unique and far-reaching cosmic powers" (CF 3.330). The occupation of a female's body obviously has no effect on Ephraim's opinion of femininity or the female subject. The old man is convinced that the body he is occupying is greatly inferior to the one he occupied before because it is a female body, proclaiming loudly that he will, if "Given a man's brain [. . .] not only equal but surpass [his previous] mastery of unknown forces" (CF 3.330). And there is plainly nothing "performative" about gender here; no matter how Ephraim-like Asenath becomes (typically expressed in activities usually reserved for men, like driving), "she" (who the story no longer considers a "she" at all) never appropriates masculinity as an identity category. Rather than complicating Ephraim's understanding of sex, the switch into Asenath's body seems to solidify it, and the old man unambiguously sees gender as an inherent part of the mind, even to the point that the physical brain in which the mind is housed has an effect on the ability to perform certain tasks.[14]

Moreover, Lovecraft's story does not indicate at any point that gender is socially constructed; mind is to gender as body is to sex in 1:1 ratios that are never called into question by Upton. Never afraid to note the old man's flaws, our narrator does not raise this issue, and there is no reason to think that he accepts (or is even conscious of) third wave feminism's notion of gender as a thing that is *made* and can be *re-made* in a different way, even if we feel that Upton rejects Ephraim's positioning of the feminine/female as subaltern. Lovecraft's story, rather than transcending constructed notions of gender, reinforces the male/masculine and female/feminine binary categories, even as it allows for the switching of bodies and minds between them.

---

14. Joshi and Schultz have rightly noted that "this sentiment is clearly expressed as Asenath's (who, let us recall, is only Ephraim in another body) and need not be attributed to [Lovecraft]." Aside from reinforcing the idea that Lovecraft's story uses the mind rather than the body to determine identity, this note reminds one to avoid a reductionist collapsing of the story into the author. I have marked my own work as distinctly non-biographic, but even a reading of "The Thing on the Doorstep" that approaches the work through Lovecraft's biography should not lead one to conclude that Ephraim's thoughts are Lovecraft's, particularly since former is the story's antagonist. That anyone with any sort of background in critical discourse could make such a mistake is astonishing to me, and the authors above-mentioned were correct to call such readings "silly" (Joshi and Schultz 265).

Knowing this, it is impossible to see the phallus in Lovecraft's story as "lesbian." Instead, it is the Lacanian phallus that Lovecraft seems to be the closest to employing. Recall that Lacan's phallus is phallogocentric, primarily deriving its power from words as singular entities. So too does the knowledge-power of Ephraim center around words, the words in the "forbidden tomes" of the Miskatonic University library, and the disturbing and cryptic language in which he is given a new name ("Kamog") and is brought closer to the undefined power he is seeking. Furthermore, this knowledge-power in "The Thing on the Doorstep" has shades of poststructuralist linguistic relativism; the ability to have "mastery in unknown forces" comes through knowledge through language, but it does not have applications outside of those of the dark arts (e.g., controlling the weather, mind-body switches, taking part in forbidden rituals). Just as language is a closed system for Lacan, and the Lacanian phallus is simply the height of power within that system, so too is the knowledge-phallus in "The Thing on the Doorstep" part of a closed system of dark arts. Though Upton is often subject to these forces, he is never envious of them or desirous of acquiring them, and Edward too longs to give up his studies at various points during the story. Unlike the Freudian and Butlerian phalluses, both of which undergird all social interactions, the Lacanian phallus is centered in language-as-words and is "trapped" within that system; so too is the phallus in Lovecraft's story "trapped" within the system of the dark arts.

The phallus is, even when "purely" linguistic, still a marker of sexuality, and so Lovecraft's story also approaches issues of personal identity is through its play with sexuality. Waugh calls "The Thing on the Doorstep" "Lovecraft's study of erotic love" (130), and Phillip A. Shreffler argues that "The Dunwich Horror" and "The Thing on the Doorstep" are "as close to eroticism as anything Lovecraft wrote" (12). Shreffler appropriately sees Lovecraft as primarily "lukewarm on the subject of human sexuality" (12), and Joshi's remark that "One must look very hard even to find hints of sex in [Lovecraft's] fiction" (*H. P. Lovecraft: A Life* 582) also seems correct to me, but the presence of sexual intercourse in the story is worth discussing, particularly a type of intercourse that may be read as uniquely homosexual. Though all the characters in the story are, by way of heteronormativity, presumed to be heterosexual, sexuality in the story is used in a way that is more complex than a cursory reading might indicate. The only sexual relationship present in the story is between Asenath and Edward, although there is vague mention of Upton's wife ("always shunned, evanescent, ethereal, never [appearing] in the body throughout the story": Matalcsy 172), with whom he has a son.

But Asenath's body is under control of Ephraim for the entirety of her courtship of Edward, adding an interesting (and decidedly non-heteronormative) dynamic to their romantic and sexual relationship. Though we as readers know that Ephraim's intention in using Asenath's body to marry Edward is to gain control over his body (which Ephraim considers superior because it is male), Edward is unaware of this when entering into a sexual and romantic partnership with a physical woman who has the mind of an old man. In fact, it seems to be Asenath's mind, and particularly the qualities of it that are characteristic of Ephraim, that attract Edward to his soon-to-be wife in the first place. It is her "interests and erudition which engrossed him most" (CF 3.330).[16] This relationship, an intimacy that is "beyond untangling" (CF 3.331), is defined by the ways in which Ephraim uses Edward's romantic and sexual attraction against him: Asenath "[eyes] him continually with an almost predatory air" and the relationship is the product of "the woman's [sic] strong will" (CF 3.331).

But the part of the story that leads most directly to a "queer" reading involves the marriage and honeymoon of Asenath and Edward. It is Joshi, as always, who asks the most important question: "Is this marriage homosexual?" (*H. P. Lovecraft: A Life* 582). Asenath and Edward's honeymoon points most clearly to a reading of "The Thing on the Doorstep" as, in part, a story about homosexuality and its status as a taboo subject for discussion in literature.[17] A dramatic and awful change occurs in Asenath and Edward's relationship during their honeymoon, and the text leads one to believe that it centers around one particular event. Edward calls on Upton immediately after the honeymoon, and his friend looks "soberer

---

16. It is worth mentioning that Upton does note that Edward is also taken in by Asenath's appearance, if for no other reason than to justify my assumption that the sexual matrix of the "The Thing on the Doorstep" is a heteronormative one. Pace, who has already suggested that "it is not outside of the realm of possibility that the reader is meant to understand that this married couple is sexually active," would remind readers here that "Ephraim is in full possession of Asenath for nearly the entire story" (106, 125).

17. Though he does not explicitly say so, I believe that Pace invokes Sedgwick in his analysis.

and more thoughtful, his habitual pout of childish rebelliousness being exchanged for a look almost of genuine sadness" (CF 3.332). This "new sadness or understanding" (CF 3.334) coincides with Edward's now frequent mind-body exchanges to and from his own body facilitated by Ephraim, but it is hard to ignore the homosexual undertones of a honeymoon in which two bodies are intermingled (echoing the biblical notion of marriage as "two becoming one"), and the fact that Edward, believing at this point that Ephraim-Asenath is a woman (and, beyond that, knowing for sure that she possesses the body of one), would have desired and expected sexual intercourse with the woman he has just married. Given the fact that such an event as intercourse between a man (in body and mind) and a man (in mind only) would have been practically unspeakable in the early part of the twentieth century, it is not out of question to imagine that homosexuality could be, in the terms of Eve Kosofky Sedgwick, an "open secret" in the story.[18] This "queer" reading of "The Thing on the Doorstep" would partially attribute Edward's personality change to sexual union with what turns out to be his father-in-law in his wife's body (and the realization that he has been courted by that same father-in-law all along) and would add yet another layer of phallic interpretation (with the literal phallus of Edward's penis being conquered by the knowledge-phallus of Ephraim's mind) to Lovecraft's story.

Regardless of the legitimacy of a "queer" reading, "The Thing on the Doorstep" is clearly a story that plays with Descartes's mind-body dualism, gender, sexuality and the concept of the phallus in ways that are quite advanced for its date of composition. The knowledge-phallus in "The Thing on the Doorstep," connected most closely with Lacan's phallogocentric phallus, ends up destroying its wielders, as it does in many of Lovecraft's stories. Ephraim, at times in possession of three different bodies, is even-

---

18. Lovecraft's own commentary on the story has erotic undertones of its own: "Indeed, Ephraim-Asenath probably took a grim pleasure in the idea of thrusting Edward's consciousness down into that corpse-pit of horror" (*Lord of a Visible* 275). Ephraim may have found the act (in which he is the penetrator in the theoretically phallic sense, rather than the physically phallic sense) "grimly pleasurable" in terms of its power exchange. That this leads Edward to a "corpse-pit of horror" lends further credence to a reading of their sexual union as homosexual in a sense that is disturbing for him.

tually murdered at the story's conclusion (which is, in a reversal that has its own poststructural resonances, placed at the beginning). All these points of entrance into "The Thing on the Doorstep" (and many not dealt with here, including an approach to the "Innsmouth Waites" through racial philosophy, as Pace suggests, and Marxist criticism) show Lovecraft to be an advanced and complex author, capable of creating intricate and theoretically rich literary puzzles that have to this day still not been entirely solved.

Works Cited

Airaksinen, Timo. *The Philosophy of H. P. Lovecraft: The Route to Horror.* New York: Peter Lang, 1999.

Butler, Judith. *Gender Trouble: Feminism and the Subversion of Identity.* New York: Routledge, 1990.

———. *Bodies That Matter: On the Discursive Limits of Sex.* New York: Routledge, 1993.

Cannon, Peter. *H. P. Lovecraft.* Boston: Twayne, 1989.

de Camp, L. Sprauge. *Lovecraft: A Biography.* Garden City, NY: Doubleday, 1975.

Descartes, René. *Meditations on First Philosophy.* Tr. George Hefferman. Notre Dame, IN: University of Notre Dame Press, 1992.

Felluga, Dino Franco. "Introduction to Jacques Lacan, Module on Psychosexual Development." Introductory Guide to Critical Theory, Purdue University. http://www.cla.purdue.edu/english/theory/psychoanalysis/lacandevelop.html Accessed 7 March 2014.

Gallop, Jane. *Reading Lacan.* Ithaca, NY: Cornell University Press, 1985.

Joshi, S. T. *H. P. Lovecraft: A Life.* West Warwick, RI: Necronomicon Press, 1996.

Joshi, S. T., and David E. Schultz. *An H. P. Lovecraft Encyclopedia.* Westport, CT: Greenwood Press, 2001.

Lacan, Jacques. *Ecrits.* Paris: Seuil, 1996.

Lovecraft, H. P. *Lord of a Visible: An Autobiography in Letters,* Ed. S. T. Joshi and David E. Schultz. Athens: Ohio University Press, 2000.

Matolcsy, Kálmán. "'The Innsmouth Thing': Monstrous Androgyny in H. P. Lovecraft's 'The Thing on the Doorstep.'" *Gender Studies* 1, No. 3 (2004): 171–79.

Pace, Joel. "Queer Tales? Sexuality, Race, and Architecture in 'The Thing on the Doorstep.'" *Lovecraft Annual* 2 (2008): 104–37.

Shreffler, Phillp A. *The H. P. Lovecraft Companion*. Westport, CT: Greenwood Press, 1977.

Waugh, Robert W. "'The Ecstasies of 'The Thing on the Doorstep,' 'Medusa's Coil,' and Other Erotic Studies." *Lovecraft Annual* 4 (2010): 136–62.

Wisker, Gina. "'Spawn of the Pit': Lavina, Marceline, Medusa, and All Things Foul: H. P. Lovecraft's Liminal Women." In *New Critical Essays on H. P. Lovecraft*, ed. David Simmons. New York: Palgrave Macmillan, 2013. 31–54.

The Shadow of His Smile: Humor in H. P. Lovecraft's Fiction

Stephen Walker
University of Central Missouri

In 1921 John Ravenor Bullen wrote of H. P. Lovecraft's stories: "the reader, search and probe as he may, is unable to discover any trace of humor . . . Can a view of the universe which does not take humor into consideration be complete or correct?" (cited in CE 5.68).

Lovecraft responded to his transatlantic colleague:

> I observe Mr. Bullen's complaint that no humour enters into my tales; which omission he deplores, assuming that these tales are designed to present a view of the universe. In reply, I would suggest that none of my narratives aims at scientific accuracy and inclusiveness, each being rather a mere transcript of an isolated mood or idea with its imaginative ramifications. Moreover, humour is itself but a superficial view of that which is in truth both tragic and terrible—the contrast between human pretence and cosmic mechanical reality. Humour is but the faint terrestrial echo of the hideous laughter of the blind mad gods that squat leeringly and sardonically in caverns beyond the Milky Way. It is a hollow thing, sweet on the outside, but filled with the pathos of fruitless aspiration. All great humorists are sad— Mark Twain was a cynic and agnostic, and wrote "The Mysterious Stranger" and "What Is Man?" When I was younger I wrote humorous matter—satire and light verse—and was known to many as a jester and parodist . . . But I cannot help seeing beyond the tinsel of humour, and recognising the pitiful basis of jest–the world is indeed comic, but the joke is on mankind.[1] So when

---

1. Lovecraft's "the joke is on mankind" echoes Herman Melville in *Moby-Dick*: "There are certain queer times and occasions in this strange mixed affair we call life when a man takes this whole universe for a vast practical joke, though the wit thereof he but dimly discerns, and more than suspects that the joke is at nobody's expense but his own." This is a continuance of, for example, John Gay's epitaph: "Life is a jest, and all things show it, / I thought so once, and now I know it." Like the regression of

I delineate an intense mood I plough down to the subsoil and do not try to trifle with the layer of levity on top. [asterisk shows footnote: "I have the sanction of the best models—Poe's intense tales are wholly humourless."][2] Humour is the whistling of man to keep up his courage as he travels the dark road. I once wrote:

> The wise to care a comic strain apply,
> And shake with laughter, that they may not cry.[3]

Let it not be thought that I fail to appreciate humour—indeed, I employ it in discourse; being regarded as satirical and given to repartee." (CE 5.54)[4]

Perhaps Lovecraft's analytical remarks about humor were affected during this period by the somber circumstance that his mentally ill mother

---

Jonathan Swift's fleas, the supposition that life-is-a-joke must flow back to the beginning of human reflection, saturated with all its skepticism, if not cynicism.

S. T. Joshi derives Lovecraft's consideration of existence as a joke from scientists such as Haeckel and philosophers such as Schopenhauer. Several points apply to the philosophy of Lovecraft and its relation to the joke. Consider the structure of the stories whose climax is akin to a joke's punch line, though a shiver replaces a laugh. Obvious examples are the final words in "Pickman's Model" and "The Dunwich Horror," where for good measure italics have heightened the text, almost as a physical prod. Jokes and fantasy share some of the same ground. Like myths and fairy tales, jokes have an "indifference to reality, possibility, and probability" (Heller 131).

A case can be made that the foundation of the Cthulhu Mythos is a joke. In a letter about various fantasy places and characters including his own Cthulhu Lovecraft writes, "Who can disprove any such concoction, or say that it is not 'esoterically true' even if its creator did think he invented it in jest or fiction?" (*Lord of a Visible World* 222).

2. Cf. "Many of the most significant and substantial Poe scholars of the twentieth century have held that a comic element runs throughout Poe's fiction" (Poe 182). If true of Poe, could the same apply to Lovecraft?

3. A long held observation that has been preceded, for example, by lines from Lord Byron's satire *Don Juan*: "And if I laugh at any mortal thing, / 'Tis that I may not weep."

4. Cf. "I have no opinions—I believe in nothing—but assume for the time whatever opinion amuses me or is opposite to that of the person or persons present . . . There are no values in all infinity—the least idea that there are is the supreme mockery of all. All the cosmos is a jest, and fit to be treated only as a jest, and one thing is as true as another. I believe everything and nothing" (SL 1.231). And he speaks of man, the world, the cosmos: "It is all a jest and a delusion—a struggle that can bring no reward, and that has no meaning or merit in the cosmic chaos" (SL 1.284).

was in a hospital, where she would die soon. Even so, as if acknowledging that humor was intrinsic to his character and a coping necessity, a few weeks after her death he wrote: "I am as active as possible . . . and externally appear as usual; since I never display emotion, but prefer to be calm or slightly satirical" (*SL* 1.139). Five years before he had written in a letter: "A sense of humour has helped me to endure existence; in fact, when all else fails, I never fail to extract a sarcastic smile from the contemplation of my own empty and egotistical career!" (*SL* 1.27).[5]

The year 1921 also saw Lovecraft starting on what would become his first professionally published story, "Herbert West–Reanimator." It and the subsequent "The Lurking Fear" would appear not in the dark fantasy magazine *Weird Tales*—still a Gothic gleam in the eye of founder J. C. Henneberger[6]—but in a humor magazine published by George Julian Houtain who, knowing that Lovecraft had a talent for comedy, "wanted me to turn out some samples of my adapting of jokes for his proposed magazine [*Home Brew*]" (*SL* 1.351). Called by one observer "a slightly saucy humor magazine," it boasted a cover with an anthropomorphic full moon, wrapped round with the words "full of moonshine," and showed at the bottom "America's Zippiest Pocket Magazine."[7]

A number of critics—led by S. T. Joshi—see the story as a spoof of Mary Shelley's *Frankenstein*, with the voltage cranked up.[8] It certainly could be construed as over the top, but if it is a kind of parody, is it intentional? Keep in mind that it was a work for hire, the antithesis of how Lovecraft liked to compose. Knowing that this story was to go into a humor magazine, he may have written it with tongue in cheek. Since its 1985 movie

---

5. And elsewhere: "I shall never be very merry or very sad, for I am more prone to analyse than to feel." (This is reminiscent of Horace Walpole's "The world is a comedy to those that think, a tragedy to those that feel.") Lovecraft continues his thought: "What merriment I have is always derived from the satirical principle, and what sadness I have, is not so much personal, as a vast and terrible melancholy at the pain and futility of all existence in a blind and purposeless cosmos" (*SL* 1.132).

6. "Henneberger had already achieved great success with the magazine *College Humor*" (Joshi, *I Am Providence* 451).

7. Quoted from http://www.philsp.com/data/data195.html. "Herbert West–Reanimator" was serialized under the title "Grewsome Tales."

8. Joshi has since softened his view.

adaptation *Re-Animator* found a lot of humor in the horror hijinks, perhaps it is deftly woven into the original story.

As for "The Lurking Fear," its theme of people degenerating, de-evolving into ape-like predecessors could be a critique of mankind in the same way that Jonathan Swift's yahoos represent man-as-beast, the horse Houyhnhnms being the superior race (see Nelson). In Lovecraft probably the scientist and scholar come closest to this ideal of the Houyhnhnms.

Lest it appear that the theme of human beings devolving into apes is innocent of satire, let us call to mind the tone of the statement in *At the Mountains of Madness* where aliens, the masters of the earth, represent in their sculpture "a shambling, primitive mammal, used sometimes for food and sometimes as an amusing buffoon by the land dwellers, whose vaguely simian and human foreshadowings were unmistakable" (CF 3.100).

Man's importance—not just self-importance—when scaled against the cosmic was ridiculous. Lovecraft wrote in a letter: "I cannot help laughing at the claim of human interests to paramount notice" (SL 1.172). This meant whatever people held precious—ambition, love, anything. To Lovecraft, "One should come to realise that all life is merely a comedy of vain desire, wherein those who strive are the clowns, and those who calmly and dispassionately watch are the fortunate ones who can laugh at the antics of the strivers" (SL 1.111). In Lovecraft's fiction little tolerance is given to striving, with the narrator frequently passive in the unfolding of events. Elsewhere, Lovecraft speaks of his outlook as "impersonalism" (SL 1.129).

It is not humanity alone that is ridiculed, but life itself. One scientist in *At the Mountains of Madness* mentions "Elder Things supposed to have created all earth-life as jest or mistake" (CF 3.40). As he did in various stories—"The Silver Key" may be the salient example—Lovecraft is dramatizing his own philosophy or viewpoint.[9] In 1922 he had written: "I could not take humanity seriously if I wanted to" (SL 1.172); and in 1923, "There are no values in all infinity—the least idea that there are is the supreme mockery of all. All the cosmos is a jest, and fit to be treated only as a jest, and one thing is as true as another" (SL 1.231).

The idea that Elder Things created life as a joke or in error seems a satiric commentary on creation stories. Humorists had considered this before Lovecraft. "Man was made at the end of the week's work, when God

---

9. In "The Silver Key" the philosophy jeopardizes the dramatic narrative.

was tired," said Mark Twain. Lovecraft's outlook shared an attitude in particular with the later, dark Twain, the country's then and still preeminent humourist. Lovecraft spoke of "perusing some of the pessimistical writings of S. L. Clemens, which I find much to my taste. 'What is Man' is a veritable masterpiece" (SL 1.119).

Several critics have considered humor in Lovecraft's fiction. At least one agrees with Lovecraft that humor is "Totalement inexistant dans l'univers lovecraftien (excepté dans certaines de ses lettres)" (Foresti 137). On the other hand, in his dissertation Sean Elliot Martin found that "The erroneous generalization that Lovecraft's work is straight 'horror' also led readers to miss the humor in his writing, which is a key to understanding his absurdist approach to paradigm shifts and the nature of knowledge. Those who go looking for serious horror and find 'weird' fiction with absurdist humor thrown in can easily mistake absurdist commentary for a failed attempt to inspire fear" (211). And there is the revealing title of a recent book: Gavin Callaghan's *H. P. Lovecraft's Dark Arcadia: The Satire, Symbology and Contradiction*.

Much must be abridged in any brief look that compares the literary forms of humor and of horror, whether or not of the Lovecraft variety.[10] "There is often," writes S. T. Joshi, "a very thin line separating humor from horror" ("Humor/Satire" 582).[11] Both humor and horror are subversive, showing a new and uncomfortable light on truth.[12] They provide a shock of recognition, with "shock" the operative word in the case of horror. Noël Carroll states: "In literature, there has been a strong correlation between horror and comedy since the emergence of the horror genre." He goes on to cite the movie *Re-Animator* as an example and quotes Robert Bloch: "Comedy and horror are opposite sides of the same coin. . . . Both

---

10. Obvious humor in horror is part and parcel of the oeuvre of writers such as Ambrose Bierce. In other media it informs *Los Caprichos* of Goya and the illustrations of Gahan Wilson and Charles Addams; it was in the patter of television horror hosts (cf. Watson), emerged as unrelenting puns in Forrest J Ackerman's *Famous Monsters of Filmland*, etc.

11. In his "Humour and Satire in Lovecraft" Joshi divides Lovecraft's humor into three forms—puns, in-jokes, and bitter satire, although he has examples that don't fit in these classifications. He concludes that the reputation for a lack of humor in Lovecraft's fiction is a myth.

12. Horror films are "the most subversive of genres" (Clarens 336).

deal in the grotesque and the unexpected, but in such a fashion as to provoke two entirely different physical reactions" (Carroll 145, 146).[13] Humor and horror are individual and subjective apprehensions of an onlooker and their success depends on efficiency of effect.

An horrific concept may be treated as horror or comedy. Take for example the literary treatment of cannibalism. In one classic work children are to be eaten by adults; in another people are raised as livestock; in a third, being snowbound reduces the stranded to cannibalism; and in a fourth people on a raft consume one another. The first (children being eaten) is in the Jonathan Swift satire *A Modest Proposal*; the second (people raised as livestock) is in Lovecraft's "The Rats in the Walls," a husbandry horror tale; the snowbound misadventure is the comedic "Cannibalism in the Cars" by Mark Twain; the fourth (shipwreck) is "The Yarn of the 'Nancy Bell,'" a jocular poem by William Schwenck Gilbert. Horror can become comedy, comedy horror.

Lovecraft is associated with horror that is cosmic rather than comic. Though not the first response that comes to the mind when thinking of his stories, under various guises humor appears in a number of them. It can be sorted into a tentative (though hardly exhaustive) typology: name puns and word play; satire; parody; and observations on humanity.

Name Puns and Word Play

The pun might not be so alien to Lovecraftian horror as one might think. Edmund Leach calls the pun "a familiar type of purely linguistic taboo . . . The pun seems funny or shocking because it challenges a taboo which ordinarily forbids us to recognize that the sound pattern is ambiguous" (25).[14]

Some of the puns and word play take the form of in-jokes. Complicated by the decades that have passed, their relevance for newcomers to Lovecraft is further overwhelmed by the prominent creepy atmosphere. Without sufficient knowledge of background information about Lovecraft's friends and acquaintances, the in-jokes go over a reader's head. But after multiple

---

13. For more on Bloch and humor, see Schweitzer.

14. Stark confrontation with taboos is implicit in horror. Set in a half dozen of Lovecraft's tales, the phrase "forbidden things" is one way of describing what is taboo.

perusals, and horror fatigue sets in, the constant reader may start appreciating the layered shadows—the intimations—designed in the writing.

Lovecraft finished his career—which he may not have acknowledged, but his career *qua* career has been chiefly a posthumous success—with the last professionally published story during his lifetime, "The Haunter of the Dark" (written November 1935, published in *Weird Tales*, December 1936). Composed in the spirit of playful one-upmanship, it is Lovecraft's answer to a story by Robert Bloch, his young and gifted correspondent whose serious aptitude for humor showed off in his later work and in his own emcee duties at science fiction conventions. In Bloch's short story "The Shambler from the Stars" (*Weird Tales*, September 1935)—dedicated to Lovecraft—a character with more than a few nods to its dedicatee is dispatched. Before doing this Bloch had received Lovecraft's permission for the fictional slaughter, Lovecraft signing not only his name but that of Abdul Alhazred and other characters.

In Lovecraft's story a "Robert Blake" is a writer of weird fiction who lives at the same Wisconsin address as the real Bloch—a subtle wink that the average *Weird Tales* reader couldn't appreciate. The fate of Robert Blake would be to lose his mind (literally) and his life.[15]

Prior to Robert Bloch, Lovecraft had incorporated other friends into his fiction. Fellow fantaisiste Clark Ashton Smith was a recipient in several works of what in 1924 Lovecraft called "free advertising." Smith's name was mentioned in an altered form in "The Whisperer in Darkness," where amid the litany of made-up names of monstrous beings and books is "the Atlantean high-priest Klarkash-Ton" (CF 2.519).[17] Not only has Smith's first and second name been transformed into something that seems exotic (especially when seen spelled out), but the bit of business about "Atlantean" refers to the Atlantis theme in Smith's poetry and prose. If not the

---

15. Years after Lovecraft's death Bloch wrote a sequel, "The Shadow from the Steeple" (*Weird Tales*, September 1950), but by then the fun was out of the game.

17. This was one of Lovecraft's play-names for Smith in their correspondence. Lovecraft often assigned humorous names to his correspondents: Texan Robert E. Howard, known for his action and western stories, was "Two-Gun Bob," while fellow weird writer Donald Wandrei became Melmoth the Wandrei (after the epic Gothic novel *Melmoth the Wanderer*).

Weird Tales readers, many of Lovecraft's and Smith's correspondents would have appreciated the allusion.

Such a playful *roman à clef* was also used satirically. "In the Walls of Eryx"[18] identifies various fauna of Venus, where the story unfolds. Two of these are "farnoth flies" and "ugrats," derived from editors who caused Lovecraft grief. Farnsworth Wright ("farnoth flies"), now known as the legendary editor of *Weird Tales*, could be arbitrary in rejecting Lovecraft submissions, such as "The Call of Cthulhu." "Ugrats" might seem prescient of "rugrats," but the neologism comes from Lovecraft's pet nickname for the father of science fiction, Hugo Gernsback, whose payment for "The Colour out of Space" had been reluctant and stingy (one-fifth of a cent a word). Lovecraft referred to him as "Hugo the Rat," which became the portmanteau word "hugrat."

Other people in Lovecraft's sphere involuntarily lent their names to Venusian entities. Super-fan Forrest J Ackerman had criticized Smith and exchanged heated words with Lovecraft in the magazine *The Fantasy Fan*,[19] who had his explorer find "slimy akmans" as well as "efjeh-weeds," "Efjay" being a moniker that FJA claimed.

In cahoots with young friend R. H. Barlow, Lovecraft sported with the names of more than thirty associates in the 1934 prank story "The Battle That Ended the Century." Writer and poet Frank Belknap Long Jr. became Frank Chimesleep Short; Ackerman again is commemorated as Effjay of Akkamin; *Weird Tales* cover artist Margaret Brundage shows up as "the eminent magazine-cover anatomist Mrs. M. Blunderage." etc. (see CF 4.521).

---

18. Co-authored with Kenneth Sterling, it appeared in *Weird Tales* (October 1939) after Lovecraft's death in 1937. In his letters Lovecraft has many humorous takes on his stories. For the Harry Houdini ghostwritten "Under the Pyramids" (a.k.a. "Imprisoned with the Pharaohs," *Weird Tales*, May–June–July 1924) Lovecraft summarized the story to a friend: "when Hoodie takes the police to the scene, I'll have the guides found dead—strangled—chok'd lifeless in that antient necropolis of the regal stiffs—*with marks of claws on their throats* . . . claws . . . claws . . . principle and subordinate clawses" (SL 1.313). This is an example of bathos, here through use of a pun to undermine an intentional melodramatic effect. The "principal and subordinate clawses" is the sort of jest one literature professor might make to another.

19. For documentation on the Ackerman-Lovecraft feud, see Clark Ashton Smith, Forrest J Ackerman, and H. P. Lovecraft, *The Boiling Point* (West Warwick, RI: Necronomicon Press, 1985).

Whether Lovecraft chose to pun on names other than as in-jokes is debatable. Still, critic Christopher L. Robinson finds that in "The Shadow over Innsmouth," where human amphibian hybrids have gills, a family with the name Gilman "is a fitting pun" (133).

Satire

Of types of humor categorized here, satire has the most in common with horror. For Gilbert Highet, "Satires are not horror stories. They nearly all appeal, closely or distantly, to our sense of humor; and the great satirists are those who have been best able to convey a disgusting or ghastly message, and make it palatable by making it ridiculous" (212). As already suggested, Swift's *A Modest Proposal* could have been a horror story. Aggression or disdain redeemed by wit, satire puts humankind in its place, and fits with the Lovecraftian view, e.g., "all mankind forms but a transient, negligible atom" ("Idealism and Materialism: A Reflection"; *CE* 5.38).[20]

Lovecraft recognized satire's value. In 1922 he wrote that one of his literary idols, Lord Dunsany, never departs "from a cosmic and gently satirical realisation of the true microscopic insignificance of the man-puppets and their relations to one another" ("Lord Dunsany and His Work"; *CE* 2.61).[21] He could also speak critically of satire. In science fiction "Social and political satire are always undesirable" ("Some Notes on Interplanetary Fiction"; *CE* 2.181).[22]

Parody

One of satire's weapons, parody figures in Lovecraft.[23] For Dustin Geeraert, "Lovecraft's work may be understood as parodic. His fiction

---

20. Cf. the 1899 poem "A Man Said to the Universe" by Stephen Crane.

21. However, Dunsany's newer work had less appeal because of its "increasing note of visible irony, humour, & sophistication" (*SL* 1.203). The stories he wrote under the spell of Lord Dunsany have not been reckoned in this brief survey of his fiction.

22. Curiously, Highet sees voyages into the future as failed satires: "These it is difficult to describe as satires, since they usually arouse neither laughter nor contempt nor disgust, but merely wonder or horror" (Highet 171).

23. Lovecraft seems the most parodied writer in the English language, and the imitators started early. In the same year (and perhaps even the same month) as the Bullen response, an amateur press association member, Edith Miniter, published "Falco Os-

portrays events which transcend the laws of space and time, and which confirm in the process abstract and absurd ancient doctrines about incomprehensible deities." He interprets the narrative of "The Dunwich Horror" as "Lovecraft's direct parody of the life of Christ in which a half-'divine' man seeks to bring his 'kingdom' to the earth" (16, 62)[24] Similarly, Donald R. Burleson suggests that the entity calling on his father during the story's climax is a parody of the crucifixion (119). Novelist and gadfly Michel Houellebecq judged this ending "une répugnante parodie de la Passion" (139). But is "Dunwich" a Christian parody—and if so, is it designed to mock, or to shock?

To other critics parody may be less about theology than philosophy, something embedded in Lovecraft's perspective, say in the very existence of his monsters. Concerning the cone- shaped aliens in "The Shadow out of Time," Roger B. Salomon found that "The avatars of the 'Great Race' deny all human possibility; indeed, their actions constitute a relentless dark parody of such possibility" (25). Some monsters come much closer to human parodies. "Under the Pyramids" mentions "the most leeringly blood-congealing legends [. . .] *composite mummies* made by the artificial union of human trunks and limbs with the heads of animals in imitation of the elder gods" (CF 1.439).[26]

Perhaps Lovecraft's creation of Miskatonic University was also a form of parody. Novelist and essayist Angela Carter speculates that since Lovecraft was a high school dropout, he "revenged himself" by creating the university (445).

When it comes to Lovecraft and parody, it is possible that occasionally

---

sifracus," a good-natured send-up of Lovecraft's weird fiction work.

24. Geeraert finds—or claims to find—other comparisons. The hired boy Luther Brown (in "The Dunwich Horror") is a "deliberate reference to the most famous figure of early Protestantism, Martin Luther, [and] supports the notion that Lovecraft is condemning Protestant Christianity specifically" (67). Moreover, the aim of aliens to return "earth to another dimension or plane of existence is Lovecraft's version of *Revelations*" (68).

26. Cf. Salomon on Lovecraft's story "The Horror at Red Hook": "Lovecraft suggests that horror narrative is fundamentally parodic," and quotes from the story: "the paintings were appalling—hideous monsters of every shape and size . . . parodies on human outlines" (124–25).

he lost control of his material, that it careened from horror to parody.[27] The Prussian protagonist of "The Temple" has been judged a character parody of the iron-willed, patriotic soldier who had recently been defeated in the Great War.[28] Was Lovecraft being satirical in "The Temple" or was he reflecting the unprecedented and controlling propaganda—the war fever—marshaled by the United States to establish the villainies of the Hun in the Great War?

Human Observation

A Lovecraft story is deliberately, if occasionally, humorous when dealing with humanity and its behavior. For example, in "The Haunter of the Dark" there is the detail, "Blake wondered how the obscurely painted panes could have survived so well, in view of the known habits of small boys the world over" (CF 3.456). The mild humor comes from omitting the obvious: boys break windows. This follows the method Lovecraft uses to create the atmosphere of dread; by hinting at something that terrifies, with carefully calculated implications that the reader is led to deduce. Consider "The Dunwich Horror," where a Rev. Hoadley "preached a memorable sermon on the close presence of Satan and his imps." The sermon is quoted, and then the reader is told almost in an aside: "Mr. Hoadley disappeared soon after delivering this sermon" (CF 2.420). Here is a conjuring up of an insidious, subliminal world that eventually vanishes into what, in Lovecraft's thematic language, is the indescribable and unspeakable. Humor and horror use the same tactics, but for different ends.

A key type in Lovecraft is the outsider, who has the potential of a droll figure through challenging norms that society has established. Think of the character Mork in the comedy show *Mork and Mindy* or the slapstick extraterrestrial villain of *Men in Black* or the title character in Larry Shue's play *The Foreigner* and apply that fish-out-of-water to Nathaniel Wingate Peaslee from "The Shadow out of Time," who wrote: "I seemed anomalously avid to absorb the speech, customs, and perspectives of the age around me; as if I were a studious traveller from a far, foreign land" (CF

---

27. Cf. Poe's "Eulalie" for an example of his great predecessor's unconscious parody.
28. "Lovecraft mars the story by crude satire on the protagonist's militarist and chauvinist sentiments" (Joshi and Schultz 261).

3.367) and "They noticed that my chief efforts were to master certain points in history, science, art, language, and folklore—some of them tremendously abstruse, and some childishly simple" (CF 3.367). His predicament could have made a sitcom.

That H. P. Lovecraft's greatest influence has been on the horror tale is beyond gainsay, and indeed, perhaps his writing is a brand unto itself, as distinct as science fiction or supernatural fiction. However, Lovecraft's second greatest influence has been on humor. His fiction has created a boutique humor industry (Christmas carols, Cthulhu toys, political slogans, etc.), which subverts horror—itself a subversion—through incongruity.

There remains much to explore in the area of Lovecraft and the comic in his fiction (not to mention the vast potential in his letters).[29] The subject of humor is an ocean, a panthalassa, and although narrowing it to the fiction of H. P. Lovecraft, this investigation, however aspiring, must be seen as a drop in Narragansett Bay.[30]

Works Cited

Burleson, Donald R. *Lovecraft: Disturbing the Universe*. Lexington: University Press of Kentucky, 1990.

Callaghan, Gavin. *H. P. Lovecraft's Dark Arcadia: The Satire, Symbology and Contradiction*. Jefferson, NC: McFarland, 2013.

Carroll, Noël. "Horror and Humor." *Journal of Aesthetics and Art Criticism* 57, No. 2 (Spring, 1999): 145-60.

Carter, Angela. "The Hidden Child." In *Shaking a Leg: Collected Journalism and Writings*. New York: Penguin, 1998.

Clarens, Carlos. *Crime Movies: From Griffith to the Godfather and Beyond*. New York: W. W. Norton, 1980.

Foresti, Guillaume. *Corman Lovecraft: La Rencontre Fantastique*. Paris: Dreamland, 2002.

---

29. There is, for example, the opportunity to benchmark or compare his use of humor against standards represented by Juvenal, Swift, Pope—who perhaps had the most literary influence on his writing—and Mark Twain.

30. The literature on humor is large. A 1992 bibliography on American humor contains more than 1200 entries (see Nilsen). A casual search in the *MLA Bibliography* for post-1992 items yields more than 800 results.

Geeraert, Dustin. "Spectres of Darwin: H. P. Lovecraft's Nilhilistic Parody of Religion." M.A. thesis: University of Manitoba, 2010.

Heller, Agnes. *Immortal Comedy: The Comic Phenomenon in Art, Literature, and Life.* Lanham, MD: Lexington Books, 2005.

Highet, Gilbert. *The Anatomy of Satire.* Princeton: Princeton University Press, 1962.

Houellebecq, Michel. *H. P. Lovecraft: Contre le monde, contre la vie.* Paris: Editions J'ai Lu, 1999.

Joshi, S. T. "Humor/Satire." In *Supernatural Literature of the World: An Encyclopedia,* ed. S. T. Joshi and Stefan Dziemianowicz. Westport, CT: Greenwood Press, 2005. 2.582-84.

———. "Humour and Satire in Lovecraft." In *Lovecraft and a World in Transition: Collected Essays on H. P. Lovecraft.* New York: Hippocampus Press, 2014. 308-21.

———. *I Am Providence: The Life and Times of H. P. Lovecraft.* New York: Hippocampus Press, 2010.

Joshi, S. T., and David E. Schultz. *An H. P. Lovecraft Encyclopedia.* Westport, CT: Greenwood Press, 2001.

Leach, Edmund. "Anthropological Aspects of Language: Animal Categories and Verbal Abuse." In *New Directions in the Study of Language,* ed. Eric H. Lenneberg. Cambridge, MA: M.I.T. Press, 1964. 23-63.

Lovecraft, H. P. *Lord of a Visible World: An Autobiography in Letters.* Ed. S. T. Joshi and David E. Schultz. Athens: Ohio University Press, 2000.

Martin, Sean Elliot. "H. P. Lovecraft and the Modernist Grotesque." Ph.D. diss.: Duquesne University, 2008.

Nelson, Dale J. "Arthur Jermyn Was a Yahoo: Swift and Modern Horror Fiction." *Studies in Weird Fiction* No. 7 (Spring 1990), 3-7.

Nilsen, Don L. F. *Humor in American Literature: A Selected Annotated Bibliography.* New York: Garland, 1992.

Poe, Harry Lee. *Evermore: Edgar Allan Poe and the Mystery of the Universe.* Waco, TX: Baylor University Press, 2012.

Robinson, Christopher L. "Teratonymy: The Weird and Monstrous Names of HP Lovecraft." *Names* 58, No. 3 (September 2010): 127-38.

Salomon, Roger B. *Mazes of the Serpent: An Anatomy of Horror Narrative.* Ithaca, NY: Cornell University Press, 2002.

Schweitzer, Darrell. "The Lighter Side of Death: Robert Bloch as a Humorist." In *The Man Who Collected Psychos: Critical Essays on Robert Bloch,* ed. Benjamin Szumskyj. Jefferson, NC: McFarland, 2009. 57–67.

Watson, Elena M. *Television Horror Movie Hosts: 68 Vampires, Mad Scientists, and Other Denizens of the Late-Night Airwaves Examined and Interviewed.* Jefferson, NC: McFarland, 1991.

Monstrous Modernism: H. P. Lovecraft's Theory of the Aesthetic in Modernity

Jason Ray Carney
Christopher Newport University

In an essay titled "Heritage or Modernism: Common Sense in Art Forms," published in a 1935 issue of Hyman Bradofsky's amateur journal, the *Californian*, H. P. Lovecraft puts forth an argument in defense of traditional art styles and thereby censures those he characterizes by their pretensions to intense levels of novelty. As a shorthand he refers to these innovative styles and productions as "modernism," and as concrete examples of the "art" he means to refer to by this term he cites Gertrude Stein, Picasso, James Joyce, Frank Lloyd Wright, and others. He criticizes these artists for their belief that "all art ought to be divorced completely from tradition and from earlier art-forms" (*CE* 5.120). In response to the belief attributes these innovators of art, he scolds, "Remove all sources of familiarity—all the subtle landmarks supplied by what we know of the past—and no phase of art or life can have more than the slenderest vestige of appeal, beauty, or meaning" (*CE* 5.120). Lovecraft aligns the subjective quality of familiarity and the intersubjective one of formal convention with traditional art-forms, and in his enthusiasm elevates them to existential proportions: "There can be no such thing as value, purpose, direction, or meaning, or even interest, except in a strictly local and relative sense" (*CE* 5.119).

In large part, Lovecraft's scarecrow modernism in "Heritage or Modernism" is a caricature based less on an actual understanding of historical modernism—a largely academic creation fraught with contradictions—and more on a stereotype inevitably derived from experiencing modernist works out of their contexts, dissociated from the interpretative communities that understood their unique idiom.[1] For example, one of Lovecraft's essay's central premises, modernism's antagonistic relationship to tradition, is problematic. It does not take into consideration the extent to which many of the artists typically designated as "modernists" in classic and contemporary studies were concerned primarily not with severing their ties to artistic tradition, but with the problem of reinvigorating that tradition.[2] But Lovecraft's inaccurate rendition of historical modernism is of scant interest here when compared to his fictionalized modernism, a fiction that, when properly scrutinized, yields a rich theory of art.

As we know, many of Lovecraft's short stories feature artists as characters who produce art clearly marked as severed from established aesthetic traditions and can, in this way, be interpreted as quasi-modernists; furthermore, unlike Lovecraft's many expository-style polemics and humorous parodies where he censures modernism directly, this literary discourse featuring fictional "modernists" allows him to preserve the rich complexities of his reflections on modernist art. But unlike critical discourse, generally taken on the level of the denotative, literary discourse, operating through connotation and allegoric resonances, asks for responsible translation.[3] This is what I propose to do. I highlight a few key examples of what I call Lovecraft's quasi-modernists (I drop the "quasi" for convenience) and the modernist art they create at their (and our) peril. I then trace a loose aesthetic theory these fictional artists and art objects outline.[4]

---

1. For a brief overview of the etymology and history of the term "modernism" as applied to specific groups of experimental artists working in the early twentieth century, see Matai Calinescu, *Five Faces of Modernity: Modernism, Avant-Garde, Decadence, Kitsch, Postmodernism* (Durham, NC: Duke University Press, 1987). Of particular relevance is his chapter on "The Idea of Modernity" (13-92).

2. For an overview of key modernist writings on the relationship of their work to tradition, see Richard Ellmann and Charles Feidelson, Jr., *The Modern Tradition* (New York: Oxford University Press, 1965).

3. My idea of literature as a type of discourse that asks for translation into critical discourse is informed by Northrop Frye's now classic description of the literary arts in the introduction to his *Anatomy of Criticism* (Princeton: Princeton University Press, 1957).

4. See Kenneth Burke's "Literature as Equipment for Living" in *Philosophy of Literary Form* (New York: Vintage, 1957), 251-62, for a classic description of how literature communicates ideas in excess of its surface, denotative content. In this brief essay, Burke proposes that literature should be considered sociologically/rhetorically, as

I argue that modernist artistic effort in these key instances is portrayed as a form of occult research, a struggle to perceive the cosmos-at-large, to bring its telescopic and microscopic scales into human context. In briefly concluding, contra his statements in "Heritage and Modernism," I argue that these stories betray a hitherto undocumented intimacy linking the aesthetic strategies typically associated with modernist aesthetics with those associated with cosmic horror, of which Lovecraft is master.

Although many characters featured in earlier Lovecraft stories manifest the acute sensibilities of artists or are directly portrayed as artists—e.g., Jervas Dudley of "The Tomb," Joe Slater of "Beyond the Wall of Sleep," Crawford Tillinghast of "From Beyond," Randolph Carter of the Dream Cycle, Iranon of "The Quest of Iranon"—none of them can be interpreted firmly as quasi-modernists until the strange violist of "The Music of Erich Zann." In this story, the narrator, lodging on the fifth story of a house on the strange "Rue d'Auseil," comes into contact with a decrepit hermit, Erich Zann, a violist who lives in attic garret of the same house, who is described as possessing "highly original genius" (175). Consider how Zann's music is described as being disconnected from all previous traditions of music familiar to the narrator: "I was haunted by the weirdness of his music. Knowing little of art myself, I was yet certain that none of his harmonies had any relation to music I had heard before" (175). It is implied that Zann's strange musical enterprise is a kind of transgression that has attracted the attention of a hostile force manifested as a kind of horrible dissonance, a force that can only be kept at bay (but never defeated) by Zann's playing. And when it arrives, it threatens to drown out Zann's music. Whereas Zann's music is complex, this opposing non-musical dissonance is cruelly simple, is described as "a shriller, steadier note not from the viol; a calm, deliberate, purposeful, mocking note from away in the west" (179). At the end of the story, Zann fails in warding off the entity, and, as a result, something horrible happens that the narrator registers as a visual phenomenon beyond the attic window:

> When I looked from the highest of all gable windows, looked while the candles sputtered and the insane viol howled with the night-wind, I saw no

---

"strategies for selecting enemies and allies, for socializing losses, for warding off the evil eye, for purification, propitiation, and desanctification, consolation, vengeance, admonition and exhortation, implicit commands or instructions of this sort or another" (262).

city spread below, and no friendly lights gleaming from remembered streets, but only the blackness of space illimitable; unimagined space alive with motion and music, and having no semblance with anything on earth. (179)

Here we have displayed in literary discourse an idea Lovecraft proposed elsewhere in a critical register: "There can be no such thing as value, purpose, direction, or meaning, or even interest, except in a strictly local and relative sense" ("Heritage and Modernism," CE 5.119). This story is an inaugural instance of Lovecraft's fictionalization of the modernist artist who, striking out into new, original aesthetic realms, transgresses. And through the transgression of his artistic enterprise, Zann has brought upon himself and the narrator the reality of humanity's existence in a hostile universe, for which the terrible anti-musical entity stands as avatar. This entity's presence in the story conveys a universe where the local and relative fictions of our significance, morality, and personal projects lose much of their validity. And yet, in a thinly allegorical register, Lovecraft frames the artist as a steward of human meaning in a cosmos hostile to it. From this perspective, the figure of Zann holds in tension an idealized and a cynical vision of the artist typically associated with modernism, particularly James Joyce: (1) the idealized vision of the artist as antagonist to chaos, and (2) the cynical vision of the artist an impotent in a standoff with chaos.[5] Consider the narrator's description of Zann as he plays in agonizing opposition to the musical entity that heralds the hostile cosmos: "It would be useless to describe the playing of Erich Zann on that dreadful night. It was more horrible than I had ever overheard, because I could now see the expression on his face, and could realise that this time the motive was stark fear" (178-79).

---

5. Consider T. S. Eliot's comment's (originally published in the *Dial* in 1923) on James Joyce's *Ulysses* in "'Ulysses,' Order and Myth," in *Selected Prose of T. S. Eliot* (London: Faber & Faber, 1975): "In using the myth, in manipulating a continuous parallel between contemporaneity and antiquity, Mr. Joyce is pursuing a method which others must pursue after him. They will not be imitators, any more than the scientist who uses the discoveries of an Einstein in pursuing his own, independent, further investigations. It is simply a way of controlling, of ordering, of giving a shape and a significance to the immense panorama of futility and anarchy which is contemporary history" (177). In framing Joyce as writing in antagonistic relationship to "the immense panorama of futility and anarchy" of modernity, Eliot coincidentally prefigures the figure of Zann playing feverishly in antagonistic stance toward cosmic chaos.

Many stories following "The Music of Erich Zann" feature artists whose artistic enterprise takes them beyond established aesthetic traditions. Artists like the unnamed narrator of "Hypnos" (a sculptor) and his companion (who is transformed into a statue) instill intense subjective feeling into an kind of scientific project referred to as "impious exploration[s]" that are indescribable "for want of symbols or suggestions in any language" (207). The narrator of "The Hound" and his companion, St. John, construct grotesque art objects out of skeletons, play music on "nauseous musical instruments" that produce "dissonances of exquisite morbidity and cacaodamoniacal ghastliness," embark on "predatory excursions" to gather "tomb-loot," described as "artistically memorable events;" and it is significant that these transgressive activities are undertaken in response to their boredom with previously established aesthetic movements (217). Of course, the figure of Randolph Carter can be brought up, and by slightly reframing his fictional theory of indescribability depicted in "The Unnamable," he can be seen as struggling with the same exigencies as those frequently cited as those of the modernists: the challenges associated with the task of aestheticizing or even describing novelty as such in a disenchanted modern world pervaded by novelty.[6] But I would move on to another fictional modernist whose strange sculpture holds in tension familiarity and novelty, Henry Anthony Wilcox of "The Call of Cthulhu."

Wilcox is introduced as an intensely innovative artist, a radical figure who has been expelled from the Providence Art Club because it was "anxious to preserve its conservativism" (358). The narrative of "The Call of Cthulhu" begins to unfold when Wilcox brings a "singular bas-relief" sculpture adorned with strange hieroglyphics to an archaeological expert. It is in this fictional exchange between Professor Angell, the archaeologist, and Henry Wilcox, the modernist, that we can see that Lovecraft has fully sharpened his idiom for reflecting on modernist art, the modernist artist, and the relationship of the artist-in-general to human society and the cosmos at large. Let us begin with Wilcox's strange art object. Wilcox's sculp-

---

6. Consider Ezra Pound's essay, "'How I Began" (*T.P.'s Weekly*, 6 June 1913), in which he describes the challenge to create novelty faced by his peers in this way: "Any work of art which is not a beginning, an invention, a discovery is of little worth. The very name Troubadour means a 'finder,' one who discovers" (707).

ture holds, in vibrating tension, antiquity and novelty. It is equally ancient and modern, deriving from the "just now" of the night before (it is described as "exceedingly damp and fresh") and yet manifesting dreams "older than brooding Tyre" (358). Now let us turn to Wilcox. He describes himself as "psychically hypersensitive" (357) and in response to certain geologic disturbances has a "dream of Cyclopean cities of titan blocks and sky-flung monoliths, all dripping with green ooze and sinister with latent horror" (358).

Professor Angell, after analyzing Wilcox, undertakes a broader study of other artists similarly affected, and in this way he makes the discovery that during the length of the geologic disturbance that inspired Wilcox, many other sensitive people were affected, particularly in Paris. It is related that "a famous fantastic painter named Ardois-Bonnot hangs a blasphemous 'Dream Landscape' in the Paris spring salon of 1926" (361). The Left Bank of Paris was, of course, one of the epicenters of Anglo-American modernist artistic production in the early '20s, as well as an important headquarters of the continental European avant-garde.[7] Although this extra-literary fact of history should not bear much interpretative weight in the context of translating properly literary discourse, it is nevertheless suggestive, I am convinced, that Lovecraft triangulates Wilcox in relation to what the author and other cultural elites would have understood as a hotbed of experimental artistic activity.

Following the narrative logic of the story from beginning to end, Wilcox's fevered midnight aesthetic enterprise, his creation of sculptural art disconnected from previously established tradition, results in the terrible revelation of Cthulhu we are familiar with. Like the single dissonant note that conquers Zann, Cthulhu is an avatar who indexes the cosmos-at-large and thereby scales humanity down, shatters its notions of importance and claims to significance. Thus, like Erich Zann, the unnamed artists of "Hypnos," the artists of "The Hound," and others, Wilcox is a modernist

---

7. Many classic accounts of the Left Bank of Paris during this era are available, a key one being Malcolm Cowley's celebrated *Exile's Return* (New York: Viking, 1934), a memoir/critical account of many of the expatriates who would later be considered modernists. A more recent revisionist account, Shari Benstock's *Women of the Left Bank: Paris, 1900–1940* (Austin: University of Texas Press, 1987), unearths the roles many women artists played in this community.

who appears to break with all aesthetic traditions in the task of creating create novelty. But Wilcox's art is marked in a way that diverges from previous fictional modernist art; unlike the fictional art treated earlier, Wilcox's strange sculpture binds together geologic time and human time. Put another way, it takes human experience based in the flow of personal time as a point of departure and in violently expands it to the levels of cosmos.

The last of Lovecraft's fictional modernists I treat is Richard Upton Pickman, an imaginary artist from which we can extract the outline of a mature and complex vision of actual aesthetic enterprise in modernity. Pickman is, for all intents and purposes, an experimental artist. Consider the narrator's, Thurber's, description of Pickman's work: "There's no use trying to tell you what they were like, because the awful, the blasphemous horror, and the unbelievable loathsomeness and moral foetor came from simple touches quite beyond the power of words to classify" (385). Like Zann's music and many other examples of the tradition-free fictional art depicted by Lovecraft, Pickman's work is unfamiliar to such a pitch that is cannot be exhibited, a situation referred to by Thurber: "As you know, the club wouldn't exhibit it, and the Museum of Fine Arts wouldn't accept it as a gift; and I can add that nobody would buy it, and so Pickman had it right in his house till he went" (382). What comes into sharp focus in this story, a point vaguely outlined in "The Call of Cthulhu," is the nature of the relationship of the modernist artist to history and tradition, a relationship that can be seen clearly in the narrator's exploration of Pickman's private collection in the North End. After a nighttime trek across Boston to Pickman's studio, the demented artist displays for Thurber his paintings depicting the witch- and ghoul-haunted New England past. After being stirred to his core by these depictions of dog-faced ghoul-changelings haunting Puritan homes and hearths, Pickman asks if Thurber would like to see his "modern studies" (386). Thurber is affected by the alteration of historical context and describes his reaction in this way:

> I'd just about recovered my wind and gotten used to those frightful pictures which turned colonial New England into a kind of annex of hell. Well, in spite of all this, that next room forced a real scream from out of me, and I had to clutch at the doorway to keep from keeling over. The other chamber had shewn a pack of ghouls and witches overrunning the world of our forefathers, but this one brought the horror right into our own daily life! (386)

What this suggests it that the modernist art Lovecraft depicts in this story only appears to be disconnected from established traditions. In this story, the bizarre, indescribable characteristics of modernist artistic production, in spite of their tradition-free appeal, actually interface with history. Their novelty is not intrinsic to their being but a function of the local and narrow perspective of the one who views them; in other words, the historical flow they are embedded in is of a cosmic and not a human context.

In the context of viewing Lovecraft's fictional artists, the modernist who deviates from established traditions of aesthetic production does not create something new at all. The novelty of their work is an illusion. Rather than create novelty, these artists turn away from what Clark Ashton Smith termed "the human aquarium" to face directly the totality of the cosmos. And in bringing the ghoul-haunted New England past into the present day, Pickman (and perhaps even Lovecraft) reveal their structural resemblance, in terms of aesthetic strategies, to the very modernists they censure (Pickman in a parodic resister, of course). They do so by manifesting acutely what T. S. Eliot famous termed "the historical sense" in "Tradition and the Individual Talent":

> The historical sense involves a perception, not only of the pastness of the past, but of its presence; the historical sense compels a man to write not merely with his own generation in his bones, but with a feeling that the whole of the literature of Europe from Homer and within it the whole of the literature of his own country has a simultaneous existence and composes a simultaneous order.[8]

---

[8] T. S. Eliot, "Tradition and the Individual Talent," in *Literary Opinion in America*, ed. Morton Dauwen Zabel (New York: Harper, 1962), 92.

Dagon and Derrida: The Modern and Post-Modern in Dialogue in the Cthulhu Mythos

Lyle Enright
Loyola University Chicago

"Once you rule out the impossible, whatever remains, however improbable, must be true," Holmes says to Watson in Steven Moffat's *Sherlock*. Attempting to explain a frightening lapse of reason, he adds, "It was more than [fear]; I felt doubt. I've always been able to trust my senses, the evidence of my own eyes, until last night."

"You can't actually believe that you saw some sort of monster," Watson counters.

"No, I can't believe it. But I did see it, so the question is how? How?"

This attitude is one that typifies the modern detective story: the ruling out of the impossible so as to uncover the improbable, mundane reality beneath the seemingly fantastic. In many ways, this has also been the program of the Enlightenment and its attempts to build an increasingly reliable model of a predictable universe. The impact of this commitment to rationalism and empiricism on literature became especially evident in the realist fiction of the 1920s and '30s. However, in the midst of this period, one little-known and impoverished author examined the changing times from a different perspective from many of his peers. In one of his letters, Howard Phillips Lovecraft explains: "The time has come when the normal revolt against time, space, and matter must assume a form not overtly incompatible with what is known of reality—when it must be gratified by images forming *supplements* rather than *contradictions* of the visible and measurable universe" (SL 3.295-96).

For Lovecraft, it is the mundane that proves improbable when one peels away the veneers of predictability. In essence, Lovecraft claims that the tools to "revolt against time, space, and matter" are contained within the very beliefs about such things, that the destabilizing agents that create the emotional spaces of horror narratives are not "overtly incompatible" with the predictability of a materialist worldview. Contradiction destroys credibility, but if the system is supplemented with more weight than it can handle it will collapse on its own and take the world with it.

Lovecraft's fiction follows this method of destabilization from within in a way that closely parallels the work of philosopher Jacques Derrida (1930-2004) and his concepts of deconstruction. However, even as Lovecraft employs what would come to be called deconstructive methods, reaching similar conclusions about language, sign patterns, and the ways in which human existence interfaces with reality, he and Derrida produce very different visions of what those projects might yield. This essay presents Lovecraft's stories—particularly "The Call of Cthulhu" (1926), "The Colour out of Space" (1927), and *At the Mountains of Madness* (1931)—as destabilizing, even deconstructive, readings of Enlightenment empiricism, as well as anticipatory critiques of Derrida's philosophical conclusions.

Derrida, Center, and Opening the Infinite

As quoted earlier, Lovecraft expressed that the most effective "revolt" against fundamental ideas of reality is in *supplementing* rather than *contradicting* knowledge in ways that are "not overtly incompatible" with what is believed to be true. The source of Lovecraft's vision of horror, then, lies *within* the rational mind; the inconsistencies that allow the familiar to yield to the unknown and the strange need not come from the blatant impositions of supernatural contradictions, but from within the very paradigm of rationalism itself. Decades later, Jacques Derrida would detail similar thoughts in his various works. The project of both writers, through their respective approaches, is in problematizing notions of acceptable "epistemic position": "the necessary conditions of interpretation—the right horizons of expectation and the right presuppositions" (Smith 49). Where Lovecraft accomplishes this via narrative, Derrida takes an analytical approach.

In "Structure, Sign, and Play in the Discourse of the Human Sciences" (1967), Derrida comments on the state of a world which has become "decentered." He argues that philosophical structures and systems of discourse operate on fundamental paradoxes. Each system works to displace the others, and they each rely on the languages of their predecessors. According to Derrida, systems of discourse are determined by a basic limiting agent: a *center* that, as the delimiter of a philosophical discourse, is not itself a part of the system: "the center is, paradoxically, *within* the structure and *outside* it" (354). This self-contradictory nature of the *center* rests, as with all concepts, on the very shaky grounds of language. Words can only take meanings by implying other words, which in turn imply other words in a chain of infinite deferrals, analogies based on differences and implied absences. This creates "a system where the central signified, the original or transcendental signified, is never absolutely present outside a system of differences. The absence of the transcendental signified extends the domain and the interplay of signification *ad infinitum*" (355). As a result of this infinite deferral, centers, and all concepts in discourse, are inevitably lost to the undecideability of language, even to the point of non-existence (*Of Grammatology* 158-59).[1] Discourses are games played in accordance with arbitrary and self-contradictory rules and, for Derrida, this leaves the free-play of language as the only thing warranting attention.

Because of this inherent instability in linguistic systems, no discourse can be held about central ideas without either attempting to reduce their inherent differences or utterly displacing them in the process. Both cases result in the irreducible paradoxes associated with the *center*. As such, Derrida's broadest claim is that language invariably folds in on itself, such that "we cannot utter a single destructive proposition which has not already slipped into the form, the logic, and the implicit postulations of precisely what it seeks to contest" ("Structure, Sign, and Play" 355). This is the dilemma of totalizing discourses—religions, philosophies, and sciences included—which Derrida terms "metaphysics" and which attempt to make sweeping claims about reality by attempting to overcome the play of language on which their positions are based, despite the fact that such reductions require the same undecidability they seek to overcome ("Structure, Sign, and Play" 355; *Of Grammatology* 70-71). Ultimately, this is Derrida's

---

1. Derrida goes on to explain that this is not to dismiss objective existence, but rather, in our conception of that existence, "there has never been anything but writing ... And thus to infinity ... for we have read, *in the text*, that the absolute present, Nature, that which words like 'real mother' name, have always already escaped, have never existed; that what opens meaning and language is writing as the disappearance of natural presence."

indictment of any system that behaves as though it exists or observes from outside that which it wishes to critique.

Similar to what Lovecraft describes, Derrida says that contradictions are not brought about by the destructive impositions of other discourses, but by a single discourse attempting to bear too much weight. Demonstrating these inherent and irreducible paradoxes in metaphysical discourses produces deconstructive readings of those discourses, and these deconstructions reach all the way into scientific methods:

> It is a question of putting expressly and systematically the problem of the status of a discourse which borrows from a heritage the resources necessary for the deconstruction of that heritage itself.... Language bears within itself the necessity of its own critique.... [One method] consists in conserving in the field of empirical discovery all these old concepts, while at the same time exposing here and there their limits, treating them as tools which can still be of use.... Thus it is that the language of the human sciences criticizes *itself*. ("Structure, Sign, and Play" 356-57)

Given the ways in which language functions in discourse, even within the sciences, Derrida argues that something similar happens in the way language facilitates the interface between human perception and reality. Language and discourse form a latticework around an objective reality, yet the inherent differences between language and reality mean that the objective is never quite touched—indeed, the central reality is banished into infinite deferral and undecidability. From this vantage, Derrida claims: *"il n'y a pas de hors-texte,"* perhaps best rendered as, "there is nothing outside context."[2] As such, the human condition, according to Derrida, is one of ubiquitous interpretation in which reality is engaged much like a literary text. Hermeneutic horizons cannot encompass a whole system, as those vantages originate and exist within the system being interpreted. Beginning from the horizons of that system, any observation then essentially constitutes an internal textual interpretation, whether it is in the realms of philosophy, science, or literature; human perception might reveal ninety-

---

2. Derrida, "Afterword: Toward an Ethic of Discussion" 136: "[There is nothing outside of text] ... in general so badly understood ... means nothing else: there is nothing outside context. In this form, which says exactly the same thing, the formula would doubtless have been less shocking. I am not certain that it would have provided more to think about."

eight percent of the world, but the remaining two percent, even half of a percent, contains infinite context and is quite capable of re-contextualizing the ninety-eight percent of reality thought secure. Derrida implies that, in a very real way, all human knowledge is fundamentally textual, even narrative, in nature: ontology and epistemology are far more dependent upon stories than they are to data derived from experiments; even interpretations of such data form stories in their own right. As such, the interpretative potentials of empiricism are no greater than those of any other narrative, being enclosed within the same sign systems and perpetuating the same attempts at reducing paradoxes.

In dealing with the "great uncertainty" that arises, Derrida presents two "interpretations of interpretation," essentially dividing the heritages of Levi-Strauss and Nietzsche. One is the continued search for Truth, the "origin which escapes play." The other affirms the dissolution of the center and the ubiquity of play and interpretation, dismissing origin and ceasing to seek a "new humanism," escaping the very concept of "man . . . that being who . . . has dreamed of full presence, the reassuring foundation, the origin and end of play" and who cannot engage in discourse without reducing differences via the totalizing constructs of metaphysics ("Structure, Sign, and Play" 362-63). While these two interpretations seem to be irreconcilable, Derrida excitedly refuses to choose, recognizing between them an "as yet unnamable which is proclaiming itself" and can only thus far be conceived "under the species of the nonspecies, in the formless, mute, infant, and terrifying form of monstrosity" (363). The uncertain relationship between language and reality becomes a singularity, something akin to Alice's rabbit-hole in which "it's language all the way down," for eternity, and the ride is meant to be enjoyed, one connection after the next (Smith 37-38).[3]

For H. P. Lovecraft, however, it may indeed be language all the way down, but the trip through the abyss is by no means survivable. For Derrida, human discourse has infinite potential for the free-play that constructs reality, but this vantage also presumes human discourse itself as a sort of *center* in its interface, and an absence of external pressures on human in-

---

3. Smith's discussion of Derrida's writing posits "interpretation as the human condition," and to think that one can read without interpretation is a naïve assumption of human perception being "normal" or "perfect." This goes along with Lovecraft's incredulity towards the human element in the various sciences.

terpretation. In Lovecraft's economy, the game of language is the human response to the pressures of a reality that demands to be interpreted; at some point, the human interpretative horizon fails to deliver on its potentials and all that remain are the impenetrable pressures of the "unnamable" and the monstrous, and their de-centering effects on human history (Schirmacher 609).[4] In Lovecraft's fiction, the "monstrous" does not represent an as-yet misunderstood potential for infinite readings and interpretations; on the contrary, *"er lasst sich nicht lesen—*it does not permit itself to be read" (Lovecraft, "The Horror at Red Hook" [CF 1.483]).

Prison-Houses and Frustrated Curiosities

In particular, these dynamics can be seen in "The Call of Cthulhu," "The Colour out of Space," and *At the Mountains of Madness* making two significant contributions to the dialogue between Lovecraft's and Derrida's critiques of empiricism and their assessments of the infinite. First they demonstrate that, as put by Erik Davis, "it is not the sleep of reason that breeds monsters, but reason with its eyes agog" ("Calling Cthulhu"). Lovecraft recognizes that, in the move from religiosity to rationalism, the Enlightenment project has in many ways replaced one tyranny with another: an empiricist paradigm confines the human understanding of reality to what Lovecraft calls, "the galling limitations of time, space, and natural law which for ever imprison us and frustrate our curiosity about the infinite cosmic spaces beyond the radius of our sight and analysis" (Lovecraft, "Notes on Writing Weird Fiction" [CE 2.175]).[5] Human knowledge is then incomplete by definition. Derrida reiterates this and goes on to demonstrate that honest critical inquiry takes to heart those evidences and

---

4. Schirmacher: "The death of metaphysics means that the life-long project of the human species has become in its historical development a suicidal enterprise. If we proceed along the way of metaphysics, only artifacts will survive, not human beings and objects." Schirmacher's assessment is, then, similar to Derrida's, and his proposed post-metaphysical project likewise does not necessarily account for the external pressures that, in Lovecraft's view, would make such an undertaking moot.

5. While the intentions of the Enlightenment project included breaking with the uncritical habits of obedience to religious precepts, Lovecraft describes similar "limitations" that make up the empiricist philosophy even as he ascribes to it, going so far as to call them "tyrannies" in "Some Notes on Interplanetary Fiction."

narratives which lie outside the criterion acceptable to the *center* of a given paradigm, which is itself founded upon paradoxes and contradictions. What's discovered in the process is, of course, another matter altogether.

Second, Lovecraft anticipates Derrida's reaction to the uncertainty that arises when the *center* collapses, and he levels any sense of optimism. The excitement of Derrida's philosophy hinges on the idea that language and context can indeed go on forever; while he acknowledges that the free-play of differences and deferrals takes place within the finite system of language, Derrida also sees this free-play as being boundless to the point of deconstructing the delimiting structures of the *center* and permitting the endless re-contextualization of reality. His horizon, then, remains one of infinity, and Lovecraft provides a skeptical view of that vision. If the human relationship with reality is fundamentally textual and based in narrative, and that relationship continues "beyond . . . our sight and analysis," then the terrors of the "as yet unnamable" described by Derrida reside in a horizon of infinity beyond even the vision he posits, pressuring the interpretative capabilities of humanity, and they are far more likely to destroy than to liberate.

As for the pressure to respond and to interpret, Lovecraft also calls into question the idea that human progress depends on the pursuit of knowledge. Rather, he suggests that these ideals are actually at odds with each other. However much may be discovered through reason, context will yet remain constant and infinite, ever threatening to re-contextualize the world, violently and finally destabilizing confidence in the predictability of experience. For this reason, Lovecraft finds it necessary to explore the concepts of weird fiction:

> It must be remembered that any violation of what we know as natural law is *in itself* a far more tremendous thing than any other event or feeling which could possibly affect a human being. . . . In relation to the central wonder, the characters should shew the same overwhelming emotion which similar characters would shew toward such a wonder in real life. ("Notes on Writing Weird Fiction" [CE 2.177])

In Lovecraft's fiction, this "real life" emotional response is invariably paralyzing fear and madness that destabilize confidence in human experience. Of course, people will also do anything they can to escape these pressures and emotions and the threats of uncertainty; they work to valorize their own interpretations and experiences, asking with Sherlock exactly *how* they see the monsters bearing down on them rather than acknowledging that they might have actually been there all along. Or, as wise men are wont to say, "stones do not shrink" ("The Colour out of Space" [CF 2.372]).

"The Call of Cthulhu"

> The most merciful thing in the world, I think, is the inability of the human mind to correlate all its contents. We live on a placid island of ignorance in the midst of black seas of infinity, and it was not meant that we should voyage far. The sciences, each striving in its own direction, have hitherto harmed us little; but some day the piecing together of dissociated knowledge will open up such terrifying vistas of reality, and of our frightful position therein, that we shall either go mad from the revelation or flee from the deadly light into the peace and safety of a new dark age. (CF 2.21-22)

Such are the first words of Francis Wayland Thurston in Lovecraft's best-known tale, which follows Thurston as he investigates his uncle's death and uncovers evidence pointing to the existence of a slumbering, godlike alien being. In "The Call of Cthulhu," empiricism is presented not only as a system of discourse for discovering truth, but as a system that *reduces* that truth into an acceptable paradigm as each of the sciences "pulls in its own direction" (or, as Derrida would describe it, paradoxically works to destroy one another). The resulting tensions tell us just enough about the universe to find our way in it. However, the sciences maintain that the only acceptable evidences are those that fit within their respective paradigms.

So, when Thurston is confronted with his great uncle's research and the existence of "Cthulhu," his initial investigations are very structured. When he begins by discounting circumstantial evidence, it is "with almost inexplicable perversity" as he works to discover hard facts relating to the case. But such evidences never turn up, and he is forced to return to the "coincidence of the dream notes and odd cuttings collected by Professor Angell." Thurston admits that the attitude that led him to dismiss such information was "one of absolute materialism, *as I wish it still were*" (CF 2.43). Thurston's prior commitments to empiricism cause him to look only to that evidence which will fit his horizon of interpretation, and Lovecraft's deconstruction demonstrates that Thurston's rationalism leads to some very *ir*rational conduct in the early stages of his investigation. Thurston's experience ultimately forces him to accept that truth discovered through text and narrative places him in better epistemic position than one arrived at through the empiricist paradigm: if Thurston had followed the scientific method to the letter, then his investigation would never have begun at all, as no lead would have been worth following.

But if empiricism is such a clearly contradictory horizon as Lovecraft and Derrida suggest, why adopt such a limiting paradigm in the first place? In her essay "Broken Knowledge," Andrea Nightingale says that "Nietzsche has reminded us that there are blind spots in all pursuits of knowledge. In these intellectual pursuits, there lurks a desire not to know certain things—a sort of passion for ignorance" (16). In "The Call of Cthulhu," Thurston is safe so long as he remains within the paradigm he has constructed and the *center* he has established; he can continue to ask *how* he sees the monster, instead of fully seeing it. But by widening the scope of acceptable evidence and permitting the resulting pressures, Thurston's world suddenly becomes much larger than he can handle, banishing the illusion that his own efforts can achieve some sort of understanding of or mastery over it. He is one step closer to complete knowledge, but at the cost of his safety and the relevance of his life.

This leads to Thurston's final, paradoxical act of the story: "With [Johansen's account] shall go this record of mine—this test of my own sanity, wherein is pieced together that which I hope may never be pieced together again" (CF 2.55). Thurston's own account now takes on the status of textual evidence, one more narrative in an incredible story. Not only does he have no empirical evidence to show for his investigation, but his reassessment of what makes for good epistemic position means that he knows of *no better evidence* than his own testimony, added to the others. No one pursuing his investigation anew, and beginning with the same interpretative horizons, would ever discover or accept his account unless they too recontextualized their paradigm of acceptable evidence—something that Thurston hopes never happens.

"The Colour out of Space"

"The Colour out of Space" follows an unnamed narrator who is canvassing a piece of old farmland before it is filled in as a lake. As he discusses the area's history with the local resident Ammi Pierce, the narrator is told of an extraterrestrial visitor from the surrounding town's past, and he begins to wonder if even an entire lake will be enough to drown whatever remains on the land.

In "The Colour out of Space," as in "The Call of Cthulhu," Lovecraft touches on the questions of empirical versus narrative evidence and inverts their values as they are held within the Enlightenment economy, with Pierce's third-hand account (post-mental break, no less) being the voice of narrative authority in the story. He also frustrates the omniscience of scientific inquiry—and reins in the excitement of encountering the "unnamable"—by presenting it with something that cannot be examined, all experiments yielding inconsistent data with no movement toward comprehension (see 597–99).[6]

But most unsettling is the description of the horror itself, or rather the lack of a description. "The Colour out of Space" is one of Lovecraft's best treatments of the "unnamable," as the human agents within the story work to describe something for which there are no words: "'it beats down your mind an' then gits ye . . . burns ye up [. . .] can't git away . . . draws ye . . . ye know summ'at's comin', but 'tain't no use [. . .] jest a colour . . . an' it burns an' sucks . . . it comes from some place whar things ain't as they is here [. . .] sucks the life out . . .'" (CF 2.387–88). It is here that Lovecraft begins to explore the limits of language that Derrida would have denied. While Derrida argued that the imprecision of language creates spaces of infinite context, even between an actual stone and the word "stone," Lovecraft explores a gulf that is even wider and darker, as the only language employed to describe the Colour is imprecise and insufficient in the extreme. To attempt any more accurate descriptions of the horror would require conceptual powers that are simply impossible for human beings; the interpretative demands of the Colour are more than humanity can muster. Taking Derrida's concept of infinite context to heart, even a better understanding of the Colour *would do nothing to bridge the gap between it and its interpreter*. It would remain alien, on the other side of infinite context. In this way, the Colour perfectly resists all "metaphysical" reductions of its differences and paradoxes, representing all concepts as they might appear in the economy of Derridean undecidability, but also embodying the destabilizing pressures of the *Other* on human epistemic position, which Derrida takes *a priori* as being the *only* epistemic position. The implications on human perception and relationship in general become very bleak in-

---

6. These passages detail the constant "baffling" of scientists as they examine the meteorite on Nahum's farm. The text contains such gems as "But the wise men answered that stones do not shrink" and "other things which puzzled men of science are wont to say when faced by the unknown."

deed: the furthest anyone ever needs to look to encounter the alien and unnamable is over their own shoulder.

Lovecraft goes further, as the agency of the Colour further deconstructs empiricist ideals and anticipates deconstructive responses. First, the Colour represents a complete denial of material laws and absolutes. It is even suggested that the entity obeys its own set of laws, but that these are something far different from those that govern humanity. As such, the line between the natural and the supernatural becomes hopelessly blurred, as human perception and experience can no longer draw any conclusions about the Colour or the laws it obeys. On the other hand, the Colour also establishes a human "niche" in reality, one that extends only as far as perception, interaction, and language. The Colour represents an endpoint to human interaction, an amoebic or selectively permeable reality where certain things such as the Colour are allowed back and forth but humanity is not. In its ability to interact and to conceive, humanity is the eternal victim of, to borrow Lovecraft's words, the "galling limitations" of its subjectivity and interpretative finitude.

At the Mountains of Madness

Detailing the events of a doomed Antarctic exploration, *At the Mountains of Madness* is Lovecraft's most cosmically unnerving piece. The explorers soon discover frozen life forms that defy their explanatory powers, but the bodies do not stay frozen and soon kill the better part of the team. The survivors track the creatures into the mountains where they discover a sprawling city, a detailed history, and a story of genocide that makes humanity's own narrative insignificant.

At the Mountains of Madness carries one of Lovecraft's most deliberate Enlightenment critiques, being in many ways a condensed retelling of Mary Shelley's *Frankenstein* (1818). The tale of the Old Ones and their destruction at the hands of their creations, the shoggoths, might perhaps be read as "The Modern Prometheus" on a cosmic scale: if even humanity's creators are capable of losing control of their experiments, then our own prospects at mastery of the universe are even bleaker. Further, the question of evidence turns up again as it does in "The Call of Cthulhu." While the central characters do, this time, find empirical evidence of alien life, their interpretations of their discoveries are guided by the narrative accounts left behind by the creatures. The very "otherness" of the Old Ones seems to lend them credibility and narrative authority.

More than being a modernist cautionary tale, however, the novella also problematizes later Derridean idealizations of free-play on two fronts: the treatment of re-contextualization and the limits of language. Despite suggesting the inefficacy or undesirability of pursuing a "new humanism," preferring a more Nietzschean embracing of context and play, Derrida's horizons remain anthropocentric, with humanity providing the horizons of interpretation that will discover new and varied connections forever; as humans will be the ones doing the interpreting, so shall they remain the focus of the "*seminal* adventure" (Derrida, "Structure, Sign, and Play" 362). However, this view in fact restricts potentiality by only anticipating a human-centered epistemic position, and Lovecraft problematizes this ideal with the presence of godlike alien beings. The pivotal "supplement" to knowledge, in this case, is the existence of the Old Ones and the interpretation of their history. The revelation that humanity was "concocted [. . .] as a joke or mistake" (CF 3.45) and designed as a slave race re-contextualizes the body of assumptions about human nature and origins, even down to Darwinian theory. Humanity is displaced as the focus and director of the system; the horizons of infinite context now rest with the Old Ones, and they are extinct. One might argue that humans have then inherited the potential and the process, but it has already been demonstrated that humans have nowhere near the capacity for conception that their masters had. They are merely the flotsam of a ship that has already attempted a descent into the maelstrom of infinity and been ruined by it.

In addition to this pessimistic look at re-contextualization, Lovecraft also plays here most deeply with the human reliance on language and how the limits of language coincide with human finitude while they also, according to Davis, "paradoxically point to the Beyond" ("Calling Cthulhu"). The existence of something that cannot be described, and so cannot enter in to human systems of discourse or understanding, is the central wonder in Lovecraft's stories, and his anticipation of the human reaction is one of mental breakdown or denial, as opposed to the adventurous pursuit that Derrida describes. In making this reaction as impactful as possible, Lovecraft maintains a methodical realism throughout *At the Mountains of Madness*, most notably in his descriptions and catalogues of the Old Ones' corpses.⁷ The amount of detail put into these descriptions maintains a mood of realism but it also quickly becomes unwieldy; despite exhaustive effort and attention to detail, the image of the Old Ones remains difficult and contradictory, indicating that human language is not quite serving its purpose. The constant addition of supplemental knowledge puts the system under strain.

By the end of the story, Lovecraft's prose becomes especially fragmented:

> [Danforth] has on rare occasions whispered disjointed and irresponsible things about "the black pit", "the carven rim", "the proto-shoggoths", "the windowless solids with five dimensions", "the nameless cylinder", "the elder pharos", "Yog-Sothoth", "the primal white jelly", "the colour out of space", "the wings", "the eyes in darkness", "the moon-ladder", "the original, the eternal, the undying", and other bizarre conceptions; but when he is fully himself he repudiates all this and attributes it to his curious and macabre reading of earlier years. (CF 3.157)

Danforth's glimpse into Unknown Kadath yields images, but no concepts; words, but no meanings. Here, Lovecraft demonstrates an odd limit to language, namely the limits of human consciousness by which its constituent pieces must function. While Derrida rightly looks toward infinite context, Lovecraft insists that humanity cannot survive the trip because it is so ill-equipped; there are words to form the phrase "windowless solids with five dimensions," but the human mind has no concepts to attach to these words. It cannot keep up with the potentials and undecidability that language permits.

Most telling, however, is the moment where the limits of language actually *cause* the re-contextualization that damns humanity, in which the narrator refers to the Old Ones as "men" (CF 3.143). This not a statement of solidarity, but a conceptual concession: all those things that make men *men*, all those concepts and values that contribute to the idea of what it means to be human, are *better represented* in the Old Ones than in the human species. They are more worthy of being called "men," and so humanity

---

7. "This [overcoming the handicap of incredibility] can be accomplished only through the maintenance of a careful realism in every phase of the story *except* that touching on the one given marvel" ("Notes on Writing Weird Fiction" [CE 2.177]). This comment further emphasizes Lovecraft's thoughts on the *supplementation* of knowledge rather than the *contradiction*.

is de-centered in a single utterance. "There is a point where the authority of final jurisdiction is neither rhetorical nor linguistic, nor even discursive," Derrida noted in his later work, yet he did not articulate any situation in which human interpretation was not somehow given precedence (quoted in Royle 62-63); in *At the Mountains of Madness*, the narrative of the Old Ones places this final jurisdiction with the aliens in such a way that humans can no longer make any claims toward mastery, knowledge, or interpretations of any kind. The pressures of infinity destroy them, and humanity inherits a world and a story for which it is deeply unprepared.

Dagon and Derrida

Any argument that Lovecraft's deconstruction of Enlightenment empiricism betrays contempt for science and reason is erroneous; these were things that Lovecraft deeply valued. What he does stress, however, is the fallibility of the human element where these things are concerned. He critiques the fundamental assumption that man is the measure of all things—the *center* of all things—demonstrating that humanity's constructs will necessarily be as finite as their creators. Lovecraft's philosophy is closely echoed by Dana Scully's musings in *The X-Files*: "If science serves me to these ends, it is not lost on me that the tool I have come to depend on absolutely cannot save me or protect me, only bring into focus the darkness that lies ahead."

Despite the promise of being able to use science to understand the natural world, Lovecraft still viewed that world as a prison limiting human engagement with the cosmos. Humanity has a place in the universe, a small niche carved out for itself, and human reason permits an understanding of that niche as though it were the whole of reality. But because the perceivers are limited, so must their perceptions be as well. Human engagement with reality is not pure science or reason; it is a faculty facilitated by paradigms that are also human constructs, and so share the same limitations. Lovecraft responds to the valorization of empiricism by asserting that no finite being can create an infinite system by which to attain absolute knowledge; the best we can do is understand our little layer of reality while acknowledging just how much will never be known.

Meanwhile, Derrida's philosophy acknowledges these same paradoxes and limitations and seeks to make such insufficiencies as "humanism" moot, yet he retains an anthropocentric horizon for his project: it is language that is infinite, and it is for humanity to sail the ocean of context forever. But Lovecraft anticipates these ideas and has already prepared a case: just as no human construct can be infinite if its creator is finite, the finitude of human beings can make no use of infinite potentials like those found in language. While Derrida anticipated humanity's journey of freeplay through infinite undecidability, Lovecraft posits a vision of humanity that cannot process infinity, and which breaks under the pressures of the confrontation and the implications.

It is this tension between the demonstrable finitude of human perception and experience and the implicit affirmation of the infinite—this critical view of both modern and postmodern ideas—that makes Lovecraft so compelling. He deconstructs empiricism as a new tyranny, a paradigm restricting the pursuit of knowledge, and reveals the central paradox of materialism, demonstrating that it can achieve absolute mastery and knowledge for humanity only by severely limiting the scope and sphere of that mastery. Simultaneously, Lovecraft marks the limits of language and in so doing points to a truly infinite cosmos. To mark the limits of language is fatally to critique Derrida's Nietzschean ideal posited at the end of "Structure, Sign, and Play," and yet it also validates Derrida's work by demonstrating the infinity of context. However, from beyond the human horizon of that infinity, Lovecraft yet sees something staring back.

Works Cited

Davis, Erik. "Calling Cthulhu: H. P. Lovecraft's Magick Realism." *Techgnosis* (13 December 2008). Web. Accessed 28 July 2013.

Derrida, Jacques. "Afterword: Toward an Ethic of Discussion." In *Limited Inc.* Evanston, IL: Northwestern University Press, 1988.

———. *Of Grammatology*. Tr. Gayatri Chakravorty Spivak. Baltimore: Johns Hopkins University Press, 1976.

———. "Structure, Sign, and Play in the Discourse of the Human Science." *Contexts for Criticism*, ed. Donald Keesey. New York: McGraw-Hill, 2003. 353-63.

"The Hounds of Baskerville." *Sherlock*. BBC. 13 May 2012. Television.

Joshi, S. T. *H. P. Lovecraft*. Mercer Island, WA: Starmont House, 1982.

Nightingale, Andrea. "Broken Knowledge." In *The Re-Enchantment of the World: Secular Magic in a Rational Age*, ed. Joshua Landy and Michael Saler. Stanford: Stanford University Press, 2009. 15-37.

"Redux." *The X-Files.* Fox. 2 Nov. 1997. Television.

Royle, Nicholas. *Jacques Derrida.* London: Routledge, 2003.

Schirmacher, Wolfgang. "The Death of Metaphysics—What Does This Mean?" *Social Science Information* 23 (1984): 603–9.

Smith, James K. A. *Who's Afraid of Postmodernism? Taking Derrida, Lyotard, and Foucault to Church.* Ada, MI: Baker Academic, 2006.

I and Cthulhu: Using Martin Buber's Ontology of Dialogue to Examine H. P. Lovecraft's Cosmic Dread

Daniel Holmes
Villanova University

There would seem, at first, to be little common ground between the horror fiction of H. P. Lovecraft and the theological work of Martin Buber. Although the two men were contemporaries, they were separated by a gulf not only of location and circumstance but also of philosophical temperament. The one was a widely respected German-Jewish professor whose works, composed under the looming shadow of Nazi tyranny, reaffirmed the ability of the human soul to meet God through love. The other was an obscure peddler of weird tales for pulp horror magazines who, haunted by far different shadows, denied not merely the existence of God but also the value and meaning of human life. A deeper examination, however, suggests a surprising connection between these two very different shades of genius. Just as the hero of Lovecraftian horror pieces together dissociated knowledge to discover some eldritch abomination, so shall this paper assemble disparate strands of philosophy to reveal a new means of approaching cosmic horror fiction. This new critical method shall interpret the weird tale as a horrific inversion of the metaphysical dialogue described by Buber, but one that proceeds according to similar principles of relation. Lovecraft's most famous short story, "The Call of Cthulhu" (1926), provides a compelling case study for this critical approach. When read through the lens of Buber's *I and Thou* (first published as *Ich und Du* in 1923), the story offers a startlingly clear glimpse at the literary and spiritual mechanics that govern Lovecraft's uninviting universe.

The chief goal of this paper is to demonstrate that Lovecraft's horror is successful because it reflects a diseased worldview back upon itself: it forces an objectifying materialist to self-objectify and take an unwilling stand in relation to an incomprehensible and indomitable *Thou* figure. The dread entities that Lovecraft warns us lurk just beyond the vistas of history and science—particularly Great Cthulhu, high-priest of the Great Old Ones—are perverted manifestations of Buber's *Eternal Thou*, which the philosopher considers to draw human life out of objective experience and into meaningful relation. Cthulhu warps this theme by simultaneously fulfilling Buber's concept of the *Demoniac Thou*: he is a creature that all humans must regard as a subject but who responds to them, if at all, as mere objects.

This establishes the fundamental relation of Lovecraft's cosmic dread, which operates as a grotesque parody of the cosmic love that Buber envisions taking place between a human and a divine subject. The link between human and elder god is neither *I-It* (objectifying) nor *I-Thou* (subjective and meaningful), but the uniquely Lovecraftian ideal of *It-Thou*, a relation in which one participant is consciously stripped of his subjectivity by an all-consuming *Thou* figure. The strain of literary cosmicism displayed in Lovecraft's story is therefore not merely a nihilistic fear of meaninglessness in an empty universe; it is rather the fear of a nihilist confronting a shockingly full universe and grappling with an awful, awesome meaning that involves but does not include him.

Perhaps "nihilist" would be too strong a word to describe Francis Wayland Thurston, the hapless narrator of "The Call of Cthulhu." Perhaps "character" would be too strong a word as well. Apart from a few peripheral references to his "ingrained skepticism" and "callous rationalism," Thurston gives the reader very little insight into his personality; indeed, he does very little to convince us that he even *has* one. This, according to Buber, is the natural state of the materialistic and objectifying *I* of the *I-It* relation. A meaningful personal identity develops through forming a relation with a given subject, the saying of *Thou*: "I become through my relation with the *Thou*. As I become *I*, I say *Thou*" (11). Thurston has no story of his own: everything important in his narration describes the actions of others, from Professor Angell to Inspector Legrasse to the sailor Gustaf Johansen.

Thurston's character is so inconsequential that his name is mentioned only once in the story, and even then it is in an impersonal, obituarial subtitle documenting where the narrative was discovered. Great Cthulhu has tendrils that anchor him to meaning; Thurston, by comparison, is a hollow ghost floating over the pages of his own story. His *I* is so weak that at the end of the story it is irrevocably blasted by the forced saying of *Thou* to an entity met through simple conjecture rather than actual lived experience. So sweeping is this destruction of established identity that Thurston may only refer to his shallow, skeptical persona in the past tense: "My attitude was one of absolute materialism, *as I wish it still were*" (CF 2.43. The Thurston who composes these reflections has lost even the imitation of meaningful identity. He has become an object—and, through a grim twist of irony, was led there by the objectifying *I-It* relation.

Although Buber describes this preoccupation with the *It* (shared by so many of Lovecraft's characters) as a sickly understanding of the world, he does not wish to disparage the *I-It* relation outright. Indeed, he recognizes that much of the necessary work of life (including business, science, and politics) may be accomplished only through the impersonal relation of using, experiencing, and organizing. The problem occurs when a subject is only capable of making these detached relations. One never says "*It*" with the whole of his or her being; therefore, anyone who only says "*It*" cannot be a whole person: "Without *It*, man cannot live. But he who lives with *It* alone is not a man" (34). A reader equipped with an understanding of Buber will recognize at once that Thurston's subjectivity has been stunted by too heavy a reliance on the primary word *It*. This sense of materialism carries with it a curious sort of cognitive dissonance: Thurston believes in a purely objective universe, but at the same time he tacitly assumes that he (who is, after all, *in* the universe) is perfectly valid as a subject. He does not seem to consider any vast meaning to the world but is paradoxically enthusiastic about the importance of his own research. Thurston, therefore, has two conflicting conceptions of the world. His conscious, philosophical self believes in a purely material universe where subjective meaning is irrelevant; his subconscious, personal self, meanwhile, clings desperately to the belief that his own subjectivity is genuinely important.

At the beginning of the story, Thurston does not recognize the contradiction between his rival worldviews. "But a time comes," according to Buber, "when the shuddering man looks up and sees both images in a flash together. And then the deeper shudder seizes him" (72). In "The Call of Cthulhu," this shudder is very deep indeed. It does not merely force Thurston to drop one image or the other, but terrorizes him by *reversing* his views of the world. His subjective worth is radically debased as the universe itself is revealed to contain a real (and revolting) meaning. Lovecraft describes this terrible anagnorisis in language that closely resembles Buber's explanation of spiritual dissonance:

> The most merciful thing in the world, I think, is the inability of the human mind to correlate all its contents. We live on a placid island of ignorance in the midst of black seas of infinity, and it was not meant that we should voyage far. The sciences, each straining in its own direction, have hitherto harmed us little; but some day the piecing together of dissociated knowledge will open up terrifying vistas of reality, and of our frightful position therein [. . .] (CF 2.21–22)

This opening also identifies the process by which Thurston is brought to his horrifying discovery. Like his recently departed uncle, Thurston is fascinated by the organization and classification of objective knowledge. Professor Angell's investigations into the Cthulhu cult have left him with disassociated elements of the *Eternal Thou*. These scraps and clues seem innocuous on their own, but impart a miserable secret when considered together. Angell, himself a slave to rational objectivity, has divided these clues into file folders, all of which are inherited by his nephew after the professor's death. Thurston, as his name might suggest, suffers from the scientific thirst for knowledge that seems to run in the family, and quickly becomes obsessed with trying to put together the pieces of the cosmic puzzle left to him by his uncle. In Lovecraft's universe, this will always be a doomed quest. Buber helps us to understand why this must be so: the philosopher says that we observe the transcendental *Thou* when we discover the true union of the separated elements of our existence. Lovecraft's scholars, almost without exception, "piece together that which [they] hope may never be pieced together again" (CF 2.55) and are shocked to their eternal core when every knowable *It* fits together to form a hideous caricature of the *Thou* behind material life. The terror that seizes Thurston is therefore not simply the nihilistic fear of becoming an object among other objects but the distinctly and disturbingly religious fear of becoming an object before a malevolent perversion of the *Eternal Thou*.

Cthulhu is not, to be sure, what Buber meant when he described God as the *Eternal Thou* in whom all lines of relation meet. By the same turn, God was not the model Lovecraft had in mind when he created his alien menace. The horror writer and atheist was quite vocal in his insistence that Cthulhu and the Great Old Ones were extraterrestrial creatures and were *not* divine or supernatural in any form. Lovecraft's labeling effort, however, is superficial. Whatever we choose to call him, it seems clear that Cthulhu functions as a dark variation on Buber's theme of the godly *Eternal Thou*: he is completely incomprehensible to the feeble minds of human beings, he is limitlessly powerful before all futile human efforts, and he reaches out to dreamers at night so that "when the world of man is silent, it hears the voice of the daimonion say *Thou*" (Buber 66). In other words, Cthulhu functions as a god because he must be addressed as a *Thou* by all humans unfortunate enough to regard him: his prodigious strength will not permit him to be dominated, his vast incomprehensibility prevents him from being objectified, and his role in the overwhelming destiny of the world will not allow him to be ignored. As to the eternality of Cthulhu as *Thou*, one need only look at that most famous couplet of the *Necronomicon*: "That is not dead which can eternal lie, / And with strange aeons even death may die" (CF 2.40).

Both Cthulhu and the *Eternal Thou* share in material causality but exist outside of its physical and temporal conventions. Cthulhu is in our world, but is not a part of it: he "had shape [. . .] but that shape was not of matter," meaning that when the stars are properly arranged he can "plunge from world to world through the sky" (CF 2.39). He does not disregard the laws of geometry and time but observes them in a frighteningly alternative fashion: he dreams away nameless eternities in a non-Euclidean corpse city whose very angles can swallow men whole. Similarly, Buber tells us that the *Thou* appears, to be sure, in space, but in the exclusive situation of what is over against it, where everything else can only be the background out of which it emerges, not its boundary and measured limit. It appears, too, in time, but of that in the event which is fulfilled in itself: it is not lived as part of a continuous and organized sequence, but lived in a 'duration' whose purely intensive dimension is definable only in terms of itself. (30)

Cthulhu, by his very nature, shatters the human understanding of the material *I-It* relation and leaves nothing but himself in its stead. We can never call Cthulhu *It*: in Johansen's manuscript, he is called "the Thing," not as a token of objectification but specifically because there are no coherent terms that will allow us to objectify Cthulhu. "The Thing cannot be described," writes Lovecraft, "there is no language for such abysms of shrieking and immemorial lunacy, such eldritch contradictions of all matter, force, and cosmic order" (CF 2.53). The *Thou* cannot be contained within the narrow confines of human language. Buber says that "we speak the primary word with our being, yet can hardly utter *Thou* with our lips" and that when we communicate with the *Thou* "our words cling to the threshold of speech" (6). This directly corresponds to the guttural, barely pronounceable chant of the Cthulhu cult, and the even more sinister secret which under no circumstances can be spoken aloud.

If, however, great Cthulhu were nothing more than the *Eternal Thou* with tentacles, Lovecraft's story would likely have had a much more cheerful ending. What makes this a tale of cosmic dread rather than a benign (if unusually cephalopodan) story of religious conversion is that Cthulhu also fulfills Buber's concept of the *Demoniac Thou*. We must, by virtue of his dread influence over us, address this alien god as *Thou*, but he will never respond to us except as objects. Rather than establishing a meaningful and loving relationship of mutual subjectivity, Cthulhu disposes of humans as objects in such a way that they are forced to recognize and despairingly accept their own objectification. So long as we know of the eldritch horror lying in wait beneath the gentle waves, we must acknowledge the world and all that is in it—including our very selves—as objects that exist for him and his dreadful brethren, all of whom will arise when the stars are right to claim us as their own. We discover the value of our life (or the lack thereof) in relation to Cthulhu, but he will by no means condescend to form a return relation with beings as pathetic as human creatures. But what of the sickening dream-visions broadcast from R'lyeh and the cults that claim a deep connection with the extraterrestrial High Priest? Do these not constitute some form of relation, tenuous and terrible though it may well be? We again find the answer in Buber:

> This demonic *Thou* to which no one can become *Thou* is the elementary barrier of history, where the basic word of connexion loses its reality.... Towards him everything flames, but his fire is cold. To him a thousand several relations lead, but from him none.... He sees the beings around him, indeed, as machines, capable of various achievements which must be taken into account and utilized for the Cause. (68)

Cthulhu does not engage in genuine relation-building with the world of men. Rather, he objectively manipulates certain sensitive human beings in order to accomplish his own dread desires. The "Cause" for Cthulhu, of course, is the resurrection of the Great Old Ones and their ensuing reconquest of the globe. This may not be accomplished until the stars are in the correct alignment, but even then it will require some form of external assistance. "[A]t that time some force from outside must serve to liberate Their bodies. The spells that preserved Them intact likewise prevented Them from making an initial move" (CF 2.39). The dead god depends on the participation of humanity for his return to power, and his nightmarish interactions with individual humans are a campaign of manipulative influence rather than forming true relations. The dependence of Cthulhu on human assistance is a monstrous rendering of Buber's statement that God needs us "for the very meaning of our lives" (82).

The philosopher meant that the dialogue between the human and the divine subject is what causes God to be God and allows us to become fully human. In the context of Lovecraft, it is clear that the dialogue between man and Cthulhu is what will revive the dead god and allow him to live out the fullness of his own reality. If we accept Buber's belief that human relational value is also derived from this dialogue, we are left with a truly awful pronouncement: our only meaningful identity in Lovecraft's works is to be found in the service of a god that wants nothing more than to devour us. Critics that consider the Lovecraftian universe as a place where human life is meaningless and irrelevant are being far too merciful. Existential dread is better expressed when a character is forced to confront a meaning that excludes him but requires his existence for its operation. The fear of a life without value is nothing compared to the fear of life with a value that cannot be redeemed by the living subject. This is the fear of final objectification, when Buber says "the continually growing world of *It* overruns [a man] and robs him of the reality of his own *I* till the incubus over him and the ghost within him whisper to each other the secret of their non-salvation" (46).

There is a fearsome corollary to this understanding of cosmic horror. If we become human through a one-sided relationship with world-consuming gods and the meaning of our lives is derived from a self-effacing dialogue, then the most genuinely human characters must be those who actively participate in the pageantry of cosmic destruction. Old Castro, the sinister cultist captured by Inspector Legrasse, gives testimony of an occult network consecrated to Cthulhu. This worldwide cult practices abhorrent rituals of human sacrifice and moral degeneracy while waiting for the stars to permit them to resurrect the Great Old Ones. Their reward for this loyalty is described in starkly Nietzschean terms: to become "free and wild and beyond good and evil" and turn the world into "a holocaust of ecstasy and freedom" (CF 2.40). This strikes an interesting concord with Buber's conception of human freedom, which was itself partially derived from Nietzsche.

Buber saw freedom as being paradoxically linked with the concept of destiny: he says that a man becomes truly free through his ability to sacrifice personal potential in order to meet destiny and live out the fullness of his own reality. In other words, actual lived existence is *becoming* by surrendering all potentially lived existences. The nightmare reflection of this are certainly the Cthulhu cultists, who freely give the meaning of their lives to the dread lord, and so stand to step into destiny—a destiny of fire and bloodshed, but a destiny all the same. Because they make the sacrifice of their selves (by which we mean to say far more than merely giving up their lives), the Cthulhu cultists are capable of acting out the fullness of their human freedom, and are therefore the most genuinely human characters in Lovecraft's story.

Buber considers the opposite of freedom to be arbitrary self-will, a condition that is suffixed not by destiny but by fate. The man of arbitrary self-will is obsessed by potentiality to the extent that he loses his ability to actualize any potential existence: he refuses to sacrifice his individual potential and correspondingly cannot *become* anything. He therefore does not live out his existence (destiny) but merely suffers it (fate). Thurston must be considered an expression of this purely potential human creature. The only motivations he ever shares with the reader are his "visions of personal fame from researches into [the] origin and connections" of the cult (CF 2.43). This is a goal of purely individual potential, and is therefore both arbitrary and manifestly laughable in a world that belongs not to man but to the abominations that lurk beneath the waves. Thurston, like the other "good" characters of the story, is to become a victim of cold and impersonal fate rather than the fires of destiny, fires hot enough to melt away the self and leave only an extension of Cthulhu. Thurston will suffer the resurrection of the Great Old Ones rather than liberate them and so step up to the only genuine meaning of human life.

The Cthulhu cult, like many of Lovecraft's villains, is described in terms of its ethnic degeneration. That this is a result of Lovecraft's documented and egregious racism is beyond argument—and beyond the scope of this paper. More to our purpose, however, is the close connection between the evil half-castes, Lascars, and mestizos of Lovecraft and Buber's gentler perception of native and primitive cultures. Buber believes that the natural state of man is in connection with the *Thou*, and that this is gradually lost because of the escalating demands of life in society. Those living outside of traditional Western civilization, he says, are blessed with the ability to see life as it is lived rather than through the lens of preconceived social notions of what life ought to be. This allows them to recognize the *Thou* in an unadulterated form, through simple lived experience.

Correspondingly, it should be no wonder that the people capable of connecting with Cthulhu are those on the fringes of or entirely cut off from Lovecraft's society, whose guiding (if contradictory) tenants are scientific rationalism and religious dogmatism. The cultists do not organize and compile knowledge and they do not seek a metaphysical explanation for the phenomena that confronts them. Instead, they meet the *Thou* in every event and element of their lives. Buber says that "all real living is meeting" (15), a statement that reads curiously once imported into Lovecraft's universe. On the one hand, the deepest characters of "The Call of Cthulhu" are those who meet the *Thou* in one form or another. Unlike the younger and happier Thurston, the cultists have real lives, not merely the superficial display of personality. But the *Thou* which they continually meet is the *Demoniac Thou*, and their lives are enriched by death. In fact, in Lovecraft's story, meeting almost inevitably results in death: Professor Angell, Gustaf Johansen, and (we may assume) Thurston himself all die from direct physical meeting with a cultist, through a mysterious form of assassination that involves the culprit "bumping into" his victim. In Lovecraft, just as in Buber, to really live is to meet with the *Thou*; Lovecraft, however, extends this relation with his sentiment that to meet with the *Thou* is to die. Simplifying along transitive lines, we are left with the essential formulation of human existence in a horrific cosmos: all real living is dying.

This is not always as dramatic as the murderous orgy Legrasse encounters in the bayou, however. There is a more subtle sort of meeting experienced by a less pronounced sort of sensitive—the "psychically hypersensitive," to be specific. Henry Wilcox, the artist and Rhode Island School of Design student, lives within the context of normal society (although he has "dropped gradually from social visibility" [CF 2.25]), but he is still capable of receiving the nightmares that emanate from R'lyeh. After an earthquake thrusts Cthulhu's non-Euclidean tomb to the surface of the ocean, a widespread delirium besets a shocking number of artists and poets (as well as primitive peoples and lunatics). Wilcox falls into a hallucinatory fever, during which he sculpts a terrifying bas-relief of the alien god, the outlines of which "formed themselves insensibly under his hands" (CF 2.42). This is directly parallel with Buber's understanding of art, which he considers to rise up to the human artist from the depths of the *Thou*: "This is the eternal source of art: a man is faced by a form which desires to be made through him into a work. This form is no offspring of his soul, but is an appearance which steps up to it and demands of it the effective power" (9). Wilcox, through his meeting with the *Thou*, surrenders his personal potentiality in order to actualize a hideous work of art in the world. In his own mild way, then, he participates in the basic function of human life: meeting with and giving the self over to the *Thou*.

Like other graven images of the elder god, Wilcox's sculpture is capable of leading a receptive beholder to the *Thou* it represents. Buber understands this as the function of art and the destiny of all created works, and he praises the artist accordingly. He sees as clearly noble anyone who can create an observable work of art leading to the invisible and loving *Thou* behind sensible life. In Lovecraft's universe, however, art is a dangerous and even depraved activity that peels back the scrim of material causality to reveal "the horrors that lurk ceaselessly behind life in time and in space" (CF 2.50). The malignancy of art (which sometimes extends to include its creators) is a recurring theme in Lovecraft's stories, exemplified not only by Henry Wilcox but even more prominently by the eponymous artists of "Pickman's Model" and "The Music of Erich Zann." In all cases, art is a threat to sane existence because it fulfills the same role that Buber appoints to it: it leads to relation with the *Thou*. The theologian sees art as engendering holy love, whereas the cosmicist views it as producing abject terror.

Considering Lovecraftian horror as a ghastly mirror-image of existential love helps us to understand why it operates on a *cosmic* rather than *personal* level. The expressions of terror that we have reviewed so far have mostly involved the individual loss of meaning and identity. Yet out of the felt experience of fear eventually arises the ontological condition of cosmic dread, just as emotional experiences with the *Thou* ultimately lead to a loving cosmic union. Buber says that "feelings dwell in man; but man dwells in his love. . . . Love does not cling to the *I* in such a way as to have the *Thou* only for its 'content,' its object; but love is *between I* and *Thou*" (14-15). Love is the space in a relation between the *I* and the *Thou*, and thus the world is the canvas and the stage of cosmic love. In exactly the same way, ontological horror develops in the space between the conscious object (the human) and the overwhelming subject (Cthulhu). Once one takes a stand in relation to the *Eternal Thou*, everything within the world—and even the world itself—becomes charged with sacred meaning as a potential vessel of God; once one takes a stand in relation to Cthulhu, one lives in perpetual anxiety of the "twisted menace and suspense [that lurks] leeringly" (CF 2.51) behind every corner of the world. Buber lives to meet the vast and mysterious grandeur flowing down to us through every facet of the loving universe; Lovecraft's narrator wishes to kill himself whenever he thinks "of the *extent* of all that may be brooding down there" (CF 2.51).

The essential exposition of cosmic dread comes when Thurston tells us that he has "looked upon all that the universe has to hold of horror, and even the skies of spring and the flowers of summer must ever afterward be poison to me" (CF 2.55), which is itself a perfect corruption of the Goethe epigram that begins *I and Thou*: "So waiting, I have won from you the end/God's presence in each element."

By way of conclusion, it is important to note that Lovecraft and Buber were almost certainly unaware of each other. Until the outbreak of World War II, Buber's academic prominence was confined mostly to the Jewish community in Germany. The first English translation of *I and Thou* did not appear until 1937, the year of Lovecraft's death. Lovecraft died as he had lived: unknown and uncelebrated. Although Buber spoke fluent English, it would be ludicrous to assume that he had ever come into contact with any of the American pulp magazines that published Lovecraft's stories. The international audience for the Cthulhu Mythos was built very gradually through the efforts of Lovecraft's surviving literary correspondents and did not come into its own until well after Buber's death. Rather than look for a direct link between the works of the two men, it is more reasonable to consider both of them as responding to the world around them. The obvious springs of meaning had dried up as the shock and horror of the First World War came to a close: the established social order was shaken, science and industry had grown to objectifying and impersonal monsters, and, as tension in Europe steadily grew, the shadow of an imminent horror seemed to hang overhead.

It seems that both men agreed to the fundamental principle Buber expresses at the end of *I and Thou*, that "there is a cosmos for man only when the universe becomes his home" (102). Buber sought to make himself at home in an uninviting cosmos by building individual relations and coming to a loving union with God through the pursuit of the *Thou*. Lovecraft, however, denied that the universe could ever become a home, and therefore concluded that the cosmos was not for human habitation. It was instead a place where the human need for meaning and identity could breed only horror. It was a place where the whispers of a dead god emanated from behind the curtain of shallow materialism, carrying with them nightmares of futility and the inconsequence of human affairs. It was a place where a sickly and sickening *Thou* lurked within the primeval ocean of human consciousness, reminding us that life was not meant for man.

Works Cited

Buber, Martin. *I and Thou*. Tr. Ronald Gregor Smith. New York: Scribner, 1958.

Thinking Ecocritically: A Look at Embodiment and Nature in the Fiction of H. P. Lovecraft

Cory Willard
University of Waterloo

In an increasingly globalized and outsourced world, questions of environment and questions of place are perhaps more relevant to academic criticism and society now than ever before. The goal of an ecocritical perspective is, ultimately, to gain a critical understanding of the history, geography, literature, and cultural meanings of places; to see the ecology, vertical depth, and interconnectedness of places and to respond with criticism that is immersed and aware of relationships between people and their ecological communities. Certain elements of H. P. Lovecraft's work have been explored from a place-based perspective, but these studies tend to be almost solely biographical rather than more broadly ecocritical. This is somewhat surprising considering that Lovecraft's fiction takes place almost exclusively within one geographical area and is bound up within the environmental, social, and cultural meanings of place. While the ecocritical discipline itself has its beginnings in the study of nature writing, it is now much more linked with ecological, political, and socioeconomic concerns regarding place in any writing, or, as Lawrence Buell puts it, to attempt "to speak in cognizance of human being as ecologically or environmentally embedded" (*The Future of Environmental Criticism* 8). Additionally, ecologist and philosopher David Abram writes that

> Humans are tuned for relationship. The eyes, the skin, the tongue, ears, and nostrils—all are gates to where our body receives the nourishment of otherness. This landscape of shadowed voices, these feathered bodies and antlers and tumbling streams—these breathing shapes are our family, the beings with whom we are engaged, with whom we struggle and suffer and celebrate [. . .] (ix)

It is, therefore, through bodily experience by way of the senses that we can make some comprehensible meaning of the universe.

H. P. Lovecraft's fiction is very much about the effects of and on place. Place becomes the medium by which the people within a story can act; places have histories, expectations, and perceivable (though not knowable) futures. As Jim Dodge notes, there is an importance in natural systems "both as the source of physical nutrition and as the body of metaphors from which our spirits draw sustenance" (355). While it would be interesting to look at Lovecraft from a purely environmentalist/activist point of view, this essay shall explore how Lovecraft makes use of that body of metaphors. To have that discussion, though, it must be asked how setting informs the narrative and, like in all rhetorical criticism, one must seek to understand the meaning of that relationship not only within the text, but beyond. Within the writing of H. P. Lovecraft, and specifically within "The Colour out of Space" and "The Whisperer in Darkness," there is a tendency toward ecocritical themes of environmental perversion, the value of local knowledge, and the importance of embodied experience—rather than just science and academia—in understanding nature and the cosmos.

It is well known that the bulk of Lovecraft's fiction takes place in New England—as Maurice Lévy put it, "the land of origins, of the first beginnings, the Promised Land of mythical times, where the American nation was born and from which it thrust out its fleshly roots" (35). It is important to understand the significance of this regional choice. Lévy further elaborates that "New England was also Lovecraft's native soil, the only point on earth with which he could totally identify. This obscure emotion of belonging, of rootedness, was for him the primordial condition of all plenitude" (36). Lovecraft does not simply just set his stories within a new England backdrop; they are an outgrowth of his own deeply embedded embodied experience within the place—bound up in all kinds of biographical, historical, and cultural meanings both conscious and unconscious. This reflects what ecocritic Lawrence Buell would call "place-connectedness." As Buell explains: "the most familiar way of imagining place-connectedness is in terms of concentric areas of affiliation decreasing in intimacy as one fans out from a central point" (*Writing for an Endangered World* 64). While there are other ways of making sense of a deeply rooted connection to place, this direct geographical affiliation is most relevant to Lovecraft. The most meaningful and important place becomes where one was born, grew up, or spent most of their life. A person's identity is rooted and entangled with that geographical location as a sense of place becomes built up in a vertical depth of history and experience like a palimpsest overwritten with layers of meanings.

Additionally, in her essay "New England Narratives: Space and Place in the Fiction of H. P. Lovecraft," Rebecca Janicker argues for the inclusion of Lovecraft among the traditionally mentioned regional writers of New England. She brings forth an argument based on the many regional aspects Lovecraft utilizes to bring his twisted version of New England to life. Janicker notes that "regionalist fiction builds up the identity of a rural area such as New England by utilising local geography and landmarks, embracing local values, establishing local ideas about identity and so on." Furthermore, she argues that "This places the fictional community of ["The Colour out of Space"] squarely in an authentic New England space, affected as it is by the historical practice of flooding land to ensure water supplies for urban areas" (58). In "The Whisperer in Darkness," Lovecraft writes that for Akeley "it was hard to leave a place where all one's memories and ancestral feelings centred" (682). This overwhelming feeling of place-connectedness expressed by Lovecraft is elaborated on in Yi-Fu Tuan's *Topophilia: A Study of Environmental Perception, Attitudes, and Values*. Tuan states that in communication about connection to place, "More permanent and less easy to express are feelings that one has toward a place because it is home, the locus of memories, and the means of gaining a livelihood" (93). This also evokes the writing of Lawrence Buell and other various bioregional scholars. Lovecraft, having such a personal embodied connection to his own New England, suffuses his writing with regional flavor that has been the subject of much biographically based criticism. What is perhaps more interesting to the ecocritic, though, is not how places in Lovecraft's own life might have some direct correlation to his fiction, but how his connection to, and feelings about, place ultimately inform and affects his fiction in a more holistic sense.

One way that Lovecraft stresses principles that the ecocritic might find interesting is the importance of a sensory or embodied knowledge regarding character, narrative action, and the environment. When discussing the importance of embodiment in having a place-based connection and understanding the ecological workings of the planet, Richard White argues that

> Humans have known nature by digging in the earth, planting seeds, and harvesting plants. They have known nature by feeling heat and cold, sweating

as they went up hills, sinking into mud. They have known nature by shaping wood and stone, by living with animals, nurturing them, and killing them [. . .] They have achieved a bodily knowledge of the natural world. (172)

In "The Whisperer in Darkness," there are several instances where a bodily knowledge of the facts at hand transgress the boundaries of academic knowledge into an embodiment that recognizes the seemingly impossible as, in fact, not only possible but real. In his initial letter to Wilmarth, Akelely mentions that Wilmarth's adversaries in the debate regarding the strange sightings in the river—as unacademic as they may be—are closer to the truth than Wilmarth is; however, Akeley also states that "they go only by theory, and cannot know what [he] know[s]" (675). The difference between academic understanding based on the transfer of knowledge through reading, writing, and lecturing and embodied knowledge through time and sensory experience becomes stressed when the subject at hand in seemingly impossible. Akeley isn't just speculating; he *knows* what the strange beings are because he is *there* in place and has amassed *experience*. Later, when contact between Akeley and the beings begins to escalate, he writes to Wilmarth: "I am telling the truth, though. It is this—*I have seen and touched one of the things, or part of one of the things*" (692). Lovecraft italicizes the text in order to enhance how terror inducing that might be, but also to further stress the power and effect of real personal experience.

Furthermore, in *The Spell of the Sensuous*, David Abram argues that "Direct sensuous reality, in all its more-than-human mystery, remains the sole solid touchstone for an experiential world [. . .] only in regular contact with the tangible ground and sky can we learn how to orient and to navigate in the multiple dimensions that now claim us" (x). While the ecocritic may champion the necessity of an embedded and embodied connection with the natural world, Lovecraft seems to also advocate the importance of the body and experience as a foundational point of understanding and terror. This is further explored in the geographic and geological descriptions Wilmarth gives of Vermont. He states:

> I knew I was entering an altogether older-fashioned and more primitive New England than the mechanised, urbanised coastal and southern areas where all my life had been spent; an un-spoiled, ancestral New England without the foreigners and factory-smoke, bill-boards and concrete roads, of the sections which modernity has touched. There would be odd survivals of that continuous native life whose deep roots make it the one authentic outgrowth

of the landscape—the continuous native life which keeps alive strange ancient memories, and fertilises the soil for shadowy, marvellous, and seldom-mentioned beliefs. (700)

This section alone contains a number of possibilities for environmental criticism: there is the separation of natural and urban, industrialization, vertical history, and the Romantic sublime. Within the context of Lovecraft, though, there seems to be a sense that as attractive as this natural rural landscape is, the urban environment somehow provides protection from ancient forces lurking deep within the Vermont hills. The sublime sensory effect Vermont has on Wilmarth is much like the existential dread felt by the confrontation with an infinite cosmos. This is an interesting mirror whereby seeing the untamed land, free of humankind's urban/industrial domination, compares similarly to the cosmic dread experienced by so many of Lovecraft's characters once they see beyond the veil. It is as if the diminishment of human importance, whether ecological or cosmic, leaves no option but some sort of existential or cosmic angst. This becomes highlighted in a later observation of Wilmarth's that "The nearness and intimacy of the dwarfed, domed hills now became veritably breath-taking. Their steepness and abruptness were even greater than I had imagined from hearsay, and suggested nothing in common with the prosaic objective world we know" (702). The hills have a quality of the Romantic and the sublime that puts them on a different level of sensory experience than the urban spaces he is used to.

The facets of embodiment are further emphasized upon Wilmarth arriving at Akeley's farm. Wilmarth notices some unusual tracks and has to stifle a scream. Even though he has seen the tracks in pictures, has been warned about the fungi from Yuggoth's activities around Akeley's farm, and is specifically going there to learn more about them, having to confront the physical existence of these beings through a sensuous connection is an entirely different form of knowing, and one that Wilmarth finds almost overwhelming. Furthermore, Wilmarth's embodied knowledge of the place and instinctual feelings that something is amiss are informed through additional sensory experience. For example, Wilmarth twice observes the lack of animal sounds—of life—in the surrounding area: "It reminded me, though, of another thing about the region which disturbed me—the total absence of animal life. There were certainly no farm beasts about, and now I realised that even the accustomed night-noises of wild living things were absent" (714). It is through an embodied connection to the world and through an instinctual understanding of nature that Wilmarth knows something evil is afoot. David Abram ties "the recuperation of the incarnate, sensorial dimension of experience" to the "recuperation of the living landscape in which we are corporeally embedded" (65). In ecocritical scholarship, an embodied connection with natural systems is often considered integral to humankind's willingness to preserve and protect the ecology of the world. In "The Whisperer in Darkness," Lovecraft seems to use embodiment as a technique to enhance the sense of cosmic dread as well as a way to synecdochically reference the same feeling of overwhelming or purposelessness his characters often feel in the face of an infinite and uncaring universe.

Moreover, this sense of an embodied connection to place and experience flows into the concept of local or traditional knowledge. Within the fiction of Lovecraft, there appears to be a recurring theme of rustics or locals having a dreaded cosmic understanding or awareness unknown to more educated scientific minds. This is evident in "The Whisperer in Darkness" through local legends and the mutterings of so-called ignorant rustics that already speak of the impossible reality found within the story. Wilmarth, the story's narrator, laughs at what he sees as their mythological explanations. He notes that different cultural groups have different understandings of the beings, but they all know that they exist. Additionally, they all unanimously agree that the beings are not from this earth, and by the end of the story we know this to be the case. These rural rustics might not have the academic background to argue for the existence of these beings in a way that an academic like Wilmarth would accept, but they do have a local knowledge and understanding embedded within the folklore, experience, and history of their home place. It is another type of embodied and regional understanding that appears so often in Lovecraft in the form of Indian tales, bizarre myths, cults, and mysterious ancient texts like the famed *Necronomicon*.

Rebecca Janicker connects the idea of the local back to Lovecraft's focus on regionalism: "It is precisely when those regional pressure-points are stimulated, when ancient fears re-assert themselves in some tangible form, that the truly horrific is encountered" (63). This also, then, ties back to the idea of Lovecraft writing about a place he himself has local knowledge about. While he might not want to identify himself with the ignorant rural folk in his stories, like them he possesses an understanding of the distinct peculiarities that can only come from being embedded in a place, its culture, and its history for an extended period of time. The stories and traditions that make up local history are an important aspect of understanding place. Through this, place making becomes a social activity; Lawrence Buell argues that building and imagining place are themselves "a power as ancient as folk stories told at bedtime" (*Future of Environmental Criticism* 72). When Lovecraft twists his own geographic region, Maurice Lévy argues that "The familiarity of places is blurred, leaving the weird to take its place" (37). In making the landscape of New England strange, Lovecraft also turns the pastoral knowledge of its rural inhabitants towards the provenance of hideous cults and terrible rituals from a time beyond memory.

"The Colour out of Space" is particularly noteworthy for its emphasis on the significance of local knowledge. Like "The Whisperer in Darkness," this story takes place in a rural setting where an alien menace has disrupted the natural way of things. There are several points in the story that bring up the idea of local knowledge. For instance, while most of the people in the general area are opposed to the flooding of the land to create the planned reservoir, Ammi Pierce doesn't protest. This is because he not only has the local knowledge that has spread in rumor, but he has the embodied knowledge of having been to the blasted heath and personal knowledge of the unearthly perversion that dwells there. The entire story is, essentially, the narrator seeking out local knowledge and history about the place following an unsettling feeling and experience. In many ways, "The Colour out of Space" is just a fantastic tale of regional peculiarity; however, toward the end of the story comes a significantly relevant passage:

> The rural tales are queer. They might be even queerer if city men and college chemists could be interested enough to analyze the water from that disused well, or the grey dust that no wind seems to disperse. Botanists, too, ought to study the stunted flora on the borders of that spot, for they might shed light on the country notion that the blight is spreading—little by little, perhaps an inch a year. (615)

This passage is important to highlight and dissect, because whereas scientists are usually employed to debunk the bizarre reports of fantastic events, in this case the events would be rendered even stranger with scientific study. This marks a point where scientific study is no longer a beneficial comfort, but beckons incomprehensible realizations and suggests a sort of confirmation that the local experience and knowledge of some rural people can be ahead of, or more in touch with, reality than the scientific and academic communities. Perhaps this is because they are not bound by an intellectual understanding of how things are *supposed* to be. The tale suggests that scientists of all stripes should descend upon the heath to study and give a more eloquent report of what the locals already know; for only when catalogued and quantified in academic language will the truth and knowledge of local experience be considered or taken seriously.

Perhaps the most obvious ecocritical thread in "The Colour out of Space," though, is that of environmental perversion, or the sanctity of the natural order. As the unnamed narrator stumbles upon the blasted heath at the beginning of the story, he observes that "Upon everything was a haze of restlessness and oppression; a touch of the unreal and the grotesque, as if some vital element of perspective or chiaroscuro were awry" (CF 2.369), and that "There was no vegetation of any kind on that broad expanse, but only a fine grey dust or ash which no wind seemed ever to blow about. The trees near it were sickly and stunted, and many dead trunks stood or lay rotting at the rim" (CF 2.369). The sense of environmental degradation is apparent and is an obvious point of exploration in itself, but in mentioning chiaroscuro, or the interplay between light and dark, the narrator takes a step further and emphasizes that beyond mere environmental decay there is also a perversion of physics as we understand it. The meteorite has poisoned the soil, water, and the very laws by which we make sense of the world around us. In "Living by Life: Some Bioregional Theory and Practice," Jim Dodge argues that "bioregionalism holds that the health of natural systems is directly connected to our own physical/psychic health as individuals and as a species" (356). This story, through the meteorite's effects, presents much the same ecological link between the health of the environment and its natural systems and the physical and psychological health of humanity. As the water and soil of the Gardners' farm becomes poisoned, the meteorite and the mysterious gaseous being it carried are responsible for a number of unnatural effects—melancholy, weirdly proportioned woodchucks, monstrous cabbages, inedible apples, trees swaying without wind, the not-quite-right arrangement of animal tracks, the complete psychosis of Mrs. Gardner, and, ultimately, the death of the entire family. Because human and environmental existences are inextricably linked, the meteorite inevitably perverts the Gardners through the disruption and perversion of the natural environmental systems around their farm.

This theme of environmental perversion also comes up in "The Lurking Fear," where "the soil is covered by a fetid and corrupt vegetation, a poisonous mold representing a type of horrible suppuration of the earth" (Lévy 38), as well as in "The Call of Cthulhu," where the impossibility of R'lyeh's architecture is a perversion of our understanding of geometric space and, therefore, a disruption of our sensuous connection to and understanding of the world. Like the geometry in "The Call of Cthulhu," environmental perversion is further emphasized in "The Colour out of Space" through the sensory disruption it causes. By being incongruous with the embodied knowledge of human existence, the meteorite inescapably causes terror. For example, even though the farm produces a "gorgeous array of specious lusciousness" in the wake of the meteorite, "not one single jot was fit to eat. Into the fine flavour of the pears and apples had crept a stealthy bitterness and sickishness, so that even the smallest of bites induced lasting disgust" (CF 2.375). The effects of the meteorite have disrupted the natural sensory connection between experiential understanding of the production of fruit and the link between sight and taste. The produce appears succulent, but instead something is wrong. Furthermore, "No sane wholesome colours were anywhere to be seen except in the green grass and leafage; but everywhere were those hectic and prismatic variants of some diseased, underlying primary tone without a place among the known tints of earth" (CF 2.378). Working with the tradition of the grotesque, Lovecraft makes his color detectible by the people in the story; however, the color is just strange and impossible enough for it to cause psychological trauma and disturbance. The plant life has been tainted and rendered alien and offensive; likewise, the experience of processing and understanding colors and shades has been made frighteningly foreign. Even language is rendered strange. As Mrs. Gardner loses her grip on sanity her ravings contain "not a single specific noun, but only verbs and pronouns" (CF 2.380). This simple yet odd development employed by Lovecraft fits with the other aspects of the story as a horrific perversion pushed one step beyond simple destruction toward an unsettling and unfathomably bizarre existence.

It would seem that in Lovecraft's fiction, once individuals are alienated from their sensory perception by incomprehensible cosmic forces, they are often left paralyzed with a sense of existential and cosmic dread—overcome by the apparent purposelessness of human existence in the face of such an infinite and uncaring universe. Cosmic horror is Lovecraft's major claim to fame; however, another way to emphasize the terror in his fiction comes from unseating humankind from the tiny region where it reigns as apex predator and placing it within the greater ecology of an infinite cosmos. While this is generally represented through the ancient vastness of the whirling cosmos, the ecology of the universe of which we are but a small part also represents the earthly ecology in which we are inextricably linked. For instance, what would it mean for the works of H. P. Lovecraft if humanity was more ecologically conscious and had a cultural and conscious perception that wasn't based on individualism or the inherent superiority of humankind? If we already considered ourselves merely part of a greater biotic whole rather than its center, would the cosmos seem so diminishing and terrifying? If the cosmic ecology can be said to reflect the earthly ecology, then how does that reflect on our own environmental practices? When reading Lovecraft this way, the ecological and ecocritical underpinnings almost leap off of the page. If the lack of care or stewardship these older and more advanced beings continually show us throughout Lovecraft's fiction causes us nothing but terror, we should consider being more empathetic and compassionate toward the other forms of life we tend to treat as nothing more than liquid inventory to be processed for monetary gain. It would seem that in this light we are the dispassionate old ones who view other life as inconsequential and deserving of our cruel tyranny. In expressing the vast and terrible potential of the cosmic, Lovecraft has made us the ants beneath the magnifying glass.

Alienation is also confronted in a couple of different ways as well. Lovecraft's tales seem to have an appreciation for wild or rural places, yet they always produce a sense of strangeness or dread. This is in part to juxtapose a romanticized pastoral ideal with terrible otherworldly forces, but there seems to be more to it. Perhaps, compared to the crowded urban spaces, these open untamed places force us to confront our smallness, loneliness, and fragility in much the same way that the infinite nature of the universe does. In "The Whisperer in Darkness," alienation is similarly confronted in a bodily sense. Akeley's ultimate victimization at the hands of the fungi is to have his brain separated from his body. He is forced to exist as a brain in a canister with his sensory perception controlled from the outside in some sort of perverse realization of Descartes's skeptical premises. Furthermore, Wilmarth's discovery of Akeley's hands and face point to another sense of natural perversion—through the disembodiment of the self.

Ultimately, this essay does not attempt to make any extensive conclusions regarding H. P. Lovecraft's writings about place, but hopefully it opens up some possibilities regarding the way in which his works may be engaged. Ecocritical scholarship has made great strides into horror and science fiction over the last decade, but to the author's knowledge has been a somewhat neglected mode of study when addressing Lovecraft. This essay has been an attempt to spark some ecocritical dialogue around this author, who himself was so bound up in and concerned with place. Within literature, genres and texts themselves are ecosystems that are environmentally embedded (Buell, *Environmental Criticism* 44). That said, "The concept of place also gestures in at least three directions at once—toward environmental materiality, toward social perception or construction, and toward individual affect or bond" (Buell, *Environmental Criticism* 63). Through this brief ecocritical study of Lovecraft, it seems arguable that a combination of the second and third direction is the most fruitful focus of applicable critical study. The second direction is particularly useful when applying a regional framework to Lovecraft's fiction, and the third when focusing on the horror aspects of dread, the cosmic, and environmental perversion in his fiction.

Lovecraft himself noted that "The Whisperer in Darkness" was in part inspired by the "general impression of weirdness in the Vermont landscape, [he] gained during a fortnight's visit near Brattleboro in 1928" ("Story-Writing" 48). Based on the writer's own affective relationship with the Vermont landscape, he structures a tale around a setting that is very much wrapped up in affect and feelings of the sublime and mysterious. Furthermore, Lovecraft argues that "The true weird tale has something more than secret murder, bloody bones, or a sheeted form clanking chains according to rule. A certain atmosphere of breathless and unexplainable dread of outer, unknown forces must be present" (*CE* 2.84). The horror found in Lovecraft's fiction is very much about what cultural geographer Yi-Fu Tuan calls "topophilia," or the "affective bond between people and place or setting" (4). As Robert Bloch notes in his essay "Notes on an Entity," Lovecraft "created a hideous, hidden history of mankind's past—and of the earth and the universe prior to the emergence of man from primordial slime" (2). Lovecraft's literary settings extend beyond the knowable bounds of time and space and are integral to achieving the sense of infinite dread that the cosmic provides.

Additionally, Suzi Gablik argues in "Connective Aesthetics: Art After Individualism" that "the boundary between self and Other is fluid rather than fixed: the Other is included within the boundary of selfhood" (84). This has significant ecocritical implications regarding Lovecraft's ascribed purposelessness to human experience when considered from the vast malevolent cosmos. His pantheon can be seen as the creation of a cosmic ecology by which the Old Ones have Othered us to the point of meaninglessness in much the same way that the industrial Western capitalist agenda has at times Othered non-human life on this planet. Fritz Leiber argues that "Such a pantheon and such a chief deity can symbolize only one thing: the purposeless, mindless, yet all-powerful universe of materialistic belief" (9); however, when filtered through the writings of David Abrams, we see that the greatest terror comes not from mindless materialism, but from conscious sensuous embodiment—and especially the sensory disruption and violation thereof. At this stage of study it would be hard to make a strong case for Lovecraft as some sort of early twentieth-century environmentalist, though his writings mentioned previously as well as his travel literature like, *A Description of the Town of Quebeck*, are a rich area for ecocritical scholars to craft criticism focussed on place, affect, and the ecological meanings found therein.

Works Cited

Abram, David. *The Spell of the Sensuous: Perception and Language in a More-Than-Human World*. New York: Vintage, 1996.

Bloch, Robert. "Notes on an Entity." In *Discovering H. P. Lovecraft*, ed. Darrell Schweitzer. Mercer Island, WA: Starmount House, 1987. 1-3.

Buell, Lawrence. *Writing for an Endangered World*. Cambridge, MA: Harvard University Press, 2001.

Buell, Lawrence. *The Future of Environmental Criticism*. Malden, MA: Blackwell, 2005.

Dodge, Jim. "Living by Life: Some Bioregional Theory and Practice." In *Debating the Earth: The Environmental Politics Reader*, ed. John S. Dryzek. New York: Oxford University Press, 2005. 355-63.

Gablik, Suzi. "Connective Aesthetics: Art After Individualism." In *Mapping the Terrain: New Genre Public Art*, ed. Suzanne Lacy. Seattle: Bay Press, 1995. 74-87.

Janicker, Rebecca. "New England Narratives: Space and Place in the Fiction of H. P. Lovecraft." *Extrapolation* 48, No. 1 (Spring 2007): 56-72.

Leiber, Fritz. "A Literary Copernicus." In *Discovering H. P. Lovecraft*, ed. *Darrell Schweitzer*. Mercer Island, WA: Starmount House, 1987. 4-17.

Lévy, Maurice. *Lovecraft: A Study in the Fantastic*. Trans. S. T. Joshi. Detroit: Wayne State University Press, 1998.

Lovecraft, H. P. "Story-Writing: A Letter from HPL." In *Discovering H. P. Lovecraft*, ed. Darrell Schweitzer. Mercer Island, WA: Starmount House, 1987. 47-53.

Tierney, Richard L. "When the Stars Are Right." In *Discovering H. P. Lovecraft*, ed. Darrell Schweitzer. Mercer Island, WA: Starmount House, 1987. 85-90.

Tuan, Yi-Fu. *Topophilia: A Study of Environmental Perception, Attitudes, and Values*. Englewood Cliffs, NJ: Prentice-Hall, 1974.

White, Richard. "'Are You an Environmentalist or Do You Work for a Living?': Work and Nature." In *Uncommon Ground: Toward Reinventing Nature*, ed. William Cronon. New York: W. W. Norton, 1995. 171-85.

Genuine Pagans: A Foray into Lovecraftian Religions

Dennis P. Quinn
California State Polytechnic University, Pomona

In "A Confession of Unfaith," published in 1922 in an amateur periodical, the *Liberal*, Lovecraft writes of his "last flickering of religious belief" as a young child, which was, rather than the Protestant Christianity of his parents, the religion of ancient Greece:

> When about seven or eight I was a genuine pagan, so intoxicated with the beauty of Greece that I acquired a half-sincere belief in the old gods and Nature-spirits. I have in literal truth built altars to Pan, Apollo, Diana, and Athena, and have watched for dryads and satyrs in the woods and fields at dusk. Once I firmly thought I beheld some of these sylvan creatures dancing under autumnal oaks; a kind of "religious experience" as true in its way as the subjective ecstasies of any Christian. If a Christian tell me he has *felt* the reality of his Jesus or Jahveh, I can reply that I have *seen* the hoofed Pan and the sisters of the Hesperian Phaëthusa. (CE 5.146)

Lovecraft would later be particularly enamored by science and disavow religion, claiming them all to be delusion of the primitive mind. As Lovecraft would soon find out, some of his readers considered that he was in reality an unwitting prophet, channeling even more powerful gods than the "sylvan creatures dancing under autumnal oaks." Such occult luminaries as Kenneth Grant, the heir to Aleister Crowley's British chapter of Ordo Templis Orientis (OTO), Anton LaVey of the Church of Satan, and many subsequent ex-Satanists, chaos magicians, and unaffiliated dabblers in the dark arts have seen Lovecraft as an agent of cosmic powers. In fact, some would question whether Lovecraft was really writing fiction at all: he was a prophet revealing sacred doctrines of the Old Ones. The fact that Lovecraft consistently emphasizes in his letters that he was throughout his adult life an atheist and "mechanical materialist" makes these apostles of Lovecraft the Prophet quite curious indeed; and just some of them are the subject of this paper.

This essay examines some of those individuals who have made Lovecraft's fictional works into religious texts and the basis for their rituals.[1] It should be emphasized that I will not argue the truth or falsity of the claims that make Lovecraft into a prophet despite his protestations—he was after all canonized by S. T. Joshi as the "patron saint of atheism" (*Against Religion* ix). For this paper, I will distance Lovecraft's own claims of atheism from the ways in which later religious enthusiasts understood Lovecraft as a prophet. In fact, all the religionists we will encounter in this paper knew very well Lovecraft's stated ant-religious position, but unanimously deny it to be important to their cultic beliefs and practices. Indeed, this fact often confirms the pure and unadulterated truth of his visions expressed in his fiction, which, as Lovecraft admits, were mainly received through dreams. Thus, I am not here to judge the validity of this hermeneutical assumption, but rather to show how it works for Lovecraftian religions and how this method of using "sacred texts" has its roots in the Western exegetical tradition.

---

1. The religious practitioners mentioned here all call on the gods of the Cthulhu Mythos in their "magickal" practices. "Magick" with the added "k" was the term popularized by Alistair Crowley (1875-1947) in his Thelemic religious system, to distinguish from parlor tricks. It should be pointed out at the outset that the distinction between magick and religion has been blurred significantly over the past several decades by scholars of religion who point out that "magic" is more of a designation of contempt by those who consider their practice "true religion." It fact, Religion is often identical to what one may consider magic, affecting change to one's wishes by evoking supernatural forces, for example. Thus, many of the individuals and groups discussed in this paper might embrace the concept of magick with the added "k" to distinguish themselves from what they consider to be fictional descriptions of the practice—graduates of Hogwarts for instance who don't embrace the "k"—and may not consider what they do to be "religion" at all. However, I will use the terms magick and religion interchangeably here without much distinction because I see practitioners of Lovecraftian magick as practitioners of religions who evoke Lovecraftian gods as the preferred supernatural beings. For the foundational text that problematizes the distinction between magic and religion, see Douglas.

I

In order to understand the beliefs and motivations behind followers of Lovecraftian religions, we should begin with what Lovecraft understood about the role religion played in history. Doing so will help us to understand the religious metaphors Lovecraft used in his works, because they are abundant. We must keep in mind that even though Lovecraft denies religious faith and scorns institutional religions, he was very knowledgeable of the Western religious tradition and this history penetrates his fiction.[2] Being a student of the history of religions, H. P. Lovecraft was well aware of the role religions play in history. Religions were established for Lovecraft as an attempt to explain the unexplainable. In a letter to Emil Pataja in 1935 he wrote: "religion was a perfectly natural thing for mankind in early ages, when nothing definite was known about the constitution of matter and the causes of natural phenomena" (*Against Religion* 31). Lovecraft believed in an evolutionary understanding of the history of thought, placing religious beliefs in an earlier and thus more "primitive" and "inferior" understanding of the cosmos. Science, on the other hand, was the pinnacle of human understanding, even though he often explored the limitations of science in his fiction. Such binary oppositions (science-religion, white-black, native-foreigner) colored his thinking throughout his life. Lovecraft saw science as the pinnacle of human progress toward understanding how the world works, even though his literary works also explore the limitations of science. In general, Lovecraft understood those who were religious as irrational, inferior, and backward-looking. Religion for Lovecraft was inferior to science. This point is key to understanding two of the important themes in this paper: 1) Lovecraft consistently denied any belief in the supernatural throughout his adult life and scoffed at any possibility that his work should ever be interpreted in a religious way, and 2) practitioners of what I term Lovecraftian Religions all confront this issue of Lovecraft's atheism in strikingly similar ways: Lovecraft either simply denied or was ignorant of his prophetic vision. As we shall see, those who evoke the gods of the Cthulhu Mythos for their rituals are well aware that Lovecraft himself would have scoffed at such use of his work, regardless of the fact that he

---

2. For Lovecraft's understanding of Roman history, see Quinn.

draws from religious imagery, principally ancient religious imagery, in some of his works (see Quinn 190-96).

Lovecraft was always clear that his mythos was supposed to be understood in a metaphorical way. But not everyone thought the same. The birth of Lovecraftian Religions occurred in Lovecraft's lifetime. We can see this in October 1933, when Lovecraft wrote to Clark Ashton Smith of the occult enthusiast William Lumley:

> [He was] convinced that all our gang [of writers who employed the Cthulhu Mythos in their tales] are genuine agents of unseen Powers in distributing hints too dark and profound for human conception or comprehension. We may think we are writing fiction, and may even (absurd thought) disbelieve what we write, but at bottom we are telling the truth in spite of ourselves—serving unwittingly as mouthpieces of Tsathoggua, Crom, Cthulhu & other pleasant Outside gentry. Indeed—Bill tells me that he has fully identified my Cthulhu & Nyarlathotep . . . so that he can tell me more about 'em than I know myself. (SL 4.271)

Lovecraft, as Robert M. Price quipped over two decades ago, "was amused that his eccentric acquaintance William Lumley believed Lovecraft to be the unwitting oracle of Cthulhu himself!" (76). If we are to understand how Lovecraft would respond to those who take his texts as some sort of arcane gospel of otherworldly entities and truths, this is the key text. However, once any author publishes a work, she or he has no control how it will be received. This fact Lovecraft knew all too well, considering the contempt, misunderstanding, or simple dismissal of his works that he often had to endure. In terms of making Lovecraftian works into a sacred text, so to speak, William Lumley was not alone. In his important work on new religions in American history, Philip Jenkins placed religious followers of Lovecraft alongside many others associated with the "cult explosion" of the 1960s (174). Amid this common pedigree, Lovecraftian Religions are unified in their belief in Lovecraft as a prophet despite his protestations to the contrary. As we shall see, this emphasis on Lovecraft the "unwitting oracle," or one who kept his secret, not only connects various disparate occultists, but also connects to the Judeo-Christian tradition (Kugel and Greer 128-36). Like the Bible for Jews and Christians, Lovecraftian religious practitioners find inspiration in the pages of Lovecraft's fiction. Practitioners of Lovecraftian Religions also maintain a similar position as the Christians concerning the Jewish scriptures—namely, that the author did not disclose the true meaning of the revelation, or that it may have been hidden.

II

Although William Lumley was certainly one of the first to espouse the religious significance of the so-called Cthulhu Mythos, he was not the last or the most important to the development of Lovecraftian religion. That was Kenneth Grant (1924-2011). British heir to Aleister Crowley's occult organization The Order of the Oriental Templars, or Ordo Templi Orientis (OTO), Grant was central to bringing Lovecraft's work into the grimoire of those walking the Left Hand Path. Grant often equated Lovecraft's insights to his former master, Crowley, and saw Lovecraft as a visionary, even if Lovecraft would never have realized or admitted it himself. In a number of his books, Grant cites Lovecraft along with an esoteric mix of ancient documents and the canon of his former master. Lovecraft's extraterrestrial deities had a particular appeal to Grant. Grant was fascinated by the possibility of interstellar dimensions and alien forces in control of the universe. But this obsession ran him afoul of his former master and mainstream OTO. It also raised the scorn of the American leader of the OTO, Karl Germer, and led to Grant's eventual excommunication.

In constructing his rationale for using Lovecraft's fiction, Grant emphasizes Lovecraft's importance to occult gnosis and set the stage for the common hermeneutic: it did not matter that Lovecraft denied the reality of his visionary work. In one of his most popular works, *Outside the Circles of Time* (1980), Grant explains:

> Lovecraft's great contribution to the occult lay in his demonstration—indirect as it may have been—of the power so to control the dreaming mind that it is capable of projection into other dimensions, and of discovering that there are doors through which flow—in the form of inspiration, intuition and vision—the genuine current of creative magical consciousness. (43)

For Grant, Lovecraft unconsciously formulated the whole Cthulhu Mythos from dreams. But he did not fully understand the larger significance of his dreams (7).[3] For Grant, Lovecraft was channeling the

---

3. Adding a challenge to checking the assertion that Lovecraft admitted that he got

same esoteric truths through his dream visions as Aleister Crowley did. But Crowley was more adept at recognizing his prophetic gift. While Crowley systematized his theology into *The Book of the Law* (1904), Lovecraft transmitted his vision through his fiction. Grant saw Lovecraft's work not as fiction at all, in fact, but works that hint at real and hidden things. For example, Lovecraft's "supposedly fictional" (35) *Necronomicon* was a real work for Grant, regardless of the fact that Lovecraft only hints at its contents. It was as filled with arcane truths comparable to the Egyptian and Tibetan books of the dead (5). Indeed, the creatures, the lore, the books of Lovecraft's fiction were all pieces of a larger truth that the magician could draw on for inspiration. The fact that Lovecraft did not recognize this is immaterial. Throughout *Outside the Circles of Time*, Lovecraft reveals truths about extraterrestrial forces and cosmic realms. But, as Grant explains,

> Conscious denial cannot hold its own against the world of subconscious certainty, which is evident in almost every line of Lovecraft's stories. His conscious utterances—his letter, his conversations with friends, etc.—are belied by his unconscious utterances, his novels and his stories, so that the split in his personality is vividly exposed, and his denials—often ludicrously exaggerated—are carried to such extremes that his eminently cool and logical mind is disturbed, and he plunges again into the morass of the irrational. (42-43)

With this sweeping statement, Grant dismisses all Lovecraft's statements about atheism as the ranting of a madman with Dissociative Identity Disorder. *Thus, it is not the conscious, skeptical Lovecraft that is Grant's prophet; it is Lovecraft the unconscious, dreaming visionary.*

Grant's version of Lovecraft as an unconscious visionary was also taken up by others. Perhaps the most famous, or infamous, proponents of Lovecraftian Religions, was the founder of the Satanic Church, Anton LaVey, and his disciple Michael Aquino, later founder of the Temple of Set. It is with these two figures that Satanism and Lovecraft's mythos become close partners. We can see this in one of its central texts, *The Satanic Rituals* (1972), which was written by Aquino under LaVey's instruction; there is a chapter entitled "The Metaphysics of Lovecraft" (Matthews 58).

---

his inspiration from dreams, Grant cites the entire five-volume set of the *Selected Letters* edited by Derleth and others, without being more specific.

Both believed Lovecraft to be channeling another dimension—that of the subconscious. But, as Eric Davis has stated, LaVey always toyed with the ritual power of fantasy: "a radical subjectivity which explains his irreverence towards occult source material." LaVey and Aquino emphasized that "fictions can channel magical forces regardless of their historical authenticity" ("Calling Cthulhu"). And this is key to understanding how the Church of Satan appropriated the Lovecraftian cosmology into its rituals. Lovecraft as an unconscious conduit for the Old Ones, Aquino makes it explicit:

> His fantasies may well have been a conscious projection of the idea expressed so eloquently by Charles Lamb in his *Witches and Other Night Fears:* 'Gorgons, and Hydras, and Chimeras may reproduce themselves in the brain of superstition-but they were there before. They are transcripts, types-the archetypes are in us, and eternal.' One cannot help speculating upon a reality suggested by the fantasy-the possibility that the Old Ones are the spectres of a future human mentality. It is as the result of such speculation that *The Ceremony of the Nine Angles* and *The Call to Cthulhu* are presented. One emphasizes potential: the other reflects the dimness of an almost forgotten past. (99)

Thus, even though Lovecraft was admittedly writing fiction, he is actually tapping into a subconscious truth—a future human potential to draw the powers from the universe as expressed in the Cthulhu Mythos. And Aquino taps into this "future human mentality" by directly quoting Lovecraft's fiction in the rituals, mixed with familiar Satanic mantras. In the ceremony called "Call to Cthulhu," participants honor the Old Ones *and* Satan in turns at various points in the ritual, chanting, "Hail Cthulhu! Hail Satan." The "Ceremony of the Nine Angles" also makes reference to the Cthulhu using what he terms the "Yuggothic language," which is an incantation taken from the tale "The Call of Cthulhu": "Ph'nglui mglw'nafh Cthulhu R'lyeh wgah'nagl fhtagn." It is hoped that the cultists would have had the opportunity to practice pronunciation first. Nevertheless, *The Satanic Rituals* actually incorporates direct quotations from Lovecraft's stories in two chapters: "Ceremony of Satanic Baptism" and "The Celebration of Death." Here, Aquino lifts directly from "The Horror at Red Hook" (in which Lovecraft himself actually cribbed the entries on "Magic" and "Demonology" from his version of the *Encyclopaedia Britannica*): "O friend and companion of night, thou who rejoicest in the baying of dogs and spilt blood, who wanderest in the midst of shades among the tombs, who longest for blood and bringest terror to mortals, Gorgo,

Mormo, thousand-faced moon, look favourably on our sacrifices!" (Aquino 615; cf. CF 1.505).[5]

Here we have Lovecraft used as ritual or sacred text. To justify its use as such, Aquino relies on the standard "unwitting oracle" argument. For Aquino, Lovecraft, though not conscious of it, broke through another realm and revealed a reality which was characterized by the stories he wrote. Aquino also laments the lack of ritual specificity in Lovecraft's tales: "Lovecraft's stories abound in references to his monstrous gods, but of actual 'nameless rites and unspeakable orgies' there are few detailed descriptions. Such rituals as are described at length—as in 'The Horror at Red Hook,' 'The Festival,' and 'Imprisoned with the Pharaohs'—are reported by horrified, ignorant onlookers" (684). To rectify this deficit, Aquino embellished Lovecraftian rituals to fit his satanic system.

The embellishing of Lovecraft's writings with more ritual specificity as begun by Aquino and *The Satanic Rituals* was taken to the extreme in Simon's *Necronomicon*, first published in 1977. This text would become very popular for budding occultists and established followers of the Left Hand Path. As B. J. Gibbons points out, the *Necronomicon* is the main source for the rise of what he terms "Lovecraftian Magic" (16). However, the Simon *Necronomicon* rarely uses actual quotations from Lovecraft at all. This makes sense since, in a way, Lovecraft's *Necronomicon* was something he would have drawn knowledge from, even if subconsciously. Similar to Grant, Simon makes much of the connection between Lovecraft's Cthulhu Mythos and Crowley's cosmology (Simon 15, 24). The scholar Gavin Callaghan cogently emphasized that the difference between the Lovecraft's works and Simon's version of the *Necronomicon* was profound:

> Crowley proclaimed a new Dionysian "Age of Horus," with himself as prophet, while Lovecraft, an extreme conservative, regarded Bacchanalian and Hellenic mysticism as a symptom of western societal denIgration and racial decay—any parallels observable between Lovecraft and Crowley deriving only from the classical traditions which influenced both writers. (14)[6]

But at an even more fundamental level, it seems that Simon misunderstood Lovecraft in a profound way. He conflated Lovecraft's mythos

---

5. See also Harms and Gonce 111.
6. See also Quinn 188–90.

with that of his continuers, such as August Derleth. Simon's version of the mythos is dualistic; Simon wrongly thinks Lovecraft's is also: "Lovecraft depicted a kind of Christian Myth of the struggle between opposing forces of Light and Darkness, between God and Satan, in the Cthulhu Mythos" (4). This dualism makes its appearance only in "The Dunwich Horror," which was something of an anomaly, while the rest of Lovecraft's mythos stories do not have similar theme of good vs. evil (see Joshi, *H. P. Lovecraft: A Life* 401–2, 449–50). However, Simon emphasizes, much like the all the others whom we have seen, that Lovecraft did not acknowledge what he was actually doing. Although Lovecraft's work was meant for entertainment, Simon insists that "Scholars, of course, are able to find higher, ulterior motives in Lovecraft's writings, as can be done with any manifestation of Art" (xiii). Lovecraft reveals a true vision of the cosmos through his fiction, though unconsciously. Simon also emphasizes the connection between Lovecraft and Crowley, ranking them as equals in their revelations: "That they should both have become Prophets and Forerunners of a New Aeon of Man's history is equally, if not more, unbelievable. Yet, with H. P. Lovecraft and Aleister Crowley, the unbelievable was a commonplace of life" (xvii). Lovecraft's fiction, like Grant before him, was identical to Crowley's magikal system.[7]

III

Since the 1980s, the Lovecraftian religious landscape has proliferated; however, it has deviated little from its predecessors. As we have seen, the first evangelists of Lovecraftian Religions all considered Lovecraft an unwitting prophet. This is still the familiar refrain. For example, on the website *The Esoteric Order of Dagon*, Frater Obed Marsh, Grand Master, states: "The Esoteric Order of Dagon (E∴O∴D∴) is a serious occult Order which has been working Lovecraftian magick for nearly 30 years. The E∴O∴D∴

---

7. Simon even holds out the possibility that Lovecraft had been familiar with Crowley, finding hints in his "The Thing on the Doorstep," claiming that "Lovecraft may have heard of Crowley is hinted at darkly in his short story 'The Thing On The Doorstep' in which he refers to a cult leader from England who had established a covens of sorts in New York. In that story, published in *Weird Tales* in 1936, the cult leader is closely identified with chthonic forces, is described as 'notorious', and linked to the strange fate that befell the protagonist, Edward Derby."

utilizes the so-called Cthulhu Mythos of the horror and fantasy writer H. P. Lovecraft as a magickal method of exploring the Collective Unconscious" (Marsh). Here we see in the E.O.D's mission statement that Lovecraft's mythos is a Jungian typology that lies under the surface. And this was unknown to Lovecraft himself:

> Lovecraft suffered from an acute inferiority complex, which prevented him from personally crossing the Abyss in his lifetime. He remained a withdrawn and lonely writer who retained a rational, skeptical view of the universe, despite the glimpses of places and entities beyond the world of mundane reality, which his dream experiences allowed him. He never learned the true origin of the tremendous vistas of cosmic strangeness that haunted his dreams. He never realized that he was himself the High Priest 'Ech-Pi-El', the Prophet of the dawning Aeon of Cthulhu. (Marsh)

Although Kenneth Grant's diagnosis of Disassociate Identity Disorder is certainly a bit less curable, Marsh emphasizes that Lovecraft's lack of self-worth *also* got in the way of completely realizing his full prophetic potential.

This trend of following the religious message but ignoring the protestations of the prophetic messenger continues with all subsequent apostles of Lovecraft, and so does the use of his fiction as sacred texts. Using Lovecraft's text in ritual practice, particularly "quotations" from the *Necronomicon*, Lovecraftian religious traditions are adept at recognizing the ritual power of words. Take for example Chaos Magician Frater Tenebrous. In "The Rite of the Communion of Cthulhu," this Lovecraftian priest provides prayer designed to take place within the "Temple of Cthulhu." Celebrants bring out the following "magickal weapons": a dagger to trace a chalice filled with salt water, and "two ritual drums." These are the only items for the ritual described, but they echo items used in the "Tale of Inspector Legrasse" section of the story, "The Call of Cthulhu," as do some of the actual quotations from Lovecraft from the ritual:

> The Priest or Priestess now resumes the seated position before the Host, and makes the Call to Cthulhu:
> "Ph'nglui mglw'nafh Cthulhu R'lyeh wgah'nagl fhtagn"
> *(In his house at R'lyeh dead Cthulhu lies dreaming.)*
> The Host and the Worshippers answer this call:
> "Iä! Iä! Cthulhu fhtagn"
> *(Yes! Yes! Cthulhu dreams!)*
> The Priest or Priestess now begins to chant the Call to Cthulhu in its shortened form, as a Mantra of Invocation:

"Cthulhu R'lyeh fhtagn"
(*Cthulhu dreams in R'lyeh*)
    The two worshippers join with this Mantra, using their drums to counterpoint the chanting, thus forming a net of rhythmic sound to draw the Presence of the Deity into the Trapezoid. (Tenebrous, "Communion of Cthulhu")

Thus we see a collection of actual quotations from Lovecraft's "The Call of Cthulhu," replete with the use of drums, no doubt echoing the ritual described in the section of that story entitled "The Tale of Inspector Legrasse." Then the participants ("the Priest or Priestess, and the two worshippers") await the possession of the host, who then moves to emphasize the main goal of bringing individual worshippers to a mystical religious experience amid the communal rite. In Chaos Magick, this personal experience of projection of their own visualizations of the deity is central; out of this personal willing-to-be comes the ability for the god to appear. When the god Cthulhu materializes, participants gain power over it so that the deity will possess them. The ritual continues:

> Once the presence of the Deity is felt within the Trapezoid (this may be noted by a marked drop in temperature), the Priest/Priestess will begin to direct its energies towards the Host, via magickal passes performed with the left hand. This is to be undertaken in sympathy with the rythyms [sic] of the Mantra—a powerful focal point is thus induced within the body of the Host, forming both a strong attraction to the God-force invoked within the Trapezoid, and a physical gateway for its manifestation.

We see in both sections see a clear allusion to another Lovecraftian work, "The Haunter of the Dark," and the "shining trapezohedron," which reveals, according the story, "black gulfs of chaos from which it was called" (CF 3.466). The ritual continues:

> At the moment of possession, the power and identity of the Great God Cthulhu will be drawn into the body of the Host. At the last instance before total possession, the Host calls forth the name of the God, and the Temple falls silent. His power is radiated forth by the Priest/ Priestess, who holds out the Chalice to collect these negatively-charged emanations (Dreams from R'lyeh).
>
> When the Dreams of Cthulhu have passed from the Host (often leaving them mentally and physically exhausted), the Priest/Priestess offers the collected emanations for consumption (via the medium of the salt water), firstly to the Host, then to the two Worshippers, and lastly partakes of the Com-

munion him/herself.

Following the giving of Communion, the Priest/Priestess repeats the Banishment, retracting the Elder Sign at the cardinal points, and repeating the respective God-names. Facing the West once more, he/she declares the Rite of Communion of Cthulhu completed, and the Temple closed. The participants may now leave the Trapezoid, infused with the trans-Yuggothian energies of the Great God Cthulhu.

An individual esoteric state is the point of the whole ritual: the direct possession by Cthulhu. Although the cult of Cthulhu in the story "The Call of Cthulhu" is not followed exactly, the general tone is the same. In the description of the celebrants, Lovecraft notes that they are "braying, bellowing, and writhing about," much as if they were in a trance-like state. The ring of worshippers "jumped and roared, the general direction of the mass motion being from left to right in endless Bacchanal between the ring of bodies and the ring of fire" (CF 2.36). In all, Frater Tenebrous looks to the text of Lovecraft as a source for ritual and sacred knowledge. Frater Tenebrous follows closely to Kenneth Grant when he stated the Lovecraft's stories:

> [Lovecraft] began to form an internally consistent and self-referential mythology, created from the literary realisation of the author's dreams and intuitive impulses. Although he outwardly espoused a wholly rational and skeptical view of the universe, his dream-world experiences allowed him glimpses of places and entities beyond the world of mundane reality, and behind his stilted and often excessive prose there lies a vision and an understanding of occult forces which is directly relevant to the Magical Tradition. (*Cult of Cthulhu* 5)

So again we see Lovecraft as a dreamer who received visions of the other worlds in spite of his outwardly espoused atheism. For chaos magicians, as Erik Davis states, "there is no 'tradition'. The symbols and myths of countless sects, orders, and faiths, are constructs, useful fictions, and 'games.' That magick works has nothing to do with its truth claims and everything to do with the will and experience of the magician" ("Calling Cthulhu"). This gets at the heart of why Lovecraft's claims have no bearing on whether his visions were true or not. The will of the magician makes the words true. The method of drawing religious ritual directly from texts, a standard of many religious traditions, permeates most Lovecraftian rituals, thus grounding these superficially radical modern religions with most other Western religions. Like them, Lovecraftian Religion often relies on a sacred text, in this case Lovecraft's fiction, as the basis of their rituals. As Chaos Magician Phil Hine notes, such works of fiction, "which are not rooted in a particular culture, but which have arisen from literature, science fiction, or modern, urban myths" (220), have become the inspiration for alternative spiritual practices in much the same way as traditional religions have used mythic texts of their own. On the subject of using Lovecraft as a basis for magick, Phil Hine points out that whether or not you believe in the gods you evoke makes little difference. All one needs to do believe:

> When practising ritual magick its [sic] generally a good idea to, whatever you think about gods being archetypes or reflections of bits of yourself or whatever, behave as if they were real. So in a Cthulhu Mythos ritual, nothing will help build the neccesary [sic] tension than the adopted belief that if you get it wrong Cthulhu will slime you! Of course, outside the ritual you don't have to believe in Cthulhu and that even now a slimy paw appears at my window . . . no! No! . . . ahem, sorry about that. Related to this approach is the idea that 'Suspension of Disbelief' can also be useful. To do this, take a book which expounds an idea that you find totally crap (every magician has their favourite 'crap' author) and try to see the writers message without your inner voice hurling abuse at the page. One of the most difficult 'suspensions' for fledgling magicians is overcoming the nagging doubt that "all this stuff doesn't work." Despite hours of talk and reading vast tomes by Crowley and his cohorts, that nagging disbelief can still be heard, and can only be really dispelled by experience—one act that shows you that MAGICK WORKS is worth a thousand arguments. (40)

Thus, faith above all guides Phil Hine in his religious endeavors. This reminds one of passage in the Gospel of Mark, "Everything is possible for one who believes" (9:23).

Hine also reads much into Lovecraft's "The Dunwich Horror," where he sees that Lovecraft "clearly illustrates that hilltop rites, associated with stone circles and strange geophysical phenomena, are a key when approaching entities such as Yog-Sothoth" (27). For Hine, these stories offer keys to ritual processes and communion with the Great Old Ones. For Hine, Lovecraft's gods are brought "into our dimension" through some sort of 'gate,' "which in mythos tales, is often a wild outdoor site, a stone circle, tower, or a similar type of power spot" (27). Later, Hine returns to the topic of the stone circles used in ritual evocations of the Old Ones:

> Lovecraft's 'frienzied [sic] rites on the hilltops', and the role that sound plays in all of this. There is a great deal of magical literature available exploring the dynamics of sound, particularly different vocal techniques used to produce an Altered State of Consciousness (ASC). One of the key factors seems to be rhythm. Rhythms carry our consciousness along, from heartbeats, to cycles of breathing, sleeping, night-day and the passage of seasons. (35)

This self-conscious adherence to the spirit of Lovecraft's text is the hallmark of Lovecraftian religions. And this is certainly the case for Hine. Later he continues: "Coming back to the Cthulhu Mythos, it seems then that Lovecraft was on the right track with his themes of weird hillregions, stone circles, barbarous words of power, and 'frienzied rites'" (38). This is an essential point about the relationship between text and religious practices. Certainly, not all Lovecraftian religionists follow the stories as literally as Phil Hine and Frater Tenebrous, but they all use the stories for religious inspiration. Chaos magicians claim they can make the Old Ones appear with the assistance of the text.

IV

We conclude this paper with a discussion of modern religions that use literature as a basis for their belief and ritual system, and suggest that it is the attitude toward Lovecraft's texts that connects these new religions to how Christians viewed the Old Testament's so-called hidden messages. As we look into Lovecraftian Religions, we notice that they are not that out of the norm. Rather, it is part of a wider phenomenon of modern religious movements inspired by popular culture, particularly modern religious movements that are a part of contemporary paganism. As the scholar Graham Harvey has shown, "the formation and development of Pagan identities almost always features significant literary sources." Postmodern or alternative spiritualities have drawn extensively upon contemporary popular culture while constructing their beliefs and ritual activities. Adam M. Possamaï, in an important work on cultural consumption and alternative spiritualties, has also shown how many neo-pagan groups look to science fiction narratives within popular culture, in a process he terms "perennism," as the basis for their own spiritual pursuits. For Possamaï, "New Age and neo-paganism are only parts of a larger spirituality that [he has] called perennism and that includes more than these two subgroups"

(204).⁸ This is also true for science fiction. Possamaï continues: "some [science fiction] narratives can be understood as cultural reservoirs for the construction of subjective myths by perennists" (204). He uses the example from Robert A. Heinlein's book *Stranger in a Strange Land* (1961), which spawned The Church of All Worlds. Also, of course, the Church of Scientology was based on the science fiction stories of L. Ron Hubbard, inspiring some scholars to term Scientology as a "Science Fiction Religion" (Possemaï 204). This is also the case for fantasy literature. "More specifically to neo-paganism, the literature labeled 'fantasy' seems to express and explore pagan issues." These include the authors J. R. R. Tolkien's *Lord of the Rings*, Marion Zimmer Bradley's *The Mists of Avalon*, Brian Bates's *The Way of Wyrd*, and Terry Pratchett's *Discworld*. There are many more examples of these spiritualities rooted in popular fiction, and thus Lovecraftian Religions are clearly part of this tradition. Citing Anton LaVey's Church of Satan, Possamaï notes that *The Satanic Rituals* use Lovecraft as a fictional mythology: "believing that 'fantasy plays an important part in any religious curriculum,' LaVey (1972) developed some rituals for his Church of Satan based on this fictional mythology" (206). As Possamaï indicates, the text is present in all these new, fiction-based spiritualities. These all contribute "to neo-pagan thinking. While there is no biblical text of reference in neo-paganism, the construction of the pagan self entails reading works of fiction" (207). Thus, they have a rather open canon.

Even more than modern fiction-inspired religions, Lovecraftian Religions also have similarities with the more mainstream religions; especially the so-called religions of the Book. In fact, this type of exegesis lies at the

---

8. Possamaï defines "perennism" in the following way: "Perennism is a syncretic spirituality with three main characteristics: (a) the world is interpreted as monistic (the cosmos is perceived as having deeply interrelated elements with a single ultimate principle, being, or force, underlying all reality). The notion of dualism, e.g. mind/body is rejected; (b) perennists attempt to develop their potential human ethic (actors working towards personal growth); (c) followers of perennism are engaged in a search for spiritual knowledge (personal development through a pursuit of knowledge, whether it is knowledge of the universe or of the self, the two being sometimes interrelated). Defining perennists as practitioners of perennism or people involved in alternative spiritualities, this article analyses their cultural consumption of indigenous culture, history in general and popular culture. By cultural consumption, I refer to practices of selectively borrowing, or even shopping for, cultural content" (199).

very root of Christianity's understanding of the Old Testament. Lovecraftian Religions, which all emphasize Lovecraft's denial of his religious revelation, remind one of early Christian writers' insistence that philosophers and the writers of the Old Testament were either unaware or unwilling to admit the true nature of their revelation, until the time was right.[9] This is the basis of Christian allegorical interpretation. The "literal meaning" of Lovecraft's texts, that Lovecraft was writing fiction, is made the lowest understanding of the texts. The allegorical meaning, emphasized from William Lumley on, was that Lovecraft's texts provides insights into true religious understanding, while some even stress some literal interpretation. Thus, the figures seen in this paper all engage in a sort of proof-texting that aims to prove that Lovecraft's fiction conforms to their own pre-espoused religious orientation. The vagueness of Lovecraft's descriptions of the various Old Ones lends itself to multiple understandings, one of which, as we have seen, is religious revelation to those predisposed to understand it. This is similar to the interpretation of the Old Testament in the Gospels. For example, the story of Jonah cited in the Book of Matthew 12:40 is interpreted as a message of the death and resurrection of Jesus Christ. At one level, the story of Jonah spending time in the belly of a fish is understood literally. But Christians saw the "real message" as anticipating the coming of their messiah. Further, the Apostle Paul in 2 Corinthians 3:12-18 explains that Moses, who was thought to have written the Hebrew Scriptures, knew the Jews were not ready for the true revelation, so Moses "put a veil over his face to keep the Israelites from gazing at the end of what was fading away." Moses knew that "their minds had become closed, for the same veil is there to this very day." Christians regard themselves as having lifted that veil and having the ability to see the true message of the Old Testament. This is not unlike Kenneth Grant's interpretation of Lovecraft's works, whose real understanding is veiled even to Lovecraft himself.

It is this very same hermeneutical assumption that underlies nearly every adherent of Lovecraftian religions. For early Christians it was the Holy Spirit that transmitted the story to the Old Testament writer, who may not have fully understood the revelation, which was often times

---

9. This is especially true for early Christian typological interpretation of the Old Testament. See Froehlich 9-10.

transmitted in dreams; adherents of Lovecraftian Religions often cite inspiration of their Prophet through dreams as well. In both Christianity and Lovecraftian Religions, the methods of justifying revelatory texts are primarily exegetical in nature. But Lovecraftian exegetes also invert that Christian hermeneutical mode by taking literally the texts that Lovecraft claimed he used as means to explore his atheistic "cosmicism," and thus making religious meaning out of elements of Lovecraft's fiction. But in the end, meaning making is separate from the literal intention of the author becomes an exegetical exercise. The influence of the Christian hermeneutical tradition of finding hidden meanings in the Old Testament that are lost even to their authors (or at least denied), can be felt in all the authors and practitioners of Lovecraftian traditions we have examined here.

Robert M. Price maintained in 1992, "No one is reading Lovecraft and becoming a *real* live Cthulhu cultist" (77). In his "Cthulhu Cult" speech delivered as a Breakfast Homily at NecronomiCon 5 in 2001, he went on to mock the prospects of anyone becoming a "literal occultists": "Of course I don't mean becoming a bunch of literal occultists. That's a blind alley for most of us. And we don't want to become half-witted zealots like those goofballs splashing around the bayou in their birthday suits till Inspector Lagrasse surprised them with his Candid Camera." However, some are coming quite close. As Price states:

> Since the original appearance of this essay, things have evolved farther in a direction that HPL certainly would have minded. There is now apparently more than one Mythos cult in which the *Necronomicon*, perhaps one of its tentacle-in-chief avatars, is solemnly cited as sacred writ, the Old Ones evoked as real deities. Lovecraft maintained that, to gain proper verisimilitude, an author must lend his fiction all the energy one might expend upon an actual hoax. It appears that in this case he may have done his work a bit too well. (77)

Professor Price saw clearly in less than a decade that the Cthulhu Cult which he presides over at many banquets and festivities, such as the celebration at this event, is not as mythical as it once was.

So what does the future hold for Lovecraftian Religions? With the popularity of the works of Lovecraft on the rise, Lovecraftian Religions too are poised to proliferate. With powerful reach of the Internet, new seekers of a true connection to the universe will certainly rise to be "e"-vangelists for the gods of the Cthulhu Mythos. The web had been a boon to Lovecraftian Religions in which most of the religious treatises based on Lovecraft are self-published on the Internet. The web allows for freedom of thought and the exchange of ideas beyond anything in all world history. And in this new reality, seekers of religious truths will find them in many forms, even in the guise of the "mechanical materialist" from Providence. Lovecraft prophesied this in his own lifetime. As it was in the beginning when Lovecraft the prophet walked the earth, so it shall be in the future as Lovecraftian religions will continue to spread the bad news of the Old Ones and their impending return when the stars are right.

Works Cited

Aquino, Michael A. *The Church of Satan*. Self-published, 2012.

Callaghan, Gavin. "The Occult Lovecraft." *Fate Magazine* (August 2007): 10-21.

Davis, Eric. "Calling Cthulhu: H. P. Lovecraft's Magick Realism." *Gnosis* 37 (1995). http://www.chaosmatrix.org/library/chaos/texts/callcth.html.

Douglas, Mary. *Purity and Danger: An Analysis of Concepts of Pollution and Taboo*. 1966. London: Ark Paperbacks, 1988.

Froelich, Karlfried. *Biblical Interpretation of the Early Church*. Philadelphia: Fortress Press, 1984.

Gibbons, B. J. *Spirituality and the Occult: From the Renaissance to the Modern Age*. New York: Routledge, 2001.

Grant, Kenneth. *Outside the Circles of Time*. London: Frederick Muller, 1980.

Harms, Daniel, and John Wisdom Gonce III. *The Necronomicon Files: The Truth Behind Lovecraft's Legend*. Boston: Weiser, 2003.

Harvey, Graham. "Fantasy in the Study of Religions: Paganism as Observed and Enhanced by Terry Pratchett." *Discus: The On-Disk Journal of International Religious Studies* 6 (2000). http://www.uni-marburg.de/religionswissenschaft/journal/diskus.

Hine, Phil. *Oven-Ready Chaos*. Self-published, 1997.

Jenkins, Philip. *Mystics and Messiahs: Cults and New religions in American History*. New York: Oxford University Press, 2000.

Joshi, S. T. *H. P. Lovecraft: A Life*. West Warwick, RI: Necronomicon Press, 1996.

Kugel, James L., and Rowan A. Greer. *Early Biblical Interpretation*. Philadelphia: Westminster Press, 1986.

LaVey, Anton. *The Satanic Rituals.* New York: Avon, 1972.

Lovecraft, H. P. *Against Religion: The Atheist Writings of H. P. Lovecraft.* Ed. S. T. Joshi. New York: Sporting Gentleman, 2010.

Marsh, Frater Obed. *The Esoteric Order of Dagon.* http://www.esotericorderofdagon.org.

Mathews, Chris. *Modern Satanism: Anatomy of a Radical Subculture.* London: Praeger, 2009.

Possamaï, Adam M. "Cultural Consumption of History and Popular Culture in Alternative Spiritualities." *Journal of Consumer Culture* 2 (2002): 197–218.

Price, Robert M. "'Lovecraftianity' and the Pagan Revival." in *Black Forbidden Things*, ed. Robert M. Price. Mercer Island, WA: Starmont House, 1992. 74–77.

———. "Cthulhu Cult? Why Not? Cthulhu Prayer Breakfast Homily 2001." http://www.cthulhulives.org/HPLHSPress/Cult.pdf.

Quinn, Dennis P. "Endless Bacchanal: Rome, Livy, and Lovecraft's Cthulhu Cult." *Lovecraft Annual* 5 (2011): 188–215.

Simon. *Necronomicon.* 1977. New York: Avon/HarperCollins, 1980.

Tenebrous, Frater. *Cults of Cthulhu: H. P. Lovecraft and the Occult Tradition.* n.p.: Daath Press 1987.

———. "The Rite of the Communion of Cthulhu." http://www.chaosmatrix.org/library/chaos/rites/cthurite.html.

Appendix: Abstracts of Papers Presented at NecronomiCon Providence—2013 Emerging Scholarship Symposium

Chair: John Michael Sefel

Editor's Note: This appendix contains the abstracts of proposed papers and the credentials of the presenters as they were at the time of the symposium. As a matter of chronicling the event as it took place, no effort has been made to update academic affiliations, paper title changes, etc., to match the contents of the rest of this publication.

Agenda

Friday, 8:00–9:15 A.M.
Forbidden Knowledge in 19th- and 20th-Century Modernism

Friday, 9:30–10:45 A.M.
Comparative Literature: Monsters and Dystopias

Friday, 11:00 A.M.–12:00 P.M.
Antiquarian Aesthetics

Saturday, 8:00–9:15 A.M.
What's Love (and Sex, and Art, and Humor) Got to Do with It?

Saturday, 9:30–10:45 A.M.
Lovecraft in Late- and Post-Modern Studies

Saturday, 11:00 A.M.–12:00 P.M.
Beyond the Esoteric Order

Friday, 8:00–9:15 A.M.
Forbidden Knowledge in 19th- and 20th-Century Modernism

"If you stare long enough into the abyss . . . the abyss eats you."

Title: Poe, Lovecraft, and "The Uncanny": The Horror of the Self | *Anthony Conrad Chieffalo, Central Connecticut State University*

Abstract: "The Uncanny" is an essay by Sigmund Freud that describes how a specific type of fear functions in horror literature. Freud defines how the sensation of the uncanny results from a specific event in which one's repressed memories or emotions, which have been relegated to the individual's subconscious mind, suddenly emerge like the sunken city R'lyeh rising from unfathomable depths. This causes simultaneous feelings of familiarity and unfamiliarity in relation to the object of the individual's fear. This intense emotional experience of uncanny dread is the result of the return of a suppressed aspect of the self. It is basically a "horror of the self" by which the character experiences fear that is derived from the recesses of his own psyche. The conflicts in these cerebral works center on the internal confrontations between the protagonists and the formerly concealed aspects of themselves that manifest in the form of literal or figurative antagonists. Two of the most prominent figures of American horror literature who used this form of horror include nineteenth-century author Edgar Allan Poe and his twentieth-century successor H. P. Lovecraft. This thesis explores occurrences of the uncanny in the works of Poe and Lovecraft and the underlying theme of self-loathing that results from the inescapable and consuming horror of the self.

Title: "A Stalking Monster": The Influence of Radiation Poisoning on Lovecraft's "The Colour out of Space" | *Andy Troy, Independent Scholar*

Abstract: H. P. Lovecraft's descriptions of sickness, deterioration, and death following the landing of a meteorite in "The Colour out of Space" (1927) are sometimes compared to those of that appear in the aftermath of detonation of the atomic bomb, although the momentous invention was eighteen years away from reaching the public eye. Lovecraft did, however, have access to a sizable body of scientific texts on radioactive elements, astronomical phenomena, and chemical experimentation. Just as Lovecraft incorporated Charles Fort's research into his story, he also used current depictions of radiation, radioactive properties, and radium poisoning to heighten the horror, and the scientific verisimilitude, of "The Colour out of Space."

This article shows a definitive link between scientific texts Lovecraft is known to have read and descriptions of the meteor and the alien being in "The Colour out of Space." Other sources of information, especially scientific journals and newspapers available to Lovecraft in the decade preceding the story's composition, influenced his depiction of the creature's effects on terrestrial life. Most importantly, the "Radium Girls" industrial poisoning scandal of the 1920s, as reported in the *New York Times* and the *Providence Evening Bulletin,* has direct parallels to key passages of "Colour" as they relate to human symptoms of radium overdoses and popular fears of an apocalyptic radioactive "Death Ray." The science depicted in media coverage of the Radium Girls is repeated almost verbatim in "The Colour out of Space," and even the thematic treatment of radiation as an invisible, predatory killer demonstrates that this portrayal is not a coincidence or accident, but a deliberate reaction to contemporary ignorance as to the hazards of chemical exposure.

Although the narrative of "Colour" takes great pains to point out the incomprehensible nature of the alien creature—and indeed, even as radiation is recognized as a key feature of its physiology—there remain terrifying questions about its nature and origins. There is nevertheless an insistence upon a linked series of symptoms that comprise a functioning etiology of the being's effect on earthly biology. The pattern of growth or stimulation, followed by a period of torpor or lethargy in which the signature "imaginary colors" and luminescence appear, and finally the graying, brittle decay that signal biologic death, is derived explicitly from documented industrial diseases of the 1920s, chiefly radiation experiments and quack medicinal cures. Although this radioactive danger remains unnamed as such in the story, Lovecraft's fictional synthesis of disparate radiological research actually *predates* the more formal, rigorous findings of his day.

Title: "Nomad of the Dreamlands": The Impact of Early Inter-Dimensional Theory and Lucid Dreaming on the Mythos 'Dream Cycle' | *Kristine Beskin, Independent Researcher*

Abstract: An "exposition," as mentioned in the Shakespeare quotation at the beginning of "Beyond the Wall of Sleep," the story, refers to the entire breadth of an idea, whose every angle and comprehensible dimension is made completely clear to an observer.

Lovecraft viewed the universe as the product, in astronomical terms, of a naked singularity, an existence usually contained by an intense gravitational field that, if released, bends space and time so extensively, found in the center of a black hole, that the laws of physics no longer apply within its domain. This parallel world could be observed through oneiric objectivism, whereby dreams and the situations that would happen in them became just as valid as reality, and that these are multiple realities superimposed on top of one another. While they mostly stay separate, the Great Old Ones are able to bleed through all universes and affect the course of various histories, existing beyond the realm of physics and standard biological limitations, especially for the time. They become the manifestations of Lovecraft's cosmic agoraphobia: a pantheon of beings that no manner of reason can bring to its knees.

In "The Tomb," Lovecraft sums up his life 'in the Dreamlands': "It is an unfortunate fact that the bulk of humanity is too limited in its mental vision to weigh with patience and intelligence, those isolated phenomena, seen and felt only by a psychologically sensitive few, which lie outside its common experience . . ."

Through the Dream Cycle ("Beyond the Wall of Sleep," "Through the Gates of the Silver Key," *The Dream-Quest of Unknown Kadath*, etc.) and the affirmation of his "god complex," Lovecraft attempts to explain the theory that the things from the proverbial "other side" have a corporeal essence and are aware of our own world. This suggests that, at some point, in the sense of the concept of infinite dimensions, the two worlds intersect and allow for multiple beings from multiple planes of existence, existing in the same point in space, to fold into each other and create an information overload and schizophrenic chain reaction as astral minds all combat one another for sovereignty over one point in space. These beings absorb all the other conscious experiences in that spot, across localized universes, which, in Lovecraftian pseudoscience, would allow for his frequent hallucinations, spurring a dive into the world of the occult, to attempt to piece together what secrets these schizophrenic dreams may hold.

Despite the metaphorical attributes of Lovecraft's extradimensional beings, for all intents and purposes, when working within the Dream Cycle, the Old Gods and Elder Things across the threshold of sleep are to be received as real. At the time Lovecraft wrote, quantum theory was a fantastical concept in pulp fiction, but during the presentation the parallels between infinite dimensions and Lovecraft's own "wall of sleep" will be drawn, and what may have been regarded as "astral projection" in his present, in which he was split into all his ideals (Joe Slater, Randolph Carter, etc.) throughout the realms, can now be explained in hard theory. Lovecraft, before his time, was postulating alien divinities that existed outside linear time, and in his own ego, imagined that he was a "nomad of the Dreamlands—a watcher in the waste," meant to carry their secrets between his realm and their own. He saw himself as a godlike figure, his thoughts captured in "Beyond the Wall of Sleep" by the being, Nemesis: since he could not find much of a connection with others, he became a distant observer of his fellow human beings, looking down on them as they lived in seemingly blissful ignorance of the magical scientific facts he was revealing.

Using quantum theory, this presentation explains how someone may, in fact, be communicating across the realms, and how much scientific fact is actually rooted in Lovecraft's fantastical postulations while staying true to the nature of how the spheres operate within the Mythos.

Title: Dead Lies Dreaming: H. P. Lovecraft and the Other Side of Modernity | *Andrew Lenoir, Columbia University*

Abstract: Four people attended Howard Phillips Lovecraft's funeral. On December 21, 2012, more than 30,000 people "attended" the "Awakening of Cthulhu" on Facebook. How has the same writer whose racism "does not endear him to the modern reader" (according to Wikipedia) become a literary phenomenon, inspiring films, video games, and countless writers since? Though some claim Lovecraft's fictions contain truths—inspiring knock-off *Necronomicons* and the IRS-recognized religion, the Cult of Cthulhu—what if his greatest contributions were not fantastical but philosophical?

By examining Lovecraft's life, letters, political essays, and stories (particularly "The Horror at Red Hook," "The Rats in the Walls," "The Shadow out of Time," *At the Mountains of Madness*, and "The Music of Erich Zann") alongside the writings of Schopenhauer, Nietzsche, and Freud, the core of Lovecraftian horror is shown to be far deeper than sunken R'yleh. Inside the mythos is a terrifyingly simple revelation: this world is wrong, and we, as a symptom of that world, are complicit in the crime of existence. This nearly Gnostic worldview, with its cosmology of ancient gods, lays bare a history impelled by inertia, not intent. As Lovecraft wrote in his essay "At the Root" (1919), the "ultimate factor in human decisions is physical force."

Lovecraft's stories contain a unique brand of socialism, owing more to Plato than to Karl Marx. The only escape in a mad world is the arts. As societal conventions become transparent in a digital age, the shiver that industrialization sent down Lovecraft's spine has spread.

In childhood, Lovecraft gave himself the name Abdul Alhazred. As an adult, he gave that name to the author of the *Necronomicon*—a book that drives its readers mad with forbidden knowledge. This is what Lovecraft sought to do through allegory: showing readers what lies beneath our cheerful fictions, the most hopeful of which is our "selves."

Friday, 9:30–10:45 A.M.
Comparative Literature: Monsters and Dystopias

Exploring thematic shades of the Lovecraftian in the supernatural entities and dystopian worlds that grip our collective imagination, from 17th-century poetry to 21th-century YouTube videos.

Title: Lovecraftian Milton: Prophetic Certainties, Romantic Rebellions, and Weird Imaginings in Milton's and Lovecraft's Cosmologies | *Marcello Ricciardi, St. Joseph's College*

Abstract: To speak of a Lovecraftian Milton is to acknowledge that Lovecraft's mythos contains Miltonic themes that run parallel to his own psychological, biographical, and spiritual life. Although both men had diametrically opposed cosmic perspectives, both were driven by a sense of the sublime—for Lovecraft the sublime as ominous Other, for Milton, the numinous as Providential Guide. Nonetheless, despite certain similarities in temperament and tendencies toward mythic self-fashioning, both men shared a similar literary trajectory. This essay explores three levels of development in the Lovecraft canon, which has as its genesis Milton's theological, poetical, and imaginative development, albeit in an inverse and, at times, paradoxical way. My initial premise was to outline all the elements of the weirdly diabolical in Milton and to apply them to selected stories in Lovecraft. However, as my research continued and I journeyed deeper into Lovecraft's psychological terrain, I realized that there were multiple levels of vision to his hierophanic tiers of being, and that his imaginative landscapes were much more nuanced and expansive than I had previously thought. In fact, as Lovecraft's world was rapidly expanding, my initial premises were subsequently contracting. Intellectual honesty demanded that I modify first impressions and accommodate my thesis in order to take into account new findings, discovering and recovering a Lovecraft who inhabits realms of greater complexity than previously imagined.

My research has led me to conclude that contained within Lovecraft are three Miltonic identities. First is the *Prophetic Milton*, a youthful visionary aspiring toward a more hallowed world, awaiting to begin a great poetical enterprise of high-mindedness and high exploits. Lovecraft, like Milton, yearns and strives to inhabit a greater world in his dream-quests, envisioning himself as a nomadic bard in exile from the obtuse populace who cannot even begin to comprehend the immensity of the reality around them. Both Milton and Lovecraft share a sense of expectancy and urgency concerning their poetical vocations. However, contained with this category is also an element of prophetic doom, a mature apocalyptic vision of final cataclysm where the forces of darkness are mustering their minions to unleash a final assault against the feeble defenses of the known world—a final conflagration of destruction and ominous power—what I would define as Lovecraft's dark theophany. Second is the *Romantic Milton*, or the Milton appropriated by the Romantic poets, although Milton's genius does contain the seeds of the Byronic hero. In this world, an Ishmaelean-Lovecraftian narrator bears witness to an Ahabian-Satanic figure bent on a monomaniacal assault against a cosmos seemingly indifferent to his plight and reeking of malevolent intent. But contained within this category is also an authorial fascination with or an evocation of the denizens of this dark world and a rueful lamentation for their passing away, a theme touched upon all too subtly by Milton himself. And lastly, the *Weird Milton*, Lovecraft's vision of the grotesque and the demonic, with denizens of the deep and air, shadowy, elusive, and clearly rooted in Milton's dark imaginings of the diabolical as portrayed in *Paradise Lost* and *Regain'd*. It is here that Milton and Lovecraft are most synonymous in their depictions of occult phenomena, appropriating Edmund Burke's definition of the sublime and stripping evil of any of its attractive and appealing pretensions. Here, the *Romantic* gives way to the *Horrific*, and the *Prophetic* finds its consummation in an inevitable Armageddon lurking at the gates of the knowable world.

Title: Weird Cosmodemonology: Tapping into the Infernal Energy of Algernon Blackwood's "The Wendigo"| *Anthony Camara, University of California, Los Angeles*

Abstract: In this paper I stress the importance of recognizing the cosmic dimensions of Algernon Blackwood's outdoor horror stories, a move that I hope will give scholars of the weird a deeper appreciation of how Blackwood's understudied fiction influenced H. P. Lovecraft's masterful tales. In *Elegant Nightmares* (1978), Jack Sullivan contends that "[a]lthough the unconscious is an active force in Blackwood's stories, it is not Freudian, not limited to human beings (or even collective human beings in a Jungian sense); it is a pre-human energy which infuses not only . . . birds, beasts, and flowers, but patches of dirt." Sullivan's remarks reveal a current of inhuman, pre-libidinal energy coursing through nature, connecting organisms to other life-forms and their inorganic surroundings. Regrettably, however, Sullivan confines this energy to Earth's ecosystems. Against this planet-bound interpretation, I turn to "The Wendigo" (1910) to emphasize the cosmic scale of Blackwood's energeticist thought. Rather than depict the Wendigo as an emaciated apparition insatiably hungry for flesh, Blackwood breaks with Algonquin folklore, describing the demon as a quantum of pure energy: a malicious flux of rays from outer space that burns out, rather than eats up, human beings. Thus Blackwood's cosmic imagination reconfigures the demon as a disembodied alien force consisting of sheer vital intensity. I argue that this innovation suggests a diabolical reading of Henri Bergson's concept of *élan vital,* in which Blackwood speculates that freely circulating energy is life itself unbound from the discrete forms imposed by matter. By recasting demonology and its possession narrative in terms of physics and vitalist philosophy, "The Wendigo" exemplifies how weird horror progresses beyond the conventional supernaturalism of theology and folklore. And here we glimpse Lovecraft's naturalistic cosmos, where demons are spawned not from hellfire, but white-hot jets of stellar plasma.

Title: The Failed Promises of Rationality: Sam J. Lundwall on the Individual Lost in an Uncaring and Soulless World | *Lars G. E. Backstrom, Kings College (United Kingdom)*

Abstract: This paper analyzes the influence of Lovecraft on the early works of Sam J. Lundwall and introduces the remarkable Swedish author of science fiction to the readers of today. Lundwall (b. 1941) is a writer, musician, publisher, editor, and translator. He has been chairperson of Worldcon twice, and also North European Coordinator for the SFWA. He introduced Lovecraft's stories to the Swedish audience in the early 1970s. To English-speaking readers Lundwall is mostly known for his nonfiction book *Science Fiction: What It's All About* (Penguin, 1971) and for his early novels *No Time for Heroes* (Ace, 1971), *Bernhard the Conqueror* (DAW, 1973), and *2018 A.D. or The King Kong Blues* (DAW, 1975).

In his novels Lundwall's relation to Lovecraft works on three levels: there is a direct influence from Lovecraft; there is an influence from the writers who influenced Lovecraft; and there is parallelism in both authors' writings. Common themes in Lundwall's novels are humanity's insignificance in the universe, humanity trapped by forces it cannot understand, a strong feeling of alienation and hopelessness, and characters who are neither heroes nor influential on the unfolding of events, even if they think they are.

No Time for Heroes and *Bernhard the Conqueror* are set in a distant post-Foundation future where too many galactic empires have come and gone, and civilization has descended into chaos bordering on total entropy. *2018 A.D. or The King Kong Blues* is set in a world frighteningly similar to our own, where failed political experiments and megacorporate greed have created a society in which the only goal for the individual is instant gratification as an escape from the horrors of daily life. In these books, not only is God nonexistent—even though many characters and machines quite happily claim godhood—but society has also collapsed, corrupting all human interactions with a twisted survival-of-the-fittest logic. With these novels Lundwall can be seen as a precursor to the French author Michel Houellebecq, himself influenced by Lovecraft.

In the novel *Fängelsestaden* (*The Prison City* [Norstedts, 1978], not yet translated into English), set in the Earth's distant past, humanity huddles in a vast labyrinthine city built neither for humans nor by humans. The city's blocks are inexplorable labyrinths, each its own microcosm of legends, history, marvels, and horrors. Only an escaped madman seems to hold a partial answer to the mystery of the city. The novel is inspired by Givanni Battista Piranesi's *Carceri d'invenzione* prints, which Lovecraft was probably familiar with.

Title: Xenophobia, Atheism, and Tentacles: The Slender Man Myth as Communal Lovecraftian Tale | *Christian Haunton, University of Iowa*

Abstract: The development of the Slender Man myth over the last four years has been a revelation in horror storytelling and postmodern folklore. From its modest beginning as two photographs posted on a forum, it has developed into a constantly expanding world of blogs, videos, games, films, and toys. As aggressively as the mythology has grown, it has remained almost exclusively in the hands of independent (typically non-professional) groups and individuals, and it has developed entirely in the communal forum of the Internet, without a central or canonical storyteller.

In examining the details of the crowd-sourced Slender Man myth, one cannot help but notice the similarities in form and content that it shares with what has commonly come to be called the "Cthulhu Mythos." While this is ultimately unsurprising (as the Slender Man was born and raised in an environment rich in Lovecraftian content), it is nonetheless quite revelatory, as it provides a window into a world of inhuman nihilism that Lovecraft himself never imagined—the Internet.

This presentation focuses on the themes of xenophobia, nihilism, and atheism explored both overtly and implicitly in the work of H. P. Lovecraft, and how those themes have shaped and been shaped by the world of twenty-first-century horror on the Internet. The genesis and ongoing development of the Slender Man myth will serve as the test case and metaphor for exploring these topics.

Friday, 11:00 A.M.–12:00 P.M.
Antiquarian Aesthetics

Lovecraft's aesthetic resurrections of days gone by

Title: New England's Curator: Colonial Revival in the Travelogues and Fiction of Lovecraft | *Kenneth W. Lai, University of California, Irvine*

Abstract: Scholarship on Lovecraft has not sufficiently dealt with Lovecraft's fascination with architecture, his existing travelogues, and the relationship between these two and his fiction. This paper proposes that both in his travelogues and in his fiction (though to better success in the latter), Lovecraft is actively applying his own method of preservation, a method of "weird curation" that rationalizes and monumentalizes both spaces of fiction and of objects. The latter term, "object," carries especially important weight in relation to recent studies in Object-Oriented Ontology, a school of philosophy that has taken a Lovecraftian focus in Graham Harman's book *Weird Realism* (2012). Harman proposes a Heideggerian relationship of self and object in the weird universe that supports a reading of Lovecraft as a curator of colonial New England objects. Although Heidegger and Harman do not explicitly discuss curation, the ambiance of great architecture to locals as a lack of "being" or presence is one that is a common thread of archaeology and thus benefits any discussion on the theory of curation. For Lovecraft, the weird atmosphere brings into the foreground the very buildings that slowly withdraw into the everyday fabric of life, the "unseen" background that becomes increasingly disposable as time progresses and new, "modern" buildings come into demand. This calculated focus on architecture in Lovecraft's works is especially important for understanding Lovecraft as an innovator in the canon of American Gothic writers, tantamount to the shift from English to American Gothic that Charles Brockden Brown made in drawing the Gothic space out of historic castles and into the modern, domestic setting.

Lovecraft's literature not only performs both functions, tapping now into the past, now into the present, but also marks the shift from the folkloric to the weird, a form of Gothic that fundamentally rejects the anthropocentric model of the universe, proposing instead an alien and entropic cosmos, all the while "preserving" historic moments of *setting* and *atmosphere*. These two key terms are channeled through Lovecraft's own aesthetic approach to the supernatural, his conception of the sublime, and subsequently constructs a curatorial link between his travelogues and his fiction. This method of the sublime is, more specifically, closest to the positive Radcliffean sublime, which "expands the soul and awakens the faculties to a high degree of life," achieving higher meaning through the atmosphere of dread and, in this case, serving as the link between real, historical objects with weird, fictional histories. Weird understood thus as a "method" of sublime and of weird curation describes the manner in which Lovecraft's fiction uses the components developed by his travelogues, which are most often structured into an overview of local history, a survey of distinguishing architecture, and a walking itinerary that immerses the pedestrian in the surrounding history and architecture. Lovecraft's experiment into weird curation, beginning at least in 1921, is best exemplified by the novel *The Case of Charles Dexter Ward*, which is this paper's focus. The novella focuses on a crumbling house in Olney Court, featured across two centuries and colored by a psychological case study, an architectural survey, various itineraries, and a weird history. Its protagonist, Charles Dexter Ward, revives the past both literally, resurrecting his evil warlock ancestor, and figuratively, as a fictionalized account of a house in Providence, Rhode Island. More generally, this paper explores the ways in which Lovecraft addresses his anxiety about architectural change and contemporary preservation methods through his own method of weird curation in both his travelogues and his fiction.

Title: Lovecraft, Fear, and the Medieval Body Frame | *Perry Neil Harrison, Baylor University*

Abstract: In the opening of his essay "Supernatural Horror in Literature" (1927), H. P. Lovecraft asserts, "The oldest and strongest emotion of mankind is fear, and the oldest and strongest kind of fear is fear of the unknown." In this essay Lovecraft traces the roots of "weird" fiction to the Gothic period, but fear he evokes in his stories is markedly older and, at its core, reminiscent of the apprehensions experienced by the populace of the medieval world. Specifically, grotesque and unnatural physical bodies in Lovecraft's tales are strikingly similar to the bizarre and often monstrous bodies seen within medieval literature and iconography.

This study explores the presence of medieval body representations within Lovecraft's work. Specific attention is given to the hybrid body form seen within "The Dunwich Horror," and to the "unknowable" forms of Lovecraft's eldritch horrors. By viewing these physical frames in light of the writings of scholars of medieval body representation such as Miri Rubin, Sarah Kay, and Jeffery Cohen, I maintain that by using the corporeal imagery used during medieval times to code the unknown, Lovecraft was better able to construct the unknowable elements of his own mythos.

Title: Lovecraft and the Great Altar Stones of New England | *David Goudsward, Independent Scholar*

Abstract: Scattered across New England are oversized, worked stones identified by amateur archaeologists as "sacrificial tables" or "altar stones." The stone tables are multi-ton flat slabs of native stone with a groove carved on the face, ostensibly to channel the flow of liquid off the surface and into a container. It has been suggested one of these slabs could have been the inspiration for the altar on Sentinel Hill in Lovecraft's "The Dunwich Horror" (1928). Lovecraft does not mention viewing any of the altar stones, and so that contention must be identified by supposition using specific search criteria.

Based on travels, dates, and accessibility, the two most likely candidates are a stone originally located in Pascoag, Rhode Island, and the North Salem, New Hampshire "sacrificial table." Investigation of Lovecraft's visits to Pascoag in 1923 with James F. Morton eliminates that location, based on routes, distances, and time constraints. Author H. Warner Munn confirms visiting the New Hampshire site with Lovecraft, but his recollection describes a visit that could not have occurred within Lovecraft's lifetime.

Munn may be blurring multiple visits to the site or confusing North Salem with an earlier visit to the Dogtown ruins outside Gloucester, Massachusetts. If Munn is confusing two visits with Lovecraft to North Salem, the lack of published reports or public awareness of the site suggests it was a return visit for Lovecraft. Munn may have asked about parts of "The Dunwich Horror" that he didn't recognize as locations in Athol and Wilbraham, Massachusetts, prompting Lovecraft to lead Munn to the North Salem site. This would be similar to Lovecraft's return visit to Boston's North End in 1927 with Donald Wandrei to see the house and neighborhood that were the described in "Pickman's Model."

Lovecraft could only have been previously introduced to the ruins by someone familiar with the site, i.e., a local resident. The site, then known as "Pattee's Caves," was a popular local picnic destination, but all but unknown outside of the town of Salem. Using the original criteria, there is one date that could mark Lovecraft's previous visit—8 June 1921, the first day of his visit with Myrta Alice Little in Hampstead, New Hampshire. The Little farmstead is less than 5 miles from the site, and the Littles had both a car and a history of taking Lovecraft on side trips.

Saturday, 8:00–9:15 A.M.
What's Love (and Sex, and Art, and Humor) Got to Do with It?

From gender identity to jokes, contemplating our image of Howard Phillips Lovecraft

Title: "One Life—Ephraim, Anseth, and Edward": Attempting to Untangle the Mind, Body, and Phallus in Lovecraft's "The Thing on the Doorstep" | *Zack Rearick, Georgia State University*

Abstract: The question of mind versus body has been mulled by centuries of philosophers—indeed, philosophy has an entire field reserved for pursuits along this line of thought: philosophy of mind. But literature too probes these questions, as in H. P. Lovecraft's "The Thing on the Doorstep" (1933). The story, which follows narrator Daniel Upton's retelling of his murder of close friend Edward Derby, raises (and occasionally answers) many compelling questions about the relationship between the mind and the body (and the relationship of the two with the theoretical phallus). The story involves many instances of mind/body switching and eventually makes clear a path of transition from Ephraim (the father of Asenath Waite, Edward's wife) to Asenath to Edward.

To begin, the story argues for the pre-eminence of the mind over the body in the establishing of identity; that is to say that, as an exchange of minds results in the creation of two entirely new entities (for example, Ephraim's-body-with-Asenath's-mind and Asenath's-body-with-Ephraim's-mind), these entities are identifiable through their minds primarily and through their physical bodies secondarily. Upton thus begins the story by remarking that though he has "sent six bullets through the head" of Edward, he is "not his murderer" because the entity he shot was not Edward but instead Ephraim in Edward's body. This may seem to some to be an obvious conclusion, but it is an area of much disagreement in the philosophical field, and Edward himself, though frequently in the grips of unimaginable horrors, seems not to agree with it, persisting in calling Asenath "she" even after he is aware that her body houses Ephraim's mind.

Perhaps more interestingly, "The Thing on the Doorstep" plays with gender and sexuality in ways that, though morbid, are quite advanced for its date of composition. Edward engages (unwittingly) in a prolonged homosexual and incestuous affair (with undertones of rape) with his own father-in-law living out of Asenath's body (resulting in a nightmarish honeymoon that turns his "immature pout" to "genuine sadness"); Asenath, forced into her father's dying body, is poisoned, a metaphor that, through its notion of the forcible entry of a harmful force into the resistant and unknowing body, mirrors possible rape by Ephraim both of Edward and of herself; the knowledge-phallus (reminiscent of Foucault's knowledge-power from *Disciple and Punish*), as in many of Lovecraft's stories, ends up destroying its wielders; and Ephraim, at times in possession of three different bodies, takes the chance to espouse his sexist views on the superiority of the male to female; views that, it must be clearly noted, were not shared by Lovecraft himself. All these points of interest (and many more) throughout the story show Lovecraft to be an advanced and complex author, capable of creating intricate and theoretically rich literary puzzles that have to this day still not been entirely solved.

Title: The Shadow of His Smile: Humor in H. P. Lovecraft | *Stephen Walker, University of Central Missouri*

Abstract: Although H. P. Lovecraft's reputation rests on his weird horror fiction, this and other writing also shows various degrees of humor.

It can be used broadly or subtly, as will be shown through various examples. Lovecraft's most obvious use of humor appears in his self-revealing correspondence and poetry (e.g., a tribute to a silent cinematic beauty, a parody of T. S. Eliot's *The Waste Land* soon after it appeared). Can a man with such a sense of humor divorce it from his writing about horror? His horror fiction is examined, and in doing so categories are assigned to the humor that he used: wordplay, satire, parody, etc. In some instances the humor can be a joke on mankind, such as the ghouls in "Pickman's Model" laughing at a guidebook; or a parody of biblical episodes in such works as *At the Mountains of Madness*. Not only does the humor at times criticize human behavior; it has been argued that Lovecraft in some of his stories sends up the very genre in which he wrote.

Title: The Shadow out of the Outsider: Lovecraft's Identity | Jesus Emmanuel Navarro-Stefanon, Benemérita Universidad Autónoma de Puebla / Universidad de las Americas Puebla (Mexico)

Abstract: Several images of Lovecraft (some of them erroneous) have emerged over the years: that he was a prisoner trapped in his own fantastic work and his own familiar ties (i.e., his sense that he was an *outsider*), or that he was an occultist and knowledgeable in forbidden lore, and also that he was xenophobic and intolerant, or a sheltered conservative with a tendency toward the extremes of the political spectrum. These images are tied to the topic of Lovecraft's identity.

This paper explores the "manliness" of the Lovecraft's generation, a concept analyzed by Gail Bederman in *Manliness and Civilization: A Cultural History of Gender and Race in the United States, 1880–1917*, which covers exactly the period in which Lovecraft lived his childhood and youth, and how this idea of "manliness" reverberated in his juvenile conduct and his later political trends, as a way of reaffirming it. Such is the case in Lovecraft's essay "The Renaissance of Manhood" (1915) and in his letters of this time.

Title: Monstrous Modernism: Lovecraft's Theory of the Aesthetic in Modernity | *Jason Ray Carney, Case Western Reserve University*

Abstract: It has become commonplace among Lovecraft critics to view his horror fiction as an attempt to portray the experience of "cosmic indifferentism" derived from a vision of the cosmos linked to science, particularly astronomy. Thus, Lovecraft's fiction is often interpreted as extended scientific allegories that function to concretize abstract insights derived from scientific knowledge: e.g., the size of the earth relative to the galaxy, the brief life-cycle of our sun relative to the life-cycle of the cosmos, the genealogical continuity between intelligent life and protozoic slime, etc. In framing Lovecraft's fiction in this way, critics have discovered a key component of its popularity and wide pop-culture uptake, namely, its usefulness as an interpretative frame, i.e., a tool to think a Modernity too complex to imagine as a totality. At the same time, scholars have emphasized science over other dimensions of Modernity, many of which Lovecraft was fascinated and disturbed by, and which he treated in his fiction. Because Lovecraft is generally relegated to narratives of genre fiction history (e.g., science fiction, fantasy, and horror), it has become difficult for critics to glimpse his deep engagement with art. Throughout Lovecraft's voluminous correspondence are references to modern art or Modernism. Experimental dance, non-representational painting, blank-verse poetry, modern architecture: these disturbed and even disgusted Lovecraft. In other academic fields there is a tendency to treat Lovecraft's disavowal of Modernist art in a reductive way, to view it, at worst, as evidence of his philistine tastes, or, at best, his misunderstanding. But I am convinced that there is much more to Lovecraft's engagement with Modernism. Throughout his many years as a working literary artist, Lovecraft developed a sophisticated theory of the aesthetic and Modernity. This paper traces out and describe this theory by treating Lovecraft's many stories of fictionalized art objects—e.g., sculptures, music, architecture—as allegories that function not only to horrify readers but to theorize the conditions of aesthetic production and the aesthetic object in Modernity.

Saturday, 9:30–10:45 A.M.
Lovecraft in Late- and Post-Modern Studies

Explorations in semiotics, post-structural linguistics, existentialism, and eco-criticism

Title: "Ph'nglui mglw'nafh Cthulhu R'lyeh wgah'nagl fhtagn": The Language of Lovecraft | *Alex Houstoun, Independent Scholar*

Abstract: In recounting his experiences on R'lyeh, the sailor Johansen states that "there is no language" capable of describing what he bore witness to. And yet, prior to this point, there has been a subtle insistence that such language is available to speak of this "immemorial lunacy"—namely, the word "Cthulhu." Does this single word really convey everything that

Johansen and the other sailors unearthed? Is it truly possible for such an experience to be rendered into a medium that humanity can process?

Using the writings of the literary critical theorist Maurice Blanchot, one can begin to deconstruct Lovecraft's language and the importance he places on characters' written accounts and begin to see just how deep his cosmicism worked to undermine the limitations of human understanding.

Title: Dagon and Derrida: The Cthulhu Mythos and Deconstructing the Rational | *Lyle Enright, Loyola University of Chicago*

Abstract: One of the most fascinating things about studying Lovecraft is the way in which his work eludes literary labels. While Lovecraft has become a pop-culture icon, his work was ill-received in its own time and is still not often considered in serious academia. When he is studied, placing him becomes an exhaustive chore. Whereas one might be able to point to James Joyce as the quintessential Modernist, Lovecraft—even as a contemporary of Joyce—escapes any attempts to place him alongside any other writers of his time.

It is this placement on the spectrum of *Modernism* that seems to cause the trouble in the first place. Lovecraft identifies himself with the "Enlightenment 'project,'" as Peter Barry calls it, and the high point of his writing—the late 1920s—coincides perfectly with the height of Modernism as it is largely understood. He declares himself, numerous times, to be a rationalist. However, Lovecraft's engagement with the literary community is far different from that of his contemporaries. While he follows many tropes of Modernism, his genre choice is decidedly pulp rather than varied or amalgamated; while other Modernists experimented with fractured and reflexive forms, Lovecraft's prose is so consistent in its style and purpose that it tends toward mythology, what Michel Houellebecq refers to as "ritual literature," approaching a more postmodern treatment of myth, language, and perception that is inconsistent with Enlightenment rationalism. Indeed, Lovecraft's treatments of texts within his stories share remarkable cohesion with the ideas of Jacques Derrida who, through deconstructionism and its implications, offered a "specific repudiation" of an Enlightenment modernity that sought to preserve the dream of progress and improve society via rationalism. Yet even as his work approaches postmodernism half a century before its time, Lovecraft does not seem to share in the same celebration of fragmentation as those who would come after him.

In determining where to place Lovecraft, and as such how to receive him as part of the literary cannon, the issue seems to become more one of philosophy than of aesthetics. Modernism and postmodernism both carry certain ontological and epistemological values that separate them, and in regard to these Lovecraft seems to touch both ends of the spectrum, step off from it, and offer something completely different.

Lovecraft's method of addressing questions of knowledge, being, and truth finds unique cohesion with the language theories of Derrida. Through his short fiction, Lovecraft displays a unique sort of postmodern attitude that understands the implications of the "unnameable," "monstrous births" that Derrida asserted could be found in all lines of thought when read against themselves. Of course, for Derrida, the result was liberty. For Lovecraft, it is unfathomable horror. The aim here is to present the Cthulhu Mythos as a deconstructive reading of Enlightenment rationalism, as well as a study in the legitimacy of textual and narrative evidence over the empirical or "scientific," as it addresses the previously unconsidered tension between human flourishing and the pursuit of knowledge.

Title: I and Cthulhu: Using Martin Buber's Ontology of Dialogue to Evaluate H. P. Lovecraft's Cosmic Dread | *Daniel Holmes, Salve Regina University*

Abstract: It might seem unlikely that we should find many commonalities between the horror fiction of H. P. Lovecraft and the philosophy of Jewish theologian Martin Buber. There is, however, a compelling thematic congruity between the two, and to understand it is to gain a dramatic new way to approach Lovecraft. Reading Lovecraft's weird tales through the lens of Buber's *I and Thou* (1923) exposes a reversed dialogic metaphysic governing the horrific laws of Lovecraft's universe. The specific interest of this paper is Lovecraft's short story "The Call of Cthulhu" (1926). Using Buber's ideas to dissect this tale of madness and intrigue reveals Cthulhu as a perverted manifestation of the Eternal Thou: a *Thou* whose existence, by its very nature, shatters the *I–It* (objectifying) relation of the material world, as well as minds and lives founded upon this understanding. The paper builds on this theme to argue that Lovecraft's cosmic dread is successful because it reflects a diseased worldview back upon itself, forcing the objectifying materialist to self-objectify and take his unwilling stand in relation. It is Great Cthulhu, whose dead dreams permeate the physical world, that marks the end of all material causality and human interaction. The sickening flood of external meaning that occurs when an undeveloped individual identity is called into relation with the elder god blasts minds and souls with a ghastly psychic brutality. This unique and philosophically grotesque vision—the concept of a world where terror rather than love forms the relation between man and god—is the cornerstone of Lovecraft's weird fiction.

Title: Thinking Ecocritically: A Look at Embodiment and Nature in H. P. Lovecraft | *Cory Willard, University of Waterloo (Canada)*

Abstract: "The rural tales are queer. They might be even queerer if city men and college chemists could be interested enough to analyze the water from that disused well, or the grey dust that no wind seems to disperse."— H. P. Lovecraft, "The Colour out of Space"

In an increasingly globalized and outsourced world, questions of environment and questions of place are perhaps more relevant to academic criticism and society now than ever before. Believing this to be the case, ecocritical scholars employ a broadly materialist and interdisciplinary approach to interpreting engagements with place and contribute to an ongoing and overlapping conversation that stresses attention to inseparable connections between texts and places, environments, and ecologies. The goal of an ecocritical perspective is, then, to get a critical understanding of the history, geography, literature, and cultural meanings of places; to see the ecology, the vertical depth, and interconnectedness of places and to respond with criticism that is immersed and aware of relationships between people and their ecological communities.

Certain elements of H. P. Lovecraft's work have been explored from a place-based perspective, but these studies tend to be almost solely biographical rather than ecocritical. This seems somewhat surprising in light of the fact that Lovecraft's fiction takes place almost exclusively within one geographical area and is bound up within the environmental, social, and cultural meanings of place. This paper employs an ecocritical approach to interpreting cultural engagements with place as seen in the stories "The Colour out of Space" and "Whisperer in Darkness," while making reference to the breadth of Lovecraft's work that might be engaged with ecocritically. Making use of several ecocritical and bioregional scholars, such as Lawrence Buell, Richard White, and Lucy Lippard, I argue that Lovecraft's writing is rife with ecocritical themes of environmental perversion, the sanctity of the natural order, the value of local knowledge, and the importance of embodied experience, rather than just science, in understanding nature and the cosmos. Ecocritical scholarship has made great strides into horror and science fiction over the last decade, but has been a neglected mode of study when addressing Lovecraft. Hopefully this essay, as modest as it may be, can help spark some ecocritical dialogue around this author who himself was so bound up in, and concerned with, place.

Saturday, 11:00 A.M.–12:00 P.M.
Beyond the Esoteric Order
Exploring the edges of Lovecraftian philosophy, occultism, and scholarship

Title: Lovecraft's Monsters: Rationalism, Anti-Rationalism and Lovecraftian Modernity | *Justin Woodman, Goldsmiths College (United Kingdom)*

Abstract: Lovecraft's secularized reimagining of "the weird" constitutes a radical break with prior genre tropes. Despite his well-documented mechanistic materialism, participants in contemporary occultural milieux—from Chaos magicians to esoteric ufologists, cryptozoologists and conspiracy theorists—continue to treat Lovecraft's work as the product of genuine encounters with non-human cosmic realities. Constructing from out his "Cthulhu Mythos" diverse alternative beliefs and pseudoscientific theories involving monstrous alien interventions within human history and consciousness, such beliefs could themselves be considered "monstrous" with regard to Lovecraft's own advocacy of rationalism and unbelief (and his desire to forge "a form of non-supernatural cosmic art"). Through insights proffered from anthropological research undertaken among "Lovecraftian" occultures (with a particular focus on practitioners of Chaos magick) within the UK—and from contemporary theories regarding the constituents of modernity and cultural constructions of the monstrous—the reasons for (pop-)occultural fascinations with Lovecraft's work (especially his monsters) are critically evaluated in relation to practitioners' own experience of modernity.

Eschewing reductionist explanations of these "Lovecraftian occultures" as the product of irrationality or ignorance, I re-examine Lovecraft's relationship with science and the rational to suggest that his own anti-modernist "revolt against time, space and matter" intimates a gnostic sensibility consonant with contemporary esoteric beliefs. Furthermore, Lovecraft's own articulation of the monstrous—while demythologized—nonetheless points to a secular conception of the sublime cognate with the central project of contemporary occultures. These occultures are shown to be thoroughly *modern* (and congruent with Copernican modernity) in their Lovecraftian synthesizing of science, religion, and magic that is at once instrumental, rationalizing, demystifying, *and* resacralizing of the cosmos. In this respect, the paper explores the claim that one of the reasons for Lovecraft's growing cultural salience is because his monsters in fact demarcate the limit of modernity's rationalizing scope. Subsequently, the conception that modernity represents the progressive fulfillment of Enlightenment reason is also challenged, citing a burgeoning body of theoretical work that acknowledges the way that occult and other "non-rational" discourses are not only central to but constitutive of "modernity."

As such, the paper goes on to suggest that the occultural deployment of Lovecraft's work offers a subcultural critique of the ways in which rational-legal and bureaucratized modern states counterintuitively create that which is counter to everyday human expectations. In other words, chaos, disorder, and the rule of unreason are produced in the attempt at delimiting a "monstrous" (but very human) heterogeneity, often through the imposition of a "rational" order that is itself dehumanizing. Lovecraft's popularity may result from the fact that the modernity of which Lovecraftian "pop culture" esotericisms form a part—governed as it is by the seemingly monolithic and inconceivably vast forces of transnational corporate and state interests—is itself conceptualized as monstrously irrational and inhumanly "Lovecraftian."

Title: It's Only Dark Because You Can't See: A Post-Human Look at Lovecraft's Cosmology | Cody Jones | *University of Chicago*

Abstract: Starting from the philosophical presupposition that any type of phenomenological perception must have at its foundation physiological correlates, this paper explores, as far as possible, a post-human phenomenological interpretation of Lovecraftian cosmology.

Post-humanism is an ill-defined category. For our purposes, it can be understood as a critical movement that seeks to deconstruct the notions of human nature that have their roots in Renaissance theologies and ontologies. This category of critique is then applied to philosophical phenomenology, seeking to produce a workable model of what experiencing would be like for a non-human or post-human entity.

Our exploration will begin with a consideration of space from a Darwinian framework: What notions of space that we take to be a form of "brute data," with roots in some type of objective reality, are actually evolutionary apperception? If an organism can be considered simply a membranous portion of the environment in which it lives, how does the environment not only affect but demand metaphors of spatiality? We will explore as an example the potential spatiality for Cthulhu's closest analogue, the squid, by using several of the ideas presented in *Vampyroteuthis Infernalis* by Vilém Flusser and Louis Bec and supplemented with brief comments on space as understood by Kant, Bergson, Blachelard, and Husserl, among others.

From here, we explore briefly the other half of the equation: time. How are metaphors of time influenced similarly to conceptions of space? Do they play as integral a role in phenomenological metaphor as space? (No doubt they do, but to what extent?) Is time as deeply connected to our physiology as space?

The conclusion of this paper will discuss the possibility of a "hermeneutics of the inconceivable": a form of interpretation by which we could potentially come to understand the inhabitants of Lovecraft's universe, Cthulhu and Dagon in particular, as functionally rational beings from the framework of an equally valid, yet difficult to conceive, existential phenomenology that further cements the commensurability of terror, rationalism, madness, and the authentic self within Lovecraft's work.

Title: Lovecraftian Religions: Yesterday, Today, and When the Stars Are Right | *Dennis P. Quinn, California State Polytechnic University, Pomona*

Abstract: The influence of H. P. Lovecraft can be felt today in almost all dark corners of modern American popular culture. Literature, film, movies, animation, video games, role-playing games, and a host of other media have all felt the impact of Lovecraft's pseudomythology. Most of these media are created with a humorous tongue-in-cheek sensibility. What is less known are the multitude of frighteningly serious devotees to the Great Old Ones, the practitioners of the Cthulhu Cult, those who give literal homage to Yog-Sothoth and his horrifying kin. This paper brings some of this dark and foreboding reality to the surface and shows that, even from the very first appearances of the so-called Cthulhu Mythos, searchers for the dark mysteries have read Lovecraft's literary beings as real entities worthy of religious reverence. From dabblers in the occult to the most infamous names in black magic and Satanism, Lovecraft has become acknowledged as a "High Priest of the Dark Arts," even though, as they all claim, he either did not venture to acknowledge this himself or was unconscious of the truth of his own revelations. Quotations from his works are evoked as incantations and prayers to the legions of Elder Gods, who, the worshippers claim, can induce trance or ecstatic states. These gods are also called upon in myriad magickal and other religious practices.

Though certainly not an exhaustive study, this paper touches on some of the prominent devotees of Lovecraft's gods in order to show what they all have in common and some of their specific devotional practices. I also argue that, far from being unique, these Lovecraftian religionists have a pedigree, not only in modern religions based on fictional works (such as The Church of All Worlds, Scientology, and those who find religious inspiration from J. R. R. Tolkien's and Marion Zimmer Bradley's works), but also with other more ancient religions that find inspiration in literature (such as Christianity). Finding secret meanings in literary texts originally written for other purposes is as old as the oldest "Religions of the Book."

The cults inspired by our honored "mechanical materialist" show another dimension of Lovecraft's ascending cultural influence in the contemporary world. In a letter to Clark Ashton Smith in 1933, Lovecraft had already seen hints of his burgeoning religious influence in which he and his "gang" were considered by a Cthulhu zealot to be "genuine agents of unseen Powers in distributing hints too dark and profound for human conception or comprehension." As this paper shows, this religious sentiment has grown beyond what Lovecraft could have ever divined, and has no signs of ever going away.

Index

Abram, David 201, 204, 206, 212
"Account of Charleston, An" 112, 113-14, 115, 119
Ackerman, Forrest J 155n10, 158
Addams, Charles 155n10
"Afterword: Toward an Ethic of Discussion" (Derrida) 176
Airaksinen, Timo 102, 109n1, 139n6
Alhazred, Abdul 71
Alice's World (Lundwall) 96
Anatomy of Criticism (Frye) 166n3
Apology for Smetcymnus (Milton) 81
Aquino, Michael 220-22
"Are Modern X-Rays a Public Danger?" (Contremoulins) 38-39
At the Mountains of Madness 70-71, 154, 174, 178, 183-86

"Background" 77
Bailey, William 40
Baird, Edwin 55, 76
Barlow, R. H. 158
Bates, Brian 229
"Battle That Ended the Century, The" (Lovecraft-Barlow) 158
Becquerel, Henri 37, 38
Benstock, Shari 170n7
Beowulf 127, 129
"Beowulf: The Monsters and the Critics" (Tolkien) 127
Bernhard the Conqueror (Lundwall) 96, 100, 103-4, 105, 106
"Beyond the Wall of Sleep" 86, 167
Bierce, Ambrose 37, 155n10
Bildhauer, Bettina 126, 129
Birdwell, Ken 10
Black Mask 55
Blackwood, Algernon 37, 83
Blair Witch Project, The (film) 83
Bleiler, E. F. 73

Bloch, Robert 155-56, 157, 211
Bodies That Matter (Butler) 141
Book of the Law, The (Crowley) 220
Bradley, Marion Zimmer 229
Bradofsky, Hyman 165
Brundage, Margaret 158
Buber, Martin 189-200
Buchanan, Carl 29, 30, 31
Buell, Lawrence 201, 202, 203, 207, 211
Bullen, John Ravenor 151
Burke, Edmund 79-80
Burke, Kenneth 166n3
Burleson, Donald R. 160
Butler, Judith 135, 141, 142-43, 145
Byron, George Gordon, Lord 152n3

Californian 165
Calinescu, Matai 166n1
"Call of Cthulhu, The" 16, 32, 69, 70, 82, 102, 158, 169-71, 174, 178, 180-81, 183, 189-99, 209, 224-25, 226
Callaghan, Gavin 155, 222
Camargo, Martin 129
"Cannibalism in the Cars" (Twain) 156
Cannon, Peter 73, 77, 137n3, 140
Carroll, Noël 155-56
Carter, Angela 160
Case of Charles Dexter Ward, The 21-23, 111, 112, 120, 121
"Cask of Amontillado, A" (Poe) 31
"Celephaïs" 50, 81
Chambers, Robert W. 125
Cixous, Hélène 137, 142
Clark, Claudia 39, 40, 41, 42, 43, 44, 46, 49, 50
Close Encounters of the Third Kind (film) 84

Cloverfield (film) 74
Cobb, Irvin S. 67
Cohen, Jeffrey Jerome 126, 129, 133
"Colour of out Space, The" 35-51, 82-83, 84, 85, 158, 174, 178, 180, 181-83, 202, 203, 207-8, 209
"Confession of Unfaith, A" 215
Contremoulins, Gaston 38-39, 43
Cowley, Malcolm 170n7
Crane, Stephen 159n19
Crowley, Aleister 215, 216n1, 219, 220, 222, 223
Curie, Pierre and Marie 37

"Dagon" 55, 85-86
"Damned Thing, The" (Bierce) 36-37
"Danger in Using Radium" 48
Dante Alighieri 127
Davis, Erik 178, 184, 226
de Camp, L. Sprague 53-54
Deadly Sunshine (Harvie) 37
Derleth, August 223
Derrida, Jacques 137n4, 141n9, 173-87
Descartes, René 138, 147, 210
Description of the Town of Quebeck, A 112, 114, 119, 212
Discworld (Pratchett) 229
Dodge, Jim 202, 208
Don Juan (Byron) 152n3
Donne, John 79
Doré, Gustave 78, 90
Dostoevsky, Feodor 137
Dream-Quest of Unknown Kadath, The 50
Drout, Michael D. C. 127n2
Dunsany, Lord 99, 100
"Dunwich Horror, The" 90-91, 128, 130-32, 152n1, 160, 161, 223, 227

Eckhardt, Jason C. 127
Egan, James 74, 84
"Eight Said to Have Died in Lead Plant" 44
Eliade, Mircea 76
Elder, Will 99
Eliot, T. S. 79, 168n5
Ellmann, Richard 166n2

Encyclopaedia Britannica 221
Esoteric Order of Dagon 223-24
Essay on the Sublime and the Beautiful (Burke) 79-80
"Eulalie" (Poe) 161n25
Evans, Timothy H. 109
Exile's Return (Cowley) 170n7

"Facts concerning the Late Arthur Jermyn and His Family" 63, 69, 87
"Falco Ossifracus" (Miniter) 159n22
"Fall of the House of Usher, The" (Poe) 31, 67
Fängelsestaden (Lundwall) 98, 100, 102, 104, 105
Fantaskiska romanen 2, Den (Lundwall) 99
Fantasy Fan 158
Feidelson, Charles, Jr. 166n2
Fellowship of the Ring, The (Tolkien) 83
"Festival, The" 222
"Five Deaths Laid to Radium Poison" 40, 44
Five Faces of Modernity (Calinescu) 166n1
Flickan i fönstret vid världens kant (Lundwall) 98, 100
Foreigner, The (Shue) 161
Foresti, Guillaume 155
Foucault, Michel 142n10
Frankenstein (Shelley) 153, 183
Freud, Sigmund 14-15, 17, 18-19, 20, 23-24, 29, 30, 60-61, 135, 141, 145
"From Beyond" 27-28, 47n4, 167
Frye, Northrop 166n3
Fuseli, Henry 90

Gablik, Suzi 211
Galpin, Alfred 136n2
Gäst i Frankensteins hus (Lundwall) 98, 100
Gay, John 151n1
Geeraert, Dustin 159-60
Gender Trouble (Butler) 141
Gerald of Wales 128, 129-30, 132, 133
Gernsback, Hugo 158

Gibbons, B. J. 222
Gilbert, William Schwenck 156
Goya, Francisco 155n10
Grant, Kenneth 215, 219-20, 222, 223, 224, 226, 230
Greene, Sonia H. 53-55, 59
Grimm, Jacob and Wilhelm 14

H. P. Lovecraft: Against the World, Against Life (Houellebecq) 59
H. P. Lovecraft's Dark Arcadia (Callaghan) 155
Haeckel, Ernst 152n1
Harman, Graham 112n7
Harvey, Graham 228
Harvie, David 37
"Haunter of the Dark, The" 100, 157, 161, 225
Heinlein, Robert A. 229
Henneberger, J. C. 153
"Herbert West—Reanimator" 153
"Heritage or Modernism: Common Sense in Art Forms" 165-67, 168
Hess, Clara 44
Highet, Gilbert 159
Hine, Phil 227-28
Hitler, Adolf 57, 58
Hobbes, Thomas 78
Hoffman, Frederick 42, 44
Hoffmann, E. T. A. 14-15, 23, 32
"Horror at Red Hook, The" 56, 60, 61, 64-65, 87, 160n24, 178, 221-22
Houdini, Harry 158n17
Houellebecq, Michel 56, 59, 62, 160
"Hound, The" 169, 170
Houtain, George Julian 153
Howard, Robert E. 157n16
Hubbard, L. Ron 229
Hussey, Derrick 7, 11
"Hypnos" 88-89, 169, 170

I and Thou (Buber) 189
Idea of the Holy, The (Otto) 78
"Idealism and Materialism: A Reflection" 159

"Imprisoned with the Pharaohs" (Lovecraft-Houdini). *See* "Under the Pyramids"
In Defence of Dagon 118n16
"In the Walls of Eryx" (Lovecraft-Sterling) 158
Irigaray, Luce 142

Jackson, Peter 83
Janicker, Rebecca 203, 206
Jenkins, Philip 218
Jesus Christ 230
Johnson, Samuel 73, 77, 79
Joshi, S. T. 7, 11, 16, 27, 28, 40, 41, 44, 47n4, 67, 75, 79, 89, 116, 127n1, 136n2, 144n14, 145, 146, 152n1, 153, 155, 216, 223
Joyce, James 168
Jung, Carl 67

King Kong Blues (Lundwall) 98

Lacan, Jacques 17-18, 135, 141-42, 145, 147-48
Lamb, Charles 221
LaVey, Anton 220-21, 229
Leach, Edmund 156
Leiber, Fritz 212
Levi-Strauss, Claude 177
Lévy, Maurice 202
Long, Frank Belknap 136n2, 158
"Lord Dunsany and His Work" 159
Lord of the Rings, The (Tolkien) 229
Lovecraft, H. P.: aesthetics of, 55, 76, 84-85, 117, 151-52, 165-66; and capitalism, 65-69; and Christianity, 74-75, 84, 90-91, 160, 215, 228-32; dreams of, 78; and environmentalism, 201-12; marriage of, 53-55; and occultism, 215-32; and racism, 53-71, 116; and religion, 217-18; travel writings of, 109-22; on weird fiction, 13-14, 15-16, 79-80, 125-28
Lovecraft's Library (Joshi) 79, 89
Lucas, George 74
Lumley, William 218, 219, 230
Lundwall, Sam J. 95-107

262 INDEX

"Lurking Fear, The" 26-27, 153, 154, 209
Lycidas (Milton) 82

Machen, Arthur 36, 125, 128, 129, 130
Mad 99
Maillefer, Sarah 43
Malory, Sir Thomas 127
"Man Said to the Universe, A" (Crane) 159n19
Mandeville, Sir John 128, 129, 130, 131, 132
Mariconda, Steven J. 36
Marsh, Obed, Frater 223-24
Martin, John 87
Martin, Sean Elliott 155
Martland, Harrison 43
Matolcsy, Kálmán 143
Meditations on First Philosophy (Descartes) 138-39
Melville, Herman 84, 86-87, 151n1
Men in Black (film) 161
Merrill, James 78
Miéville, China 60
Milton, John 73-92
Miniter, Edith 159n22
Mists of Avalon, The (Bradley) 229
Moby-Dick (Melville) 62, 84, 86-87, 89, 151n1
Modern Tradition, The (Ellmann-Feidelson) 166n2
Modest Proposal, A (Swift) 156, 159
Moffat, Steven 173
Monster Theory (Cohen) 126
"Moon-Bog, The" 87-88
Mork and Mindy (TV show) 161
Moses 230
Muller, Hermann Joseph 37
Murray, Will 50
"Music of Erich Zann, The" 29-31, 71, 100, 167-69, 170, 171, 198
Mysterious Stranger, The (Twain) 151

Nabokov, Vladimir 137
Necronomicon (Alhazred) 10, 71, 220
Necronomicon (Simon) 222
NecronomiCon Providence 9-10

Nelson, Dale J. 154
New York Times 40, 42, 43, 48
Newitz, Annalee 53, 62-63, 65
Nietzsche, Friedrich 69, 177, 184, 187
Nightingale, Andrea 181
No Time for Heroes (Lundwall) 98, 103
"Notes on an Entity" (Bloch) 211
"Notes on Writing Weird Fiction" 13, 178, 185n7
"Novel of the White Powder" (Machen) 36
"Nyarlathotep" (prose-poem) 78

Oates, Joyce Carol 78
Of Grammatology (Derrida) 175
On the Morning of Christ's Nativity (Milton) 87-88
"On the Suffering of the World" (Schopenhauer) 69
Ordway, Thomas 39
Otto, Rudolf 78
Outside the Circles of Time (Grant) 219, 220
"Outsider, The" 71, 98-99, 113n8

Pace, Joel 143, 146n16, 148
Paradise Lost (Milton) 75, 77-78, 79, 81, 82, 83, 84, 85, 86, 88, 89, 90, 91, 92
Paradise Regain'd (Milton) 89
Parker, William Riley 75
Paul, St. 230
Petaja, Emil 217
Philosophy of Literary Form (Burke) 166n4
"Pickman's Model" 71, 89-90, 152n1, 171, 198
"Picture in the House, The" 99
"Plans to Safeguard Radium Handlers" 43
Poe, Edgar Allan 14, 15, 16, 19-21, 22-23, 24-26, 28, 31, 32, 67, 73, 99, 100, 125, 138, 152, 161n25
"Polaris" 89
Popular Science 38
Possamaï, Adam M. 228-29
Pound, Ezra 169
Pratchett, Terry 229

Prelude, The (Wordsworth) 74
Pretend We're Dead (Newitz) 53, 62
Price, Robert M. 128, 218, 231
Providence Detective Agency 75
Providence Evening Bulletin 40, 44, 48

Quale, Thomas 74
"Quest of Iranon, The" 81–82, 167

Radium Girls (Clark) 39
"Radium Is Expected to Turn on Thieves" 48
Ralickas, Vivian 113n9
"Rats in the Walls, The" 66–69, 70, 99, 100, 128, 156
Re-Animator (film) 154, 155
Reflections on the French Revolution (Burke) 79
Rise and Fall of the Cthulhu Mythos, The (Joshi) 16
Robinson, Christopher L. 159
Robinson, E. Arthur 25
Rutherford, Ernest 37, 38

St. Armand, Barton Levi 78
Salomon, Roger B. 160
Samson Agonistes (Milton) 75–76
"Sand-Man, The" (Hoffmann) 14–15, 23
Satan Presiding at the Infernal Council (Martin) 87
Satanic Rituals, The (LaVey-Aquino) 220–22, 229
Schirmacher, Wolfgang 178
Schopenhauer, Arthur 69, 70, 71, 152n1
Schultz, David E. 136n2, 144n14
Science Fiction: An Illustrated History (Lundwall) 96, 99
Science fiction: från Begynnelsen till våra Dagar (Lundwall) 96
Scientific American 39, 45
"Secret Cave, The" 64
Sedgwick, Eve Kosofsky 146n16, 147
Sefel, John Michael 10
"Shadow out of Time, The" 105, 160, 161–62

"Shadow over Innsmouth, The" 62–64, 65–66, 69–70, 71, 88, 111–12, 120, 121, 132–33, 159
Shakespeare, William 73, 81, 135, 137
"Shambler from the Stars, The" (Bloch) 157
Shea, J. Vernon 79
Shelley, Mary 153, 183
Sherlock (TV show) 173
Shreffler, Philip A. 121, 122, 145
Shue, Larry 161
"Silver Key, The" 154
Simon 222–23
Skräckens labyrinter (Lovecraft) 99
Smith, Clark Ashton 56–57, 84, 99, 136n2, 157, 218
Smith, James K. A. 177
Sochocky, Sabin von 43
"Some Notes on a Nonentity" 71, 77
"Some Notes on Interplanetary Fiction" 159, 178n5, 179
Spell of the Sensuous, The (Abram) 204
Sterling, Kenneth 158n17
Stranger in a Strange Land (Heinlein) 229
"Structure, Sign, and Play in the Discourse of the Human Sciences" (Derrida) 174, 175, 176, 177, 184, 187
"Supernatural Horror in Literature" 13, 14, 15, 79, 80, 125
Swift, Jonathan 152n1, 154, 156, 159

"Tell-Tale Heart, The" (Poe) 24–26, 27, 31
"Temple, The" 161
Tenebrous, Frater 224–26, 228
Terror, The (Machen) 36
"Thing on the Doorstep, The" 135–41, 143–48, 223n6
Three Impostors, The (Machen) 130
Tolkien, J. R. R. 83–84, 127, 229
"Tomb, The" 80–81, 167
Topography of Ireland, The (Gerald of Wales) 129

Topophilia (Tuan) 203
Travels of Sir John Mandeville, The (Mandeville) 129
Tuan, Yi-Fu 203, 211
Turner, Brian G. 35n1
Twain, Mark 151, 155, 156
2018 A.D. or the King Kong Blues (Lundwall) 97, 104, 105–6

U.S. Radium Corporation 39, 40, 41, 43
"Unbroken Chain, The" (Cobb) 67
"Uncanny, The" (Freud) 14, 17, 18–19, 23, 24, 29, 30
"Under the Pyramids" (Lovecraft-Houdini) 158n17, 160, 222
"Unnamable, The" 169

Vance, Jack 99

Walpole, Horace 153n5
Wandrei, Donald 157n16
Waugh, Robert H. 143, 145
Way of Wyrd, The (Bates) 229
Weird Realism: Lovecraft and Philosophy (Harman) 112n7

Weird Tales 53, 55, 153, 157–58, 223n6
What is Man? (Twain) 151, 155
"Whisperer in Darkness, The" 40, 157, 202, 203, 204–6, 210, 211
White, Richard 203–4
"William Wilson" (Poe) 19–21, 22–23
"Willows, The" (Blackwood) 37, 83
Wilson, Edmund 35
Wilson, Gahan 155n10
Wisker, Gina 140
Women of the Left Bank (Benstock) 170n7
"Wonder of the East" 129
Wordsworth, William 74
World as Will and Representation, The (Schopenhauer) 69
Wright, Farnsworth 158

X-Files, The (TV show) 186

"Yarn of the 'Nancy Bell,' The" (Gilbert) 156
Yeats, W. B. 78

Žižek, Slavoj 60, 61, 68

www.ingramcontent.com/pod-product-compliance
Lightning Source LLC
Chambersburg PA
CBHW071329190426
43193CB00041B/1038